Question&Answer

CONSTITUTIONAL AND ADMINISTRATIVE LAW

D1350492

Develop your legal skills

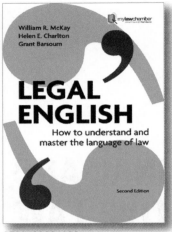

William R. McKay
Helen E. Charlton
Grant Barsoum

LEGAL ENGLISH

How to understand and master the language of law

Second Edition

9781408226100

Steve Foster

HOW TO WRITE BETTER LAW ESSAYS

Tools and techniques for success in exams and assignments

new edition

9781447905141

THE LONGMAN **DICTIONARY OF LAW**

Eighth Edition

P. H. Richards • L. B. Curzon

9781408261538

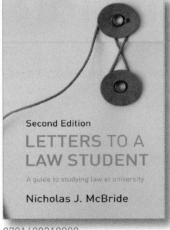

Second Edition
LETTERS TO A LAW STUDENT

A guide to studying law at university

Nicholas J. McBride

9781408218808

Written to help you develop the essential skills needed to succeed on your course and prepare for practice.

Available from all good bookshops or order online at:
www.pearsoned.co.uk/law

ALWAYS LEARNING

PEARSON

Question&Answer

CONSTITUTIONAL AND ADMINISTRATIVE LAW

2nd edition

Vicky Thirlaway

Senior Lecturer in Criminal and Public Law,
Sheffield Hallam University

Harlow, England • London • New York • Boston • San Francisco • Toronto • Sydney • Auckland • Singapore • Hong Kong
Tokyo • Seoul • Taipei • New Delhi • Cape Town • São Paulo • Mexico City • Madrid • Amsterdam • Munich • Paris • Milan

Pearson Education Limited
Edinburgh Gate
Harlow CM20 2JE
United Kingdom
Tel: +44 (0)1279 623623
Web: www.pearson.com/uk

First published 2012 (print)
Second edition published 2014 (print and electronic)

© Pearson Education Limited 2012 (print)
© Pearson Education Limited 2014 (print and electronic)

The right of Victoria Thirlaway to be identified as author of this work has been asserted by her in accordance with the Copyright, Designs and Patents Act 1988.

The print publication is protected by copyright. Prior to any prohibited reproduction, storage in a retrieval system, distribution or transmission in any form or by any means, electronic, mechanical, recording or otherwise, permission should be obtained from the publisher or, where applicable, a licence permitting restricted copying in the United Kingdom should be obtained from the Copyright Licensing Agency Ltd, Saffron House, 6-10 Kirby Street, London EC1N 8TS.

The ePublication is protected by copyright and must not be copied, reproduced, transferred, distributed, leased, licensed or publicly performed or used in any way except as specifically permitted in writing by the publishers, as allowed under the terms and conditions under which it was purchased, or as strictly permitted by applicable copyright law. Any unauthorised distribution or use of this text may be a direct infringement of the author's and the publishers' rights and those responsible may be liable in law accordingly.

All trademarks used herein are the property of their respective owners. The use of any trademark in this text does not vest in the author or publisher any trademark ownership rights in such trademarks, nor does the use of such trademarks imply any affiliation with or endorsement of this book by such owners.

Contains public sector information licensed under the Open Government Licence (OGL) v1.0.
www.nationalarchives.gov.uk/doc/open-government-licence.

Pearson Education is not responsible for the content of third-party internet sites.

ISBN: 978-0-273-78347-3 (print)
    978-0-273-78350-3 (PDF)
    978-0-273-78348-0 (eText)

British Library Cataloguing-in-Publication Data
A catalogue record for the print edition is available from the British Library

10 9 8 7 6 5 4 3 2 1
17 16 15 14 13

Print edition typeset in 10/13pt Helvetica Neue LT Pro by 35
Print edition printed and bound in Malaysia (CTP-PPSB)

NOTE THAT ANY PAGE CROSS REFERENCES REFER TO THE PRINT EDITION

Contents

Supporting resources

Visit the **Law Express Question&Answer** series companion website at
www.pearsoned.co.uk/lawexpressqa to find valuable learning material
including:

- **Additional essay and problem questions** arranged by topic for each chapter
  give you more opportunity to practise and hone your exam skills.
- **Diagram plans** for all additional questions assist you in structuring and writing
  your answers.
- **You be the marker** questions allow you to see through the eyes of the
  examiner by marking essay and problem questions on every topic covered in
  the book.
- Download and print all **Attack the question** diagrams and **Diagram plans**
  from the book.

Also: The companion website provides the following features:

- Search tool to help locate specific items of content.
- Online help and support to assist with website usage and troubleshooting.

For more information please contact your local Pearson sales representative or
visit **www.pearsoned.co.uk/lawexpressqa**

Acknowledgements

For my sister Katie.

With many thanks to Mum, and I am sorry about all the commas.

Thanks also to Christine Headley for knocking things into shape.

Vicky Thirlaway

Publisher's acknowledgements

Our thanks go to all reviewers who contributed to the development of this text, including students who participated in research and focus groups which helped to shape the series format.

The material in this guide is up-to-date and accurate as the law stood in December 2012, although some minor updating has been possible at later stages in production.

What you need to do for every question in Constitutional and Administrative Law

HOW TO USE THIS BOOK

Books in the *Question and Answer* series focus on the *why* of a good answer alongside the *what*, thereby helping you to build your question answering skills and technique.

This guide should not be used as a substitute for learning the material thoroughly, your lecture notes or your textbook. It *will* help you to make the most out of what you have already learned when answering an exam or coursework question. Remember that the answers given here are not the *only* correct way of answering the question but serve to show you some good examples of how you *could* approach the question set.

Make sure that you refer regularly to your course syllabus, check which issues are covered (as well as to what extent they are covered) and whether they are usually examined with other topics. Remember that what is required in a good answer could change significantly with only a slight change in the wording of a question. Therefore, do not try to memorise the answers given here, instead use the answers and the other features to understand what goes into a good answer and why.

The study of the British constitution poses challenges for students, as there is seldom one 'correct' answer to a question. Essay questions demand that you will be able to analyse various competing theories about the nature of the constitution, and formulate a reasoned argument. In order to be persuasive, a legal argument must be supported by evidence and, therefore, you must ensure that you are able to point to examples of the operation of the constitution drawn from historical and current events, academic argument and judicial decisions. Where you are expressing a view or opinion of your own, remember that you still need supporting evidence to show the examiner why you have reached that conclusion. You need to be specific. Comments such as 'many have argued that . . .' will not attract high marks. It is far more authoritative to say something like 'Dicey argued that . . .', as this shows your examiner that there is a source for your opinion.

Make sure that you use the terminology correctly and consistently; it is important not to say 'government' if you mean 'Parliament', for example.

Constitutional and administrative law is changing at a rapid pace. Since the last edition of this book, major developments have occurred in several areas including constitutional reform, freedom of expression, human rights law and the regulation of Parliament. To do well in this subject, you need to keep abreast of developments by paying attention to the press, the law reports and journals.

A common mistake made by students is to see the examination as a memory test. Whilst you certainly do need to remember a lot of law, take care not to make the mistake of thinking you are only required to show how much law you remember. Many students submit answers (particularly to problem scenarios) that are too descriptive. Far higher marks are given to those students who have the confidence to select the legal provisions most relevant to the facts given in the question. You should concentrate on applying the law to the facts you have been given and using this to draw conclusions about the likely outcome for the party or parties you are asked to advise. Similarly, essays require you to show the ability to use the law that you have learnt in order to formulate an answer to the specific question and marks will not be given for including irrelevant information.

Guided tour

What you need to do for every question in Constitutional and Administrative Law

HOW TO USE THIS BOOK

Books in the *Question and Answer* series focus on the *why* of a good answer alongside the *what*, thereby helping you to build your question answering skills and technique.

This guide should not be used as a substitute for learning the material thoroughly, your lecture notes or your textbook. It *will* help you to make the most out of what you have already learned when answering an exam or coursework question. Remember that the answers given here are not the *only* correct way of answering the question but serve to show you some good examples of how you *could* approach the question set.

Make sure that you refer regularly to your course syllabus, check which issues are covered (as well as to what extent they are covered) and whether they are usually examined with other topics. Remember that what is required in a good answer could change significantly with only a slight change in the wording of a question. Therefore, do not try to memorise the answers given here, instead use the answers and the other features to understand what goes into a good answer and why.

The study of the British constitution poses challenges for students, as there is seldom one 'correct' answer to a question. Essay questions demand that you will be able to analyse various competing theories about the nature of the constitution, and formulate a reasoned

What to do for every question – Identify the key things you should look for and do in any question and answer on the subject, ensuring you give every one of your answers a great chance from the start.

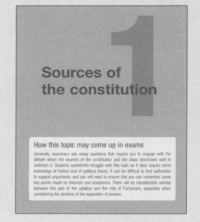

Sources of the constitution

How this topic may come up in exams

Generally, examiners ask essay questions that require you to engage with the debate about the sources of the constitution and the ideas (doctrines) said to underpin it. Students sometimes struggle with this topic as it does require some knowledge of history and of political theory. It can be difficult to find authorities to support arguments, and you will need to ensure that you can remember some key points made by theorists and academics. There will be considerable overlap between this part of the syllabus and the role of Parliament, especially when considering the doctrine of the separation of powers.

How this topic may come up in exams – Understand how to tackle any question on this topic by using the handy tips and advice relevant to both essay and problem questions. In-text symbols clearly identify each question type as they occur.

 Essay question   **Problem question**

Attack the question – Use these diagrams as a step-by-step guide to help you confidently identify the main points covered in any question asked. Download these from the companion website to use as a useful revision aid.

Answer plans and Diagram plans – A clear and concise plan is the key to a good answer and these answer and diagram plans support the structuring of your answers, whatever your preferred learning style.

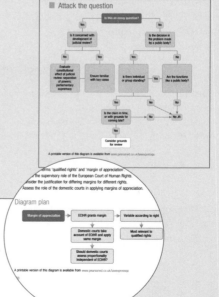

Answer plan

→ Explain the meaning of 'separation of powers'.
→ Describe the extent to which a separation of powers existed prior to the Act.
→ Outline the key provisions of the Act.
→ Consider how far there is a true separation of powers.
→ Consider whether or not a true separation of powers is possible.

Answer with accompanying guidance – Make the most out of every question by using the guidance to recognise what makes a good answer and why. Answers are the length you could realistically hope to produce in an exam to show you how to gain marks quickly when under pressure.

Case names clearly highlighted – Easy-to-spot bold text makes those all important case names stand out from the rest of the answer, ensuring they are much easier to remember in revision and an exam.

Make your answer stand out – Really impress your examiners by going the extra mile and including these additional points and further reading to illustrate your deeper knowledge of the subject, fully maximising your marks.

Don't be tempted to – Points out common mistakes ensuring you avoid losing easy marks by understanding where students most often trip up in exams.

Bibliography – Use this list of further reading to really delve in and explore areas in more depth, enabling you to excel in exams.

Answer

[1] This introduction picks out the important events from the scenario and links them to the legal issue. This is a good way to start an answer to a problem scenario. You should never begin by simply rewriting the facts of the scenario.

[ ] It is helpful to learn some definitions of key concepts, so you can give a definition of the term to be addressed.

This scenario raises issues concerning parliamentary privilege. In considering the comments made regarding Ms Turner, it is necessary to determine the extent of the privilege afforded to parliamentary proceedings, and whether or not this provides protection to Tom. Secondly, in considering the proposed action by Mr Jones, it will be necessary to determine whether records of parliamentary proceedings may be adduced as evidence in court proceedings. Lastly, it will be necessary to address the powers held by Parliament to discipline Members and non-Members alike for contempt.[1] Parliamentary privilege is a term used to describe rules protecting the House of Commons and the House of Lords from any outside interference. Privilege is enjoyed by both individual Members of Parliament and the collective

It can be one of the first times that Dicey articulated the principle of legality; therefore, it is important to recognise the importance of the case in a discussion about the rule of law.

[ ] This is a really useful authority to cite, especially alongside Entick. The two cases are, in a sense, two sides of the same coin. Whilst you should not set out the facts in any detail, you should

Dicey's first rule can be interpreted as expressing a need for protection from the arbitrary exercise of power. **Entick v Carrington** (1765) 2 Wils 275 articulated this principle of legality by holding that, in the absence of statutory or common law authority, entry to a citizen's home was unlawful.[3] It is worth noting that the requirement for legality as part of the rule of law does not necessarily mean that the judiciary will be concerned with the fairness of a particular provision. **IRC v Rossminster** [1980] AC 952 required the courts to consider powers of search and seizure that were, in the view of Lord Scarman, a 'breathtaking' interference with privacy and property.[4] As the lawful authority existed, the principle of legality was satisfied. Dicey was critical of the use of discretionary authority, and would undoubtedly

---

[11] You should not spend too much time on considering possible government responses to a declaration of incompatibility because that would be beyond the scope of the question, which focuses on enforcement.

[12] All the evidence has been presented, and a clear conclusion be succinctly set out

---

✓ Make your answer stand out

■ By spending more time considering the grounds that could be relevant to both parts of the decision. You do need to focus on irrationality because the question demands this but, if space permits, you could open up the discussion to consider whether or not a decision made solely for financial reasons could be classified as for an improper purpose. This would be impressive, as this is quite a narrow point and beyond the scope of generalist text books. It would show real confidence in analysing the law.

■ By referring to the Law Commission report (No. 322) on the issue of damages published in May 2010, *Administrative Redress: Public Bodies and the Citizen* (available at: www.lawcom.gov.uk/docs/lc322.pdf). The Law Commission propose that damages should be available as a sole remedy in review proceedings. Although you must limit your advice to the current law, you could suggest that there is a perceptible shift in favour of the award of damages, which could assist Marie. This would show the examiner that you have read around the subject.

■ By explaining the available remedies in more detail. There are a number of useful texts you could consider, including: Sunkin, M. (2010) 'Remedies available in judicial review proceedings', in D. Feldman (ed.), *English Public Law* (2nd edn). Oxford: Oxford University Press.

! Don't be tempted to . . .

■ Treat the question as an invitation to outline Dicey's theory and ignore other definitions of the rule of law. This is an area of the syllabus that students do tend to find very difficult; mainly because we would like there to be one 'correct' definition of the rule of law. If you are able to show that you understand that there are competing definitions, you will be rewarded.

■ Ignore primary sources. Although this is a very academic area of the syllabus, there are key cases that can, and should, be incorporated into your answer because they illustrate how the judiciary approach the rule of law. Weaker answers are often limited to mention of *Entick v Carrington*. Marks will be given to the answer that can refer to more recent cases such as *A v Secretary of State for the Home Department* [2004] UKHL 56.

Bibliography

Allan, T.R.S. (2001) *Constitutional Justice: A Liberal Theory of the Rule of Law*. Oxford: Oxford University Press.

Bagehot, W. (1963) *The English Constitution*. London: Fontana.

Bamforth, N. (2001) 'The True "Horizontal Effect" of the Human Rights Act 1998' 117

Guided tour of the companion website

Book resources are available to download. Print your own **Attack the question** and **Diagram plans** to pin to your wall or add to your own revision notes.

Additional Essay and Problem questions with **Diagram plans** arranged by topic for each chapter give you more opportunity to practise and hone your exam skills. Print and email your answers.

You be the marker gives you a chance to evaluate sample exam answers for different question types for each topic and understand how and why an examiner awards marks. Use the accompanying guidance to get the most out of every question and recognise what makes a good answer.

All of this and more can be found when you visit **www.pearsoned.co.uk/lawexpressqa**

Table of cases and statutes

■ Cases

■ Statutory instruments

■ International conventions and treaties

Sources of
the constitution

1

How this topic may come up in exams

Generally, examiners ask essay questions that require you to engage with the debate about the sources of the constitution and the ideas (doctrines) said to underpin it. Students sometimes struggle with this topic as it does require some knowledge of history and of political theory. It can be difficult to find authorities to support arguments, and you will need to ensure that you can remember some key points made by theorists and academics. There will be considerable overlap between this part of the syllabus and the role of Parliament, especially when considering the doctrine of the separation of powers.

■ Attack the question

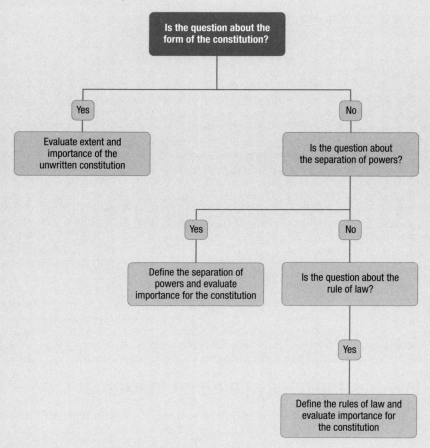

Is the question about the form of the constitution?

Yes → Evaluate extent and importance of the unwritten constitution

No → Is the question about the separation of powers?

Yes → Define the separation of powers and evaluate importance for the constitution

No → Is the question about the rule of law?

Yes → Define the rules of law and evaluate importance for the constitution

A printable version of this diagram is available from www.pearsoned.co.uk/lawexpressqa

 Question 1

The programme of reform since 1997 means it is no longer appropriate to refer to the 'unwritten constitution'.

Discuss.

Answer plan

→ Explain the distinction between written and unwritten constitutions.

→ Discuss whether or not the constitution could have been described as wholly unwritten.

→ Identify and outline major changes post-1997.

→ Consider whether unwritten sources remain relevant.

→ Argue that a written constitution demands a higher form of law.

Diagram plan

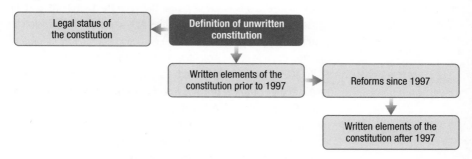

A printable version of this diagram plan is available from www.pearsoned.co.uk/lawexpressqa

Answer

[1] This definition is quite basic, but shows that you do recognise that the term constitution should be defined by its role, rather than the form it takes.

A constitution is described as a set of rules and practices that determine how power is divided within a state.[1] The UK constitution is sometimes described as 'unwritten' as there is no single written document codifying the relevant laws. This is unusual; the United Kingdom is one of only three nations without a written constitution. In 1997 the Labour government embarked on an ambitious programme of constitutional reform, with further alterations in the first years of the Coalition government. Arguably, the proliferation of statutes that now define the workings of the state means that it is now largely written. However, many aspects remain un-codified and to understand the constitution it is still necessary to refer to numerous sources. The term 'written constitution' also denotes a source of law superior to 'ordinary' law. In the United Kingdom, despite an increasing number of codified rules, the constitution has no special status.[2]

[2] The focus of the argument will be that the distinction between 'written' and 'unwritten' constitutions is not about the format as much as the notion of a superior form of law.

The UK constitution does not come from a single revolutionary point in history. Rather, the system of governance has evolved in piecemeal fashion over time.[3] It would be wrong, however, to suggest that the constitution prior to 1997 could be accurately characterised as entirely unwritten. As well as the unwritten sources of the constitution such as conventions and prerogative powers, there are important documents delineating the division of power. Statutes that could be mentioned include the Bill of Rights, which redefined the relationship between the monarch and the legislature; the various acts extending the franchise; the Parliament Acts of 1911 and 1949 which shifted the balance of power between the Commons and the Lords; and the European Communities Act, which made provision for community law to take effect in the domestic courts. Key judgments affected the role of the executive. In *Entick v Carrington* (1765) 19 St Tr 1029, the exercise of arbitrary government power was curtailed, and in *Council of Civil Service Unions v Minister for the Civil Service* [1985] AC 374 (the GCHQ case), the right of the judiciary to scrutinise the use of executive power was asserted. It is correct to say, however, that the operation of the state depended in large part on tradition and practice, and the exercise of the historical powers of the prerogative.

[3] Discussion of change to the constitution does demand that you are able to outline the historical development of the United Kingdom's arrangements. However, it is important to keep this brief, so that the balance of your answer can concentrate on the main focus of the question, which is the impact of change.

[4] As the question refers to 'rapid constitutional change', it is clearly important to be able to demonstrate knowledge of major areas of reform. These should be summarised as succinctly as possible to leave room for analysis; therefore, the paragraph following this sentence must be brief.

It is undeniable that the period between 1997 and the present day has seen immense constitutional change.[4] The Labour government steered through legislation to alter the composition of the House of Lords, devolve executive power to Northern Ireland, Scotland and Wales, ensure that the European Convention on Human Rights can be enforced in the domestic courts, and to increase access to information regarding the state. Perhaps the most systematic alteration to constitutional structures came in the form of the Constitutional Reform Act 2005. The Act was designed to strengthen the separation of powers and the rule of law through a number of measures, including reform of the office of Lord Chancellor, and the separation of the

Law Lords from the legislative assembly. The Coalition government have been responsible for the Fixed-Term Parliaments Act 2011 which abolished the prerogative power to dissolve Parliament.

Despite an increase in written sources of constitutional power, unwritten sources also remain, although the relevance of such sources is, perhaps, debatable. Prerogative powers, normally exercised by the executive in the name of the Crown, can be abolished by the creation of statute (see, for example, **Attorney General v de Keyser's Royal Hotel Ltd** [1920] AC 508[5]). It could be argued that the prerogative no longer occupies a position of constitutional importance; the supervisory role of the judiciary now seems to be entrenched in the wake of the landmark ruling of the **GCHQ case**. In addition, it appears unlikely that any government could use the full extent of powers available without fear of political consequence. For example, in 2003, the decision to declare war on Iraq was reached following a vote in the House of Commons. Strictly speaking, this was unnecessary as declaration of war is a prerogative power. Giving evidence to the Liaison Committee, the then Prime Minister stated that it was 'inconceivable' that the power would be exercised without reference to Parliament. However, since that time, three Private Members', Bills calling for the abolition of the prerogative have been tabled and have failed to gather executive support. It is fair to say that in 2007 the government stated a commitment to reform of the prerogative but, save for the minor changes introduced by the Constitution and Governance Act 2010; no sustained or substantive change has materialised.[6]

Unwritten conventions remain part of the constitution.[7] Dicey (1885)[8] defined conventions as 'understandings, habits and practices' which are considered to be binding, but have no legal force. Jennings (1959a) considered that conventions are crucial to the operation of the constitution and must be followed, arguing that their unwritten nature allows for flexibility and change in accordance with developing societal and political norms. Those who suggest codification is desirable point to the lack of consequence when a convention is ignored. Loveland (2012), for example, points to the Matrix Churchill affair of the 1990s when, in the absence of legally enforceable controls, the convention of ministerial 'responsibility' seemed to shift towards a less onerous concept of 'accountability'.

[5] Here, you are using the case simply to provide support for the proposition of law you have made. There is no need to give more detail; you have already set out the *ratio* of the case.

[6] Space doesn't allow a detailed discussion of the provisions in the CGA 2010, but the reference to the Act demonstrates awareness of relevant law. Given that the answer suggests the change is not significant, there is no need for more detail.

[7] It is important to consider the continued importance of unwritten elements of the constitution, to support the developing argument that the shift towards codification is far from complete.

[8] Reference to Dicey will be important in most essays about the nature of the constitution, as his work is still seen as the source of many of our ways of describing or explaining the system. If you are able to refer to other theorists as well (as in the remainder of the paragraph), this will increase your mark as it shows you have read around the topic.

A commitment to codification of the prerogative has not been made, but there has at least been widespread acknowledgement of the need to consider the issue. However, there has been little commitment to the codification of conventions. Indeed, the Coalition government's failed House of Lords Reform Bill expressly confirmed that many of the operational conventions should remain.[9]

[9] This is a good point to make, as it is evidence that some aspects of the unwritten constitution appear to enjoy continued support.

The significance of these issues is not simply the question of whether constitutional arrangements are written or unwritten. They are, rather, symptomatic of the fact that there is no deference to constitutional principles which will take precedence over all other forms of law.[10] There is no method of forcing compliance with constitutional arrangements governed by convention, and still some reluctance by the courts to curtail the prerogative.

[10] This is the crux of the argument that was set out in the introduction.

It cannot be said, then, that the proliferation of legislation reforming aspects of the constitution has resulted in a written constitution. It may be the case that there are a greater number of written sources of the constitution. Certainly, the Constitutional Reform Act 2005 was significant, as it expressly referred to the doctrines of the separation of powers, and to the rule of law. Constitutional lawyers have long argued that these doctrines are part of our constitution, but the Act placed this on a statutory, hence written, basis. As has been shown, however, informal, unwritten sources of power remain and these are subject to limited control. Nations described as possessing a written constitution are distinguishable not simply by the existence of a document, but rather by the acknowledgement that the constitution represents a superior form of legal power. This cannot be said to be the case in the United Kingdom, which does not afford the constitution such an elevated position.[11]

[11] This is a solid conclusion, which sets out a clear point of view; showing confidence with the subject matter.

Make your answer stand out

- By making reference to K.C. Wheare's (1966) classifications of constitutions as 'supreme' or 'subordinate' in *Modern Constitutions* (2nd edn.). Oxford: Oxford University Press.
- By developing the argument regarding 'superior law' by outlining the difference between the powers of the new Supreme Court in the United Kingdom and that of the United States, which has the power to declare legislation 'unconstitutional'.
- By suggesting that 'superior law' is impossible in light of the doctrine of parliamentary supremacy. This will show the examiner that you are able to make connections between different topics in the syllabus.

 Don't be tempted to . . .

- Try to explain the workings of the constitution in great detail. There is no need to outline the various functions of the executive, legislature and judiciary here.
- Include a detailed list of all constitutional changes since 1997, as the question requires analysis of the impact of changes rather than a descriptive account.

Question 2

'For the first time, we have a clear separation of powers between the legislature, the judiciary and the executive in the United Kingdom.' Lord Matravers, President of the Supreme Court.

To what extent has the Constitutional Reform Act 2005 been successful in achieving the aim of strengthening the separation of powers?

Answer plan

→ Explain the meaning of 'separation of powers'.
→ Describe the extent to which a separation of powers existed prior to the Act.
→ Outline the key provisions of the Act.
→ Consider how far there is a true separation of powers.
→ Consider whether or not a true separation of powers is possible.

Diagram plan

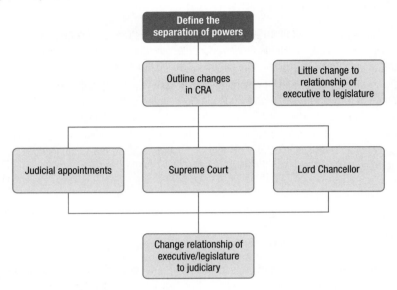

A printable version of this diagram plan is available from www.pearsoned.co.uk/lawexpressqa

Answer

[1] Reference to Montesquieu is essential, as it shows an awareness of the origins of the doctrine.

The doctrine of the separation of powers was first espoused by the political theorist Montesquieu in the eighteenth century.[1] The doctrine has been considered to be an important element of the constitution since that time. The Constitutional Reform Act 2005 (CRA) introduced changes intended to reinforce the importance of the doctrine of the separation of powers. In order to assess the impact of these changes it is necessary to first establish the pre-existing position. The success of the legislation can then be considered. It will be suggested that a complete separation of powers is neither desirable, nor possible. It will be argued that the establishment of the Supreme Court will have little impact, but that reforms to the office of Lord Chancellor are a significant step towards a greater separation of powers.[2]

[2] The introduction should outline the main argument to be adopted in the remainder of the essay; this will reassure the examiner that there will be a coherent structure to the argument.

The state can be described as consisting of three bodies which perform distinct functions: the legislature; the executive; and the judiciary. The traditional doctrine of the separation of powers states that there should be no overlap of personnel or functions between

[3] It is important to be able to succinctly explain what is meant by the term 'separation of powers' without spending too long outlining the development of the doctrine.

the institutions in order to prevent abuses of power.[3] If the separation of powers is understood in this way, then it is clear that Montesquieu (1989) must have been outlining an idealised position, for there has always been an overlap of personnel in the institutions of the United Kingdom. This does not inevitably mean that the doctrine should be dismissed, as there can still be separation of function, and a system of checks and balances between the institutions.

[4] It is not possible to deal with every aspect of the interaction between the powers in detail, so a more confident answer will highlight a few areas for discussion.

The examples of overlap prior to the CRA are numerous, but for the purpose of this discussion three will be considered.[4] First, the Law Lords sat in the House of Lords as part of the legislature. Second, the unique position of the Lord Chancellor who, as head of the judiciary, Speaker of the House of Lords, and a cabinet minister, occupied a position at the heart of all three institutions of the state. Last, and linked to the Lord Chancellor's office, was the system of senior judicial appointments which were made on his recommendation. This system had long been the subject of criticism and, certainly, the fact of executive involvement in determining the composition of the judiciary posed a challenge to claims of the existence of a separation of powers. If one role of the judiciary is to restrain executive abuse of power, then even the hypothetical possibility of executive influence can be seen to threaten the integrity of the system.[5]

[5] It will be suggested later that the CRA focused primarily on judicial independence, so it is worth stating why this is seen as critical.

In 2003, the government unexpectedly announced plans to abolish the role of Lord Chancellor. The Constitutional Reform Act did not go as far as abolition, but instead severely curtailed the role (ss. 2–22).[6] The Lord Chancellor now retains a role as government minister but no longer sits as a judge, or acts as Speaker of the House of Lords. In addition, the Law Lords now sit as a Supreme Court, which, in a visible symbol of separation, is located outside the Houses of Parliament. A new system for judicial appointments was introduced, to limit the possibility of accusations of executive influence (s. 61). Indeed, the Act specifically charges the Lord Chancellor, and all ministers, with a responsibility to uphold the independence of the judiciary, and not to seek to influence any decisions made in court proceedings (s. 3).

[6] The Constitutional Reform Act introduced many changes, so it is necessary to be able to focus on those relevant to the question, and be able to explain the effect on the office of Lord Chancellor and the House of Lords.

The pronouncement made by Lord Matravers suggests that, prior to the establishment of the Supreme Court, not only was there a lack of separation, but, more particularly, that this was evidenced by the inclusion of senior judiciary in the legislature. It is, of course, true that the Law Lords were entitled to sit in the House of Lords, and to participate in debate. By convention, however, they declined to participate in proceedings concerning legislation that they might, in future, have to adjudicate upon. It is not clear that there was any real danger of the judiciary seeking to exercise a legislative function in the creation of statute. The Supreme Court is still relatively new, but there is no suggestion that its function represents any constitutional departure from that previously exercised by the judicial branch of the House of Lords. The physical change of location and the alteration of title are perhaps better understood as being symbolic, representative of the desire to promote transparency in our constitutional arrangements.[7]

[7] Marks will be afforded for the ability to form a reasoned view about the impact of legislative change rather than simply stating the law.

Arguably, the alterations to the office of Lord Chancellor are a more systematic attempt to effect real constitutional change. At the beginning of Labour's programme of constitutional reform, Lord Irvine defended the role,[8] arguing that the unique function of the office was to allow there to be communication between the organs of state so each could understand the objectives of the other. The office was a clear example of what had been described by Bagehot in the nineteenth century as the almost 'complete fusion' between the institutions, which he considered to be the 'efficient secret' of the constitution.[9] Nonetheless, the numerous responsibilities of the Lord Chancellor in all areas of government led to the possibility of tensions between the various roles. Lord Woolf highlighted the need for statutory protection for judicial independence, rather than convention and reliance on mutual respect, and linked this to the preservation of the rule of law. The restriction of the Lord Chancellor's role, and the removal of his powers of judicial appointment, then, can be viewed as an acknowledgment of the truth of the famous maxim 'justice must not only be done, it must be seen to be done' (**R v Sussex Justices ex parte McCarthy** [1923] All ER 233).[10] The possibility of executive influence over the composition of the judiciary has, then, been diminished.

[8] This reference shows that you are familiar with the way that policy has shifted over time from defence of the office, towards reform.

[9] Inclusion of Bagehot here will be rewarded, as it shows ability to explore the topic a little more, by demonstrating awareness of the fact that it is arguable whether a separation of powers is desirable.

[10] The answer has tended towards suggesting that change has been largely cosmetic. Inclusion of this quote shows familiarity with the case, but more importantly, points towards an understanding that it is important that fairness is transparent in the organisation of the state.

The CRA focused on judicial independence. It did not address other aspects of the constitution which threaten the separation of powers such as the fact that government ministers sit as part of the legislature, or the quasi judicial function exercised by Parliament in the regulation of its own affairs.[11] It could be suggested that the judiciary had proved able to maintain independence despite their position in the Lords, under the supervision of the Lord Chancellor. There are many instances in which the Lords have been willing to confront both

[11] In the interests of balance, it is useful to be able to point to evidence that contradicts the view given by Lord Matravers.

[12] It is important not to be too descriptive when using case law. Sometimes, as here, there is no need to include any of the facts. The reference to a specific point made in the judgment shows familiarity with, and understanding of, the case.

the legislature and the executive (consider the rebuke Lord Hoffmann delivered in **A v Secretary of State for the Home Department** [2004] UKHL 56).[12] Although the CRA may be more concerned with form than substantive change, it is important to ensure that independence is protected and thus it must be seen as a step in the right direction. However, given the issues which pertain to the other institutions, the Act cannot be said to have significantly strengthened the separation of powers.

 Make your answer stand out

- By incorporating primary sources in the theoretical discussion. You could refer to additional cases in which the importance of a separation of powers has been sanctioned; see, for example, comments of Lord Diplock in *Duport Steels Ltd* v *Sirs* [1980] 1 WLR 142.

- You could argue that a view of the impact of the Act may depend on the definition of the separation of powers that is adopted. The answer has already indicated that Montesquieu and Bagehot saw the separation of powers differently, and development of this point would show the examiner that you have the ability to utilise theoretical perspectives to assess primary sources of law.

- If space allowed, reference could be made to other academic perspectives. Specifically, you could consider Marshall, who makes the point that there is no clear or consistent definition of the principle (Marshall, G. (1971) *Constitutional Theory*. Oxford: Clarendon Press).

! Don't be tempted to . . .

- Become distracted by outlining the personnel and/or functions of the institutions. There is a temptation to show 'how much you know' about the operation of the constitution and students often begin this kind of answer by describing how the different institutions operate. This approach will not gather marks and it is more important to focus on analysing the impact of the Act mentioned in the question.

- Similarly, it is not enough to outline the provisions of the CRA here. An answer which sets out the key changes and then draws conclusions about the effect of the Act will appear quite weak. This question really does require you to show that you understand some of the academic and judicial comment on the issues covered by the Act. The conclusions you draw will then be supported by evidence.

Question 3

'In the mouth of a British Constitutional Lawyer, the term "rule of law" seems to mean primarily a corpus of basic principles and values, which together lend some stability and coherence to the legal order.' (Allan (2001))

Discuss the relevance of the concept of the 'rule of law' to the United Kingdom constitution.

Answer plan

→ Try to define the rule of law.

→ Acknowledge the variety of definitions.

→ Consider the current position with examples.

→ Argue that the rule of law is relevant as an ideal.

→ Argue that the rule of law needs clearer definition and protection.

Diagram plan

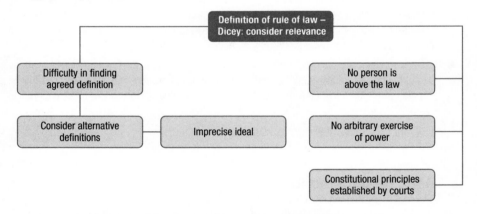

A printable version of this diagram plan is available from www.pearsoned.co.uk/lawexpressqa

Answer

The 'rule of law' is a term often invoked by politicians, judges and academics but the definition is far from certain. The lack of a clearly discernible meaning is problematic, as it has been said to underpin the organisation of the state. The Constitutional Reform Act 2005 formally recognises the importance of the rule of law (s. 1).

Dicey (1885) maintained that the rule of law was a key characteristic of the constitution, giving a three part explanation of its meaning. To assess whether or not the rule of law retains its key position, it is appropriate to consider whether the elements described by Dicey are evident today. It is necessary to acknowledge competing definitions which may be more appropriate.[1]

Dicey saw the rule of law as embodying three concepts: no person should be punished except for a distinct breach of the law; no person is above the law; and constitutional principles are established in the common courts.[2] The contemporary relevance of each of these can be assessed in turn.

Dicey's first rule can be interpreted as expressing a need for protection from the arbitrary exercise of power. **Entick v Carrington** (1765) 2 Wils 275 articulated this principle of legality by holding that, in the absence of statutory or common law authority, entry to a citizen's home was unlawful.[3] It is worth noting that the requirement for legality as part of the rule of law does not necessarily mean that the judiciary will be concerned with the fairness of a particular provision. **IRC v Rossminster** [1980] AC 952 required the courts to consider powers of search and seizure that were, in the view of Lord Scarman, a 'breathtaking' interference with privacy and property.[4] As the lawful authority existed, the principle of legality was satisfied. Dicey was critical of the use of discretionary authority, and would undoubtedly be disturbed by the range of discretionary powers now afforded to the executive, for example; in the administration of the welfare state. In reading Dicey, it is important to remember he wrote at a time when the functions of government were few. This cannot be said to be the case in the complex society we now inhabit where the job of administration would be impossible if not for the exercise of discretion.[5] A modern explanation of this part of the principle of the rule of law would perhaps not require the absence of discretionary powers but rather a robust system to regulate the exercise of discretion.[6] Therefore, judicial review of executive action can be seen as central to the rule of law. Attempts to exclude the court's power of review have been rejected by the judiciary; in the important case **R (Cart) v Upper Tribunal; R (U and XC) v Special Immigration Appeals Commission** [2009] EWHC 3052 (Admin), it was held that judicial review was available, and further is a 'principle engine of the rule of law'.

[1] This question demands that you acknowledge the difficulty in defining the rule of law, but all questions dealing with the doctrine require demonstration of understanding of the Diceyean position.

[2] You should be able to summarise Dicey's three 'rules' accurately and succinctly.

[3] *Entick* v *Carrington* is a key constitutional case, as it is one of the first times that the judiciary articulated the principle of legality; therefore, it is important to recognise the importance of the case in a discussion about the rule of law.

[4] This is a really useful authority to cite, especially alongside Entick. The two cases are, in a sense, two sides of the same coin. Whilst you should not set out the facts in any detail, you should provide enough information to demonstrate how the case shows that a law does not need to be fair.

[5] Dicey is sometimes dismissed by students as being outdated, which is a valid view, but there is a need to point to evidence of this.

[6] Here, the answer shows an ability to relate legal theory to the way the constitution operates in practice. This shows that you really understand the significance of the point Dicey was making by the first rule.

[7] Again, the case of *Entick* v *Carrington* is central to this aspect of the topic so you need to show the examiner that you are aware of this.

[8] It is always important to demonstrate knowledge of two sides of a debate, but crucial to be able to find some examples to support each side of the argument.

[9] Many commentators refer to this as an important constitutional case, and it is a useful one to be aware of for this topic area.

The notion that 'no man is above the law' seems straightforward. Dicey cited **Entick v Carrington** as support for this proposition, declaring it to be one of many instances where government officials were called to account.[7] **M v Home Office** [1994] 1 AC 377 is an example of a government minister being held in contempt of court after ignoring a court order. This would seem to suggest the truth of Dicey's statement. There are, though, examples of classes of persons who are not subject to the law in the same way such as those enjoying diplomatic immunity, or MPs protected from defamation in Parliament.[8] Part IV of the Anti-Terrorism, Crime and Security Act of 2001 attempted to create a law to which only one class of persons, foreign nationals, would be subject. The court's opposition (**A v Secretary of State for the Home Department** [2004] UKHL 56[9]) can be used to support the argument that the judiciary play an important role in preserving the rule of law. If the statement suggests there should be equality before the law, then arguably all citizens should be able to enforce their rights and there must be equal access to the courts. It is not clear that this is the case, for, despite a purported commitment to ensuring this (Access to Justice Act 1999), there have been extensive reductions in the availability of legal aid, and it is not certain that reliance on arrangements such as *pro bono* representation and no win no fee agreements can ensure that access is ensured for all.

[10] The final proposition can be difficult to explain, so you will be rewarded if you can provide a clear explanation.

The final element of Dicey's conception of the rule of law[10] expresses his belief that the common law was capable of protecting individual rights, obviating the need for a written constitution. The Human Rights Act 1998 incorporates the rights under the European Convention on Human Rights into domestic law, and therefore, arguably, the role of the courts is diminished.

[11] It is not going to be possible to consider the range of complex debate regarding the meaning of the rule of law, but ensure you are familiar with the broad differences between those who see it as linked to morality, and those who view it as a structural issue.

There have been many other explanations of the rule of law.[11] Craig (1997) argues that there are two main schools of thought. One approach is the formal conception of the rule of law, which is concerned with the process of law making, and simply demands that laws are made according to an open clear process, and that obligations imposed by the law are prospective and clear. The rule of law, on this definition, is not concerned with the content of those laws. A substantive conception of the rule of law suggest the law embodies rights, and that distinctions can be drawn between good and bad laws. Raz (1979) notes that there are numerous definitions of the rule of law, but rejects efforts to imbue the doctrine with a moral ideology. He argues that some features are required including the requirement for clear, prospective laws, an independent judiciary, and review powers available to the courts. On this simple definition, it can be argued that the rule of law remains central to the constitution.[12] The CRA explicitly protects the independence of the judiciary (s. 3) and, as discussed, powers of review remain. There are few examples of retrospective legislation. The War Damage Act is often referred to, but this was half a century ago and there are few other examples.[13] (The European Convention on Human Rights expressly prohibits retrospective criminal legislation.)

The rule of law is not a precise legal doctrine, and there are aspects of Dicey's description of its operation which seem less relevant in a modern context. If the key elements as suggested by Raz are accepted as broadly accurate, then it seems clear that the concept remains both relevant and central.[14]

[12] Here, you reassure the examiner that you are using the material to address the question.

[13] To ensure a good mark, the answer must provide evidence to support the view that the rule of law remains relevant.

[14] The conclusion may appear quite short, but the final argument was set out in the preceding paragraph. It is crucial though, to provide a direct answer to the question.

✓ Make your answer stand out

- By showing a knowledge of a broader range of academic theorists in this area. The answer references Raz and Craig, but there are many people you could mention. Some useful sources are: Allan, T.R.S. (2001), *Constitutional Justice: A Liberal Theory of the Rule of Law*. Oxford: Oxford University Press; Craig, P. (1997) Formal and substantive conceptions of the rule of law: an analytical framework *Public Law* 467; Jowell, J. and Oliver, D. (eds.) (2000) *The Changing Constitution* (4th edn). Oxford: Oxford University Press; Raz, J. (1979) *The Authority of Law*. Oxford: Oxford University Press.

- By considering the relationship between the doctrine of the rule of law, and other principles said to underpin the constitution. This answer refers to the role of the judiciary; it could be argued that a functional separation of powers is necessary to uphold the rule of law. The examiner will be impressed by an answer that demonstrates understanding of how different topics considered on the syllabus overlap.

! **Don't be tempted to . . .**

- Treat the question as an invitation to outline Dicey's theory and ignore other definitions of the rule of law. This is an area of the syllabus that students do tend to find very difficult; mainly because we would like there to be one 'correct' definition of the rule of law. If you are able to show that you understand that there are competing definitions, you will be rewarded.

- Ignore primary sources. Although this is a very academic area of the syllabus, there are key cases that can, and should, be incorporated into your answer because they illustrate how the judiciary approach the rule of law. Weaker answers are often limited to mention of *Entick* v *Carrington*. Marks will be given to the answer that can refer to more recent cases such as *A* v *Secretary of State for the Home Department* [2004] UKHL 56.

📝 Question 4

"In the determination of his civil rights and liabilities or of any criminal charge against him, everyone is entitled to a fair and public hearing . . ." (Article 6, The European Convention on Human Rights and Fundamental Freedoms).

To what extent are closed material proceedings compatible with the rule of law?

Answer plan

→ Explain the rule of law as defined by Dicey and consider where the requirement for open justice sits.

→ Demonstrate the general judicial acceptance of the principle.

→ Explain how closed material proceedings are currently utilised.

→ Outline the changes proposed in the Justice and Security Bill.

→ Consider the judicial approach to closed material proceedings (CMPs).

Diagram plan

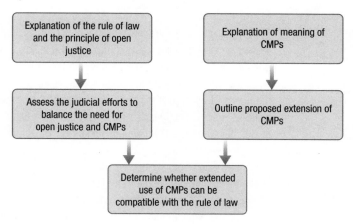

A printable version of this diagram plan is available from www.pearsoned.co.uk/lawexpressqa

Answer

[1] In any question concerning the rule of law, the temptation is to outline the debate regarding the meaning of the doctrine. Here, as the question is pointing you towards a more specific discussion of CMPs, you need to dispense with the definitions as swiftly as you can in order to focus on the real issue.

[2] The introduction to this answer is particularly important, as it is the opportunity to show an understanding of the links between the various concepts set out in the question. In order to make a detailed analysis of CMPs, you must first explain the relevance of open justice.

Although the precise requirements of the rule of law are the subject of academic debate, the centrality of the principle to the constitution is generally agreed.[1] Dicey described the rule of law as having three components: equality before the law, an absence of arbitrary justice and judicial protection of rights. Despite the fact that these maxims do not expressly refer to open justice, many argue that public hearings are required to maintain the rule of law by ensuring protection from the arbitrary abuse of power.[2] In **Scott v Scott** [1913] AC 417, Lord Shaw declared that allowing an expansion of judicial discretion to order hearings in camera would be to 'shift the foundations of freedom from the rock to the sand'. More recently Lord Neuberger (2011a) declared that court hearings conducted in public are a central part of the commitment to the rule of law. Thus, it can be seen that in seeking to protect the right to a public hearing, Article 6 of the Convention enshrines an aspect of the rule of law.[3] However, departures from the principle of open justice are not unknown. Anonymity orders can be made in both civil and criminal hearings where justice requires this. It is routine for proceedings in both family and youth courts to be closed to the public. Closed material proceedings (CMPs), though, go beyond these exclusions by

[3] As the question quotes Article 6, it is important to draw the link between the convention right and the rule of law. This will assist you later, when discussing the key cases, as the judgments discuss the right to a fair trial, rather than the doctrine.

[4] It is surprising how many students attempt to answer this question without explaining what is meant by a CMP. Make sure you define all the key legal terms in any question.

[5] Here, more detail is provided about the facts of the case than is usually required. It is included to make clear the government's rationale for seeking to change the law.

allowing for hearings to occur in the absence of a party to the case or their legal representative.[4]

CMPs are not new, but have become more prevalent in recent years. Currently, they are used in Employment Tribunals, Special Immigration Appeals Commission Hearings and the Investigative Powers Tribunals. The Justice and Security Bill introduced in 2012 proposed the use of CMPs across the civil courts system. It was drafted in the wake of the collapsed litigation concerning British citizens detained at Guantanamo Bay. The detainees commenced action against the intelligence services seeking compensation for their wrongful imprisonment and ill treatment, claiming that MI5 and MI6 had aided and abetted their detention and torture. The government requested CMPs to deal with parts of the evidence they wished to adduce in defence of the claims, arguing that disclosure would damage national security and, in particular, would involve divulging material relating to the US security services.[5] In the absence of specific statutory authority to do so, the Supreme Court held it had no power to order CMPs in the civil action. The government then settled the cases.

The Bill seeks to rectify the situation by authorising the High Court and Court of Appeal to order closed material proceedings on application by the Secretary of State where there is a risk that disclosure of information relied on could damage national security. Once authorised, this would allow the case to proceed with certain parts of the evidence dealt with in the absence of one or more of the parties and their legal counsel.

The use of CMPs in control order cases has generated a considerable amount of judicial attention since 2005, as both domestic courts and Strasbourg struggled to determine whether such hearings could be compatible with Article 6. The right to cross examine witnesses is only protected in respect of criminal proceedings (Article 6(3)), but questions remain as to whether CMPs can meet the standard of fairness required to comply with Article 6(1).[6] The government has relied upon the special advocate procedure, in which a court-appointed advocate deals with those parts of the evidence which are closed and the defendant continues to be represented by their own advocate in respect of the 'open' proceedings.[7] If enacted, the Justice and Security Bill would see the use of special advocates become more widespread.

[6] This shows awareness of the distinction drawn in the ECHR between civil and criminal proceedings.

[7] You must show that you understand the role of a special advocate.

In **A v UK** [2009] ECHR 3455/05, the ECtHR held that enough information about the closed material must be disclosed to allow the defendant to give instructions to the special advocate: a ruling accepted and confirmed by the Supreme Court (**Secretary of State for the Home Department v AF** (No 3) [2010] AC).[8] Whilst these rulings show strong support for open justice, later decisions have diluted their impact by emphasising that the amount of disclosure required by Article 6 may depend upon the nature of the proceedings and the likely impact upon the defendant.[9] It appears that an enhanced amount of disclosure is necessary where liberty is at stake, but where the incursion upon the defendant's rights is not as grave, the use of the special advocate may be less problematic (for example, the case of **Home Office v Tariq** [2011] UKSC 35 dealing with covert surveillance).[10] Special advocates have expressed misgivings regarding the procedure on more than one occasion (Chamberlain (2009a).

The balance between procedural fairness and national security is undoubtedly difficult. If it were to be the case that proceedings had to be dropped to avoid court-ordered disclosure of damaging and sensitive evidence, then it could be argued that the rule of law would be undermined, as a class of persons may be able to evade its reach.[11] In considering the Binyam Mohammed case (**R (on the application of Mohammed) v Secretary of State for Foreign and Commonwealth Affairs** [2010] EWCA Civ 65), however, Otty (2012) argues that settlement occurred not because of the refusal of the courts to endorse CMPs, but because the state could not have won the case.

Government proposals, if accepted, will allow CMPs to be ordered in respect of a broad range of 'sensitive' information, a term given a broad definition at clause 13 of the Bill. It could be argued that potential injustice is avoided as after all, even if the defendant's advocate does not see all the evidence, the judge will be able to provide the constitutional protection from executive abuse that Dicey warned against.[12] Lord Kerr, however, warned against this assumption in **Al-Rawi and others v Security Services and others** [2011] UKSC 34, calling the argument 'a fallacy'. He reiterated the common law principle, now enshrined in Article 6, that evidence must be capable of withstanding challenge if it is to be relied upon.[13]

[8] These are key authorities on the issue of CMPs and must be included. There is no need to give further detail about the facts.

[9] This is an important point and demonstrates an understanding of how the law is developing.

[10] Although you do not need to explain the facts of this case, it is really important you cite at least one case to support your claim.

[11] This is a good point to make, as it demonstrates awareness of both sides of the arguments regarding the collapse of the Guantanamo cases.

[12] The answer has dealt with a wide range of issues: make sure that you take care to link back to the question's focus on the rule of law.

[13] This is a useful paragraph, as an alternative point of view is noted, but the inclusion of Lord Kerr's view is a persuasive argument against the position.

It is clear from the authorities that CMPs are not by definition incompatible with the rule of law, provided that the "gist" of the evidence is disclosed. The spread of such proceedings in the absence of enhanced safeguards to govern disclosure, however, threatens the important principle of open justice which is so central to the doctrine.

✓ Make your answer stand out

- By keeping up to date with the progress of legislation. At the time of writing, the Justice and Security Bill 2012 is still being considered by the Lords. It is not clear whether the proposals for CMPs will remain in their present form if the Bill is enacted. You do need to make sure that you are prepared to adapt your arguments in light of significant changes.
- By considering the relationship between the rule of law and the separation of powers. The reference to comments made by Lord Kerr could be the starting point for this part of the discussion. This seems to suggest that the ability of the judicial system to hold the executive to account is not solely the responsibility of the judges, but is to a certain extent a result of the litigation process.
- By providing more detail about opposition to the proposals concerning CMPs in the Justice and Security Bill. You could refer to reports by organisations such as the Equality and Human Rights Commission, or Liberty. Ensure your answer is balanced, so you would need to address the arguments put forward by proponents of the Bill who argued that CMPs will increase the accountability of the secret service.

! Don't be tempted to . . .

- Write a general answer discussing the rule of law and the right to a fair trial. There will be few marks awarded here for arguing that the rule of law demands an impartial tribunal and equal treatment for all citizens. The question makes it clear that your answer should concentrate solely on CMPs and open justice.
- Make general statements about CMPs without reference to any decided cases. Here, you will need to show some knowledge of the case law both in the domestic courts and Strasbourg.
- Ignore the need to provide a balanced argument. A number of answers failed to examine the points made by those who support the extension of CMPs. In order to be persuasive, an answer must consider opposing views and explain why the reader should reject them.

 # Question 5

The legislative response to terrorism has brought the executive and judicial arms of the state into a conflict which threatens the separation of powers.

Discuss.

Answer plan

→ Briefly outline the doctrine of the separation of powers.

→ Explain the history of judicial deference to executive decisions.

→ Focus the discussion on key cases concerning terrorism.

→ Assess the impact of the HRA on the judicial approach to terrorism.

→ Analyse the extent to which the doctrine remains in force.

Diagram plan

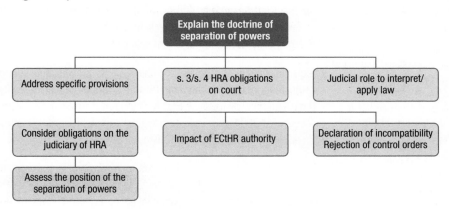

A printable version of this diagram plan is available from www.pearsoned.co.uk/lawexpressqa

Answer

The doctrine of the separation of powers is recognised as a key feature of the UK constitution. According to the doctrine, the three branches of government have separate roles and responsibilities, and operate a system of checks and balances to prevent the arbitrary use of power by any organ of the state. The threat of international terrorism has led to a series of high profile cases addressing the compatibility of legislation with commitments under the European Convention on Human Rights. It will be argued that the Human Rights Act imposes an obligation on the judiciary to take a more robust approach to matters affecting the liberty of citizens. To suggest that this threatens the separation of powers is to overstate the case. Conversely, the willingness of the judiciary to scrutinise executive action could be seen as evidence of the strength of the doctrine.[1]

[1] The introduction has shown awareness of the key elements of the question, and signalled to the examiner the direction that the argument will take.

The doctrine of the separation of powers, the sovereignty of Parliament and the rule of law are seen as the theories that underpin the organisation of the state. Using these models, the role of the judiciary is to apply legislation made by Parliament, and to ensure that the executive uses discretionary powers lawfully.[2] The judiciary have, however, traditionally been unwilling to interfere with executive policy in sensitive areas, in particular, national security.[3] In the seminal **GCHQ case (*Council of Civil Service Unions* v *Minister for the Civil Service*** [1985] AC 374), the court asserted the right to review the exercise of prerogative power, but accepted that areas of 'high policy' would remain 'non-justiciable'.

[2] The answer needs to demonstrate understanding of the doctrine of the separation of powers, but this is not the main focus of the question so there is a need to be brief.

[3] This is an important point, as anti-terrorism measures certainly concern national security, so the traditional approach of the judiciary needs to be examined in order to evaluate whether there has been a change.

Legislation conferring powers on the state to prevent and control terrorism is, of course, concerned with matters of national security. The discussion will focus on Part IV of the Anti-Terrorism, Crime and Security Act 2001, now repealed, and the control order regime introduced by the Prevention of Terrorism Act 2005.[4]

[4] There has been a lot of legislation in this area, and the answer cannot possibly consider all the measures. It is important to pinpoint those measures that will be the basis for the discussion.

The Human Rights Act 1998 has incorporated the European Convention of Human Rights into domestic law and requires all public bodies to act in accordance with convention rights.[5] The courts are required to interpret all legislation in accordance with those rights 'in so far as it possible to do so' (HRA, s. 3). If such an interpretation cannot be found, then a declaration of incompatibility can be made (s. 4). Part IV of the Anti-Terrorism, Crime and Security Act (ACTSA) made provision for the indefinite detention without trial of foreign nationals suspected of involvement in terrorism. The individuals concerned could not be deported to their country of origin, as there was a risk that they could be subject to torture or inhuman and degrading treatment; therefore deportation would be a violation of the government's obligations under Art. 3. The UK government accepted that the provisions were an infringement of the right to

[5] As the argument will suggest that the HRA has affected the judicial approach to 'national security', a brief explanation of the relevant part of the legislation is required.

liberty, but had applied a derogation from Art. 5 in accordance with Art. 15; due to the state of emergency posed by the threat of terrorist action.[6]

The matter fell to be considered by the House of Lords in **A v Secretary of State for the Home Department** [2004] UKHL 56.[7] The Lords accepted that a state of emergency existed justifying the derogation, in accordance with the conventional acceptance of executive judgment on such matters. However, Convention jurisprudence emphasises the need for proportionality, and their Lordships found that the measures were disproportionate, and further, discriminatory; as they applied only to foreign nationals.[8] A declaration of incompatibility was made. The case is highly significant, as it signalled a readiness to review executive actions in areas previously considered to be non-justiciable.

The offending legislation was repealed by the Prevention of Terrorism Act 2005, which created the system of control orders, used to monitor individuals within their own homes.[9] The system of control orders has been analysed for Convention compatibility in a number of cases. As Walker (2010) has pointed out, although the initial cases considered Art. 5 and the acceptable limitations on liberty, the more contentious matters have related to the compatibility of the regime with Art. 6 rights to a fair hearing. Hearings concerning control orders routinely rely upon 'closed' evidence, material that cannot be disclosed to the individual concerned due to security or intelligence risks. Such material is dealt with by a 'special advocate' appointed to represent the interests of the individual. In **Secretary of State for the Home Department v MB** [2007] UKHL 46, the majority held that special advocates could, in principle, counter the risk of procedural unfairness in all but the most exceptional of cases. The matter was considered again in **Secretary of State for the Home Department v AF** (No. 3) [2009] UKHL 28, which followed a determination in Strasbourg that such procedures violated Art. 6 (**A v UK** [2009] ECHR 301). Lord Hoffmann regarded that decision as wrong, but the majority appeared to accept that they were bound by judgment; as Lord Rodger remarked: 'Strasbourg has spoken, the case is closed.'[10] As a result, the government were forced to decide whether to revoke existing control orders, or make further evidence available to achieve the required degree of fairness. (Human Rights Joint Committee (2010)).

[6] This is an important point, as the case law on the area is not, in fact, focused on liberty, but the legality of the derogation.

[7] This is a crucially important case, and should be included in the answer as, arguably, it marked a real shift in the relationship between the judiciary and the executive.

[8] The judgment in this case is complicated, and credit will be given for the ability to summarise the key points clearly.

[9] As this question is concerned with the relationship between the judiciary and the executive there is no need to give detail about the nature of control orders.

[10] It is not essential, or even expected, that students will include many direct quotations in examination answers but a short phrase is useful to include as it makes the answer appear confident, and also neatly expresses the fact that the judiciary appear to feel that they are bound by the European Court of Human Rights.

It can be seen, then, that the Human Rights Act has empowered the judiciary to engage in consideration of matters previously considered to be within an area of executive competence. The structure of the Human Rights Act, however, limits the extent to which these developments can be seen as an alteration to the separation of powers.[11] As McKeever (2010) points out, the judiciary can criticise policy, and indeed legislation, but are powerless to change it. A declaration of incompatibility does not affect the validity of legislation; following the judgment in **Secretary of State for the Home Department v AF** (No. 3), the individuals remained in detention until ACTSA was repealed by the legislature.[12] Similarly, despite the ruling that the procedure for obtaining control orders is flawed, they remained in force unless and until the executive instigated change.

[11] Having explored the judicial response to anti-terrorism measures, the answer needs to return to the issue of the separation of powers.

[12] This is an important point to make, as the HRA was drafted to preserve parliamentary supremacy.

The readiness to address executive decision-making in these cases can be seen as evidence of the strength of the doctrine of separation of powers, as the judiciary operate to check the use of executive powers. The preservation of parliamentary supremacy, however, ensures that the basic shape of the constitution remains unchanged.

✓ Make your answer stand out

- By discussing in more detail how judicial review of anti-terrorism measures forms part of a system of checks and balances to prevent the arbitrary exercise of power. This could make reference to some of the theorists who have commented on the separation of powers. The last chapter in Vile, L. (1998) *Constitutionalism and the Separation of Powers* (2nd edn). Indianapolis: Liberty Fund Inc provides an overview of the changing role of the judiciary.

- By staying up to date. It cannot be stressed enough how quickly this area of law develops. Check important judgments and recent academic comment so that you can include matters that are not yet in the textbooks. The journal *Public Law* is a good starting point and should be checked regularly.

- Expanding the discussion regarding the decision in *Secretary of State for the Home Department* v *AF (No. 3)* [2009] UKHL 28, and in particular the fact that the courts feel bound by the ECtHR. This could be contrasted with the decision in *R (GC and C)* v *Commissioner of the Police for the Metropolis* [2010] EWHC 2225 (Admin), in which the courts appeared to prefer a more traditional approach to parliamentary supremacy. This could show an ability to address the complexities of the argument.

! Don't be tempted to . . .

- Attempt to outline all 'terrorism' legislation that has been enacted since 2000. If you do this, you will end up with an answer that lists a lot of law, but which includes little analysis. The answer should concentrate on one or two provisions that allow for analysis of the relationship between government and the judiciary.

- Spend too much time explaining the structure of the constitution and the meaning of the separation of powers in general terms. Discussion of the doctrine must be focused on the issue of anti-terrorism measures. Weaker answers tend to approach this question as if it were a question about constitutional doctrines.

www.pearsoned.co.uk/lawexpressqa

 Go online to access more revision support including additional essay and problem questions with diagram plans, You be the marker questions, and download all diagrams from the book.

Parliament and parliamentary supremacy

2

How this topic may come up in exams

Examiners may require you to demonstrate knowledge about how Parliament is regulated. This necessitates an understanding of parliamentary privilege, and could be either a problem scenario or an essay question. Here, you will be rewarded for an ability to draw on current examples to support your arguments. Alternatively, you may be asked to discuss the position of Parliament within broader constitutional arrangements and in particular, to discuss the relevance of the doctrine of parliamentary sovereignty. This aspect is commonly tested by essay questions requiring a focus on one or more issues affecting the constitutional position of Parliament.

■ Attack the question

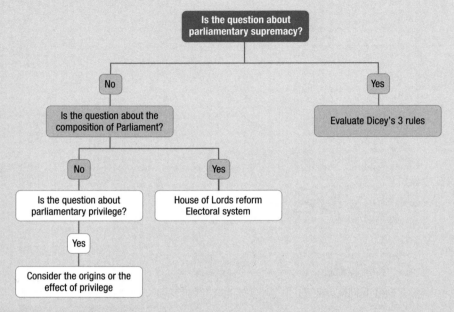

A printable version of this diagram is available from www.pearsoned.co.uk/lawexpressqa

❓ Question 1

Tom, the editor of the student union newspaper, seeks your advice. He recently published an article concerning a local MP, Mr Jones, which reported that the MP had strongly opposed an increase in fuel tax in parliamentary debates. The article paraphrased the questions that were asked and recorded in *Hansard*. The article reported that Mr Jones had referred to a prominent environmental campaigner, Natalie Turner, as a 'blithering idiot'. The proposals were defeated. The article alleged that two months later the MP was rewarded with a place on the board of a fuel company. Mr Jones has commenced libel proceedings against Tom. Tom has also received a summons to attend the House of Commons for 'contempt of the House', and a letter from Ms Turner's solicitor complaining about the inclusion of reports of comments about her in the article. Tom wants to know if he will be able to defend the court proceedings by using records of the debates, and what the summons to the House of Commons means.

Advise Tom.

Answer plan

➜ Identify that the problem concerns the regulation of parliamentary proceedings.

➜ Explain the privilege awarded to 'parliamentary proceedings, and the defence of qualified privilege'.

➜ Refer to the Defamation Act 1996, section 13.

➜ Explain the meaning of 'contempt of the House'.

Diagram plan

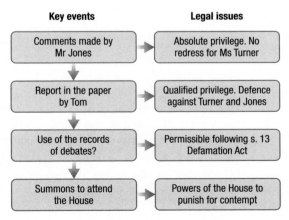

Key events	Legal issues
Comments made by Mr Jones	Absolute privilege. No redress for Ms Turner
Report in the paper by Tom	Qualified privilege. Defence against Turner and Jones
Use of the records of debates?	Permissible following s. 13 Defamation Act
Summons to attend the House	Powers of the House to punish for contempt

A printable version of this diagram plan is available from www.pearsoned.co.uk/lawexpressqa

Answer

¹ This introduction picks out
the important events from the
scenario and links them to
the legal issue. This is a good
way to start an answer to a
problem scenario. You should
never begin by simply rewriting
the facts of the scenario.

² It is helpful to learn some
explanations of key concepts,
so that you can give a
succinct definition of the
topic area to be addressed.

³ Rather than listing every
example of privilege that you
can remember, be specific
in identifying those that are
relevant.

⁴ Article 9 of the Bill of Rights
is central to a question
concerning parliamentary
privilege, so it is useful to
be able to give a concise
explanation.

⁵ When using case law, it is
vital that you explain how
the legal principle identified
impacts on the facts of the
scenario you are dealing with.
Here, it is important to explain
that the ruling in *A* v *UK*
means that there is an
absolute bar on an action
for defamation against the
Member of Parliament.

⁶ The answer does need to
set out the law relating to
absolute privilege, but here
you remind the examiner that
you have not lost focus on
the specific questions asked.

This scenario raises issues concerning parliamentary privilege. In considering the comments made regarding Ms Turner, it is necessary to determine the extent of the privilege afforded to parliamentary proceedings, and whether or not this provides protection to Tom. Secondly, in considering the proposed action by Mr Jones, it will be necessary to determine when records of parliamentary proceedings may be adduced as evidence in court proceedings. Lastly, it will be necessary to address the powers held by Parliament to discipline Members and non-Members alike for contempt.¹ Parliamentary privilege is a term used to describe rules protecting the House of Commons and the House of Lords from any outside interference. Privilege is enjoyed by both individual Members of Parliament and the collective institutions and, as *Erskine May* explains, to a certain extent provides exemption from the general law.² Relevant to this scenario are the privileges afforded to Parliament to regulate its own affairs, and the protection given to freedom of speech during parliamentary proceedings.³

Article 9 of the Bill of Rights states that freedom of speech in Parliament is protected from impeachment or question by any body; this includes the judiciary.⁴ Therefore, parliamentary privilege protects a Member of Parliament from civil actions for defamation in respect of comments made during parliamentary proceedings. The case of ***A* v United Kingdom (Application 35373/97)** [2002] All ER (D) 264 (Dec) confirmed the existence of this absolute privilege. In that case, a Member of Parliament made comments about a constituent during a debate which was reported in the press. She claimed that the fact she was unable to challenge the remarks in court breached her Art. 6 right to a fair trial, as well as her rights under Art. 8 (respect for her private life) and Art. 13 (right to a remedy). The European Court found that despite the 'regrettable' nature of the comments, there was no breach of Convention rights as Art. 9 was necessary to protect the freedom of speech in Parliament. Therefore, it is clear that Ms Turner cannot bring a claim for defamation against the MP Mr Jones.⁵ However, the scenario asks us to consider whether or not Tom could be liable for libel in reporting the comments made.⁶

Should court proceedings be instigated, Tom would be able to claim the defence of qualified privilege. The report of the debate in *Hansard* attracts absolute privilege due to the Parliamentary Papers Act 1840.

It is accepted that there is a public interest in the business of Parliament, and there can be no successful action for defamation against a 'fair and accurate' report of parliamentary proceedings (**Wason v Walter** (1868) LR 4 QB 73). We are told that Tom has 'paraphrased' the proceedings, but there is no requirement for the report to be verbatim in order for it to attract qualified privilege. This was confirmed in the case of **Cook v Alexander** [1974] QB 279, where a 'Parliamentary sketch' was held not to be defamatory, despite the fact it was a selective account, as it conveyed the general tenor of the debate. In order to succeed against Tom, Ms Turner would have to prove that the report was malicious. On the facts given, this does not appear to be a sustainable claim and Tom should be advised that should an action be brought, he will have a valid defence.[7]

[7] Having set out the relevant law, it is important to then apply this to give advice to Tom, as the question requires.

Tom also includes in the report allegations about the conduct of Mr Jones. This has resulted in an action from the MP as an individual, but also from the House. Dealing first with the action by Mr Jones, these facts appear to recall the events surrounding the libel action brought by the MP Neil Hamilton against the *Guardian* newspapers following the allegation that he took cash for questions in the 1990s.[8] This case demonstrated that in providing protection for MPs from actions in defamation, Art. 9 also limited the ability of members to sue when libellous statements were made about them. To defend the claim, the *Guardian* wished to adduce evidence of questions asked in the House in order to demonstrate the truth of the allegations. Article 9 prevents proceedings in Parliament being questioned in court, and **Prebble v Television New Zealand** (1995) 15 LS 204 confirmed that, where a party's defence depended on such inadmissible material, proceedings should be stayed as it would be unjust to deny the defendant the ability to properly present their case. Accordingly, Hamilton was unable to bring his claim. This resulted in the passing of the Defamation Act 1996 which, at section 13, amends the Bill of Rights by allowing an individual MP to waive privilege so that an action can proceed. Tom should be advised therefore, that he will be able to adduce evidence of parliamentary proceedings if the records of the debate will help him argue that the claims made about Mr Jones are correct.[9]

[8] Although you should generally refrain from giving too much factual detail concerning cases, where there are analogous facts, then it is worth highlighting them in order to point out the similarity because this means the ratio is clearly applicable to the scenario.

[9] The information given regarding the Hamilton affair is only useful if it is used to provide a solution to the problem set out in the question.

Parliamentary privilege also allows both Houses to discipline Members and non-Members alike for 'contempt' of the House. 'Contempt' is a poorly defined term but would cover any conduct which brings the

[10] In this answer, you don't need to provide a list of examples of behaviours that could be contempt, but this general definition makes it clear that you know the meaning of the term.

[11] This is one of the instances in which it is helpful to briefly refer to the facts; you are using this case to show that there is a historical precedent for the House taking action against journalists for contempt.

[12] It is easy to highlight the various methods of punishment that exist for contempt, but it is important to try to assess whether it is really likely that these would be invoked.

[13] It is useful to conclude by providing a summary of the advice to the client to ensure that it is clear all points have been covered.

reputation of the House into disrepute.[10] These matters would be investigated by the Committee on Standards and Privileges acting on the advice of, in this case, the Speaker of the Commons. If it is found that the publication of allegations regarding Mr Jones constitute contempt, then Tom could face censure. *Junor's Case* (HC 38 1956–57) concerned a *Sunday Express* article suggesting that MPs afforded themselves preferential treatment in respect of fuel allowances, and the editor was summoned to appear before the house to be admonished.[11] Theoretically the House has powers to punish for contempt, including the power to imprison offenders, although this has not been invoked since 1880. The Joint Committee on Privileges has stressed that the power to punish should only be used in extreme circumstances where absolutely necessary for the protection of Parliament. Therefore, it is unlikely that Tom would face any penalty.[12]

It should perhaps be noted that, should the allegations be correct, then Mr Jones would clearly be in contempt, as it is not permitted for any MP to participate in a debate in which he or she has a financial interest.

It can be seen then that the newspaper report may expose Tom to three distinct proceedings. First, Ms Turner could bring an action for libel. However, Tom will be able to claim qualified privilege. Mr Jones could bring libel proceedings and, following the Defamation Act, Tom can adduce records of the debate in his defence. In theory, Tom could be punished for a contempt, but it is doubtful that any penalty would be applied.[13]

✓ Make your answer stand out

- By giving more attention to the legal effect of qualified privilege. You should refer to *Reynolds* v *Times Newspaper Ltd* [2001] 2 AC 127, which remains the key authority.

- By referring to the Convention rights which could be in issue and discussing whether or not Art. 10 can assist Tom. This will show the examiner an ability to draw links between different parts of the syllabus.

- When considering whether or not the House might censure Tom for contempt, this could be assessed in the light of ongoing publicity given to issues such as MP's expenses. You could argue that it is highly unlikely action would be taken given the public opprobrium. This would show the examiner an ability to make connections between current affairs and constitutional issues.

! Don't be tempted to . . .

- Give generalised information about parliamentary privilege; the answer needs to focus on solving the problems outlined in the scenario. You do need to outline that the MP enjoys absolute privilege, for example, as this is the background to Tom's potential defence of qualified privilege. However, you should avoid the temptation to spend too long looking at this issue.

- Write a detailed history of the Hamilton affair, or indeed, the other cases you mention. This can be a difficult balance to strike, but, as a rule of thumb, you should only mention the facts to demonstrate that you understand the *ratio*; or to highlight a similarity, or significant difference, from the scenario given.

? Question 2

The Minister for Housing, Mrs Taylor, has recently introduced a Bill to the Commons proposing a simplification to planning procedures which would make it easier for landlords to convert properties into houses for multiple occupation. An MP, Mr Rafiq, receives a letter from his constituent Alexia Clements, alleging that Mrs Taylor has been bribed by a student housing company who would benefit from the change, and that the company provide Mrs Taylor's daughter with rent-free accommodation whilst she is at university.

Mr Rafiq forwards the letter to the Commissioner for Parliamentary Standards, and to the Shadow Minister for Housing. In a debate on the Bill, Mr Rafiq reads out the letter, including a passage which describes Mrs Taylor as an 'odious, slippery character who cannot be trusted'.

Later on, whilst in a Commons cafeteria, Mr Rafiq is asked about the matter by a fellow MP and reads the letter out again. This is overheard by several of Mrs Taylor's colleagues.

Mrs Taylor is informed, and storms in. She pours a jug of water over Mr Rafiq's head.

Advise Mr Rafiq, Ms Clements and Mrs Taylor about the possible consequences of these events.

Answer plan

→ Explain privilege protecting Mr Rafiq from defamation action.

→ Consider definition of 'parliamentary proceedings'.

→ Discuss different position of Ms Clements – qualified privilege.

→ Consider whether privilege extends to cover criminal activity.

→ Explain the requirements of the Register of Members' Interests and the sanctions for failing to comply.

Diagram plan

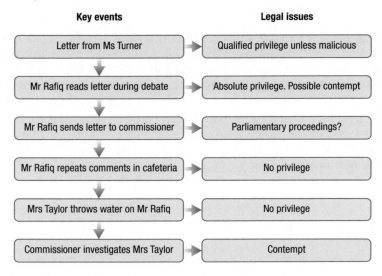

Key events		Legal issues
Letter from Ms Turner	➡️	Qualified privilege unless malicious
Mr Rafiq reads letter during debate	➡️	Absolute privilege. Possible contempt
Mr Rafiq sends letter to commissioner	➡️	Parliamentary proceedings?
Mr Rafiq repeats comments in cafeteria	➡️	No privilege
Mrs Taylor throws water on Mr Rafiq	➡️	No privilege
Commissioner investigates Mrs Taylor	➡️	Contempt

A printable version of this diagram plan is available from www.pearsoned.co.uk/lawexpressqa

Answer

The scenario raises questions about how far Members of Parliament (MPs) can claim the protection of privilege to excuse conduct which may breach civil or criminal law, and whether non-Members enjoy any similar protection. In addition, the allegations made about Mrs Taylor require consideration of the mechanisms which exist to ensure Members of Parliament comply with ethical standards.[1]

The allegations made in the letter received by Mr Rafiq may be libellous. Mrs Taylor may be able to bring civil proceedings in respect of some of his actions. When Mr Rafiq reads the contents of the letter during a debate, he enjoys absolute privilege. Article 9 of the Bill of Rights enshrined the protection of freedom of speech in Parliament, and no action for defamation can arise in respect of any remarks made during parliamentary proceedings. This would be the position even if Mr Rafiq knew the allegations were false, on the authority of **Wason v Walter** (1868) LR 4 QB 73.[2] However, the protection of absolute privilege only protects Members engaged in parliamentary proceedings. When Mr Rafiq repeats the comments in the cafeteria,

[1] You might be tempted to answer this question by focusing exclusively on the privilege of free speech, but the conduct of Ms Taylor should alert you to the need to consider regulation of conduct.

[2] It is unnecessary to give any details about this case, as the only important issue here is the ratio, which means that the advice given to Mr Rafiq about this part of the incident can be given with certainty.

3 Here, you have shown
that you understand that the
issue here is whether or not
privilege affords a defence,
and have done so briefly and
with reference to the facts.
This shows knowledge, and
an ability to apply it.

[3] Here, you have shown
that you understand that the
issue here is whether or not
privilege affords a defence,
and have done so briefly and
with reference to the facts.
This shows knowledge, and
an ability to apply it.

[4] This is an important case
to revise, as the issue of
whether or not an event will
be considered to be part of
'parliamentary proceedings'
is a common area for
examination. The additional
cases are useful, but this is
probably essential.

[5] Here the answer has shown
knowledge of case law and
academic opinion, and used
this to address the problem.

[6] Again, you can gain
extra marks by considering
the privilege of exclusive
cognisance, noting here that
the use of 'unparliamentarily
language' can lead to
a Member being rebuked.

[7] Whilst the position of
Ms Clements needs to be
addressed, you should not
need to spend too long on
considering this aspect of
the scenario, as the position
is fairly simple. There is much
more debate around the extent
of parliamentary proceedings
in relation to the letter, and
you should concentrate more
on that issue.

[8] There is no need to give any
more detail about the criminal
offence, it is simply important
to recognise that a crime has
occurred.

it appears that he is not engaged in the business of Parliament and therefore he would not be able to claim immunity from a civil action in respect of this part of the incident.[3] A question arises as to whether any action can result from the forwarding of the letter to third parties, which is, on the face of it, republication of the libel. It is debatable whether or not this would enjoy the cloak of privilege, as it is not clear that this could be considered to be 'parliamentary proceedings'. The issue was considered in **Strauss and the London Electricity Board Case** [1958] PL 80 which concerned a letter sent by the MP to the Paymaster General, complaining about methods employed by the London Electricity Board.[4] The Committee of Privileges concluded that the letter was covered by privilege, although a subsequent Commons vote rejected this view. The more recent case of **Rost v Edwards** [1990] 2 QB 460 saw the courts refuse to accept evidence of a letter sent to the Speaker, as it was accepted this did constitute 'proceedings in Parliament'. In any event, the point is perhaps rather academic as, even if absolute privilege does not apply, Mr Rafiq would almost certainly be able to claim qualified privilege. This protects him from an action unless Mrs Taylor can prove that he was malicious. The case of **Breech v Freeson** [1972] 1 QB 14 provides support for the suggestion that sending a letter to the minister on a matter of interest to parliamentary business would attract qualified privilege, although Bradley and Ewing (2010) do suggest that passing a constituent's letter on to a minister without any inquiry as to its truth could be considered malicious.[5] Mr Rafiq should also be advised that, irrespective of any civil action, he may also fall to be censured for contempt as a result of his comments during the debate.[6]

The position in respect of Ms Clements is less secure as non-Members do not enjoy the protection of absolute privilege. She may, however, be able to claim qualified privilege provided the letter is sent without malice, on a matter of public interest.[7]

Mrs Taylor has committed the criminal offence of battery when she throws water over Mr Rafiq.[8] Although parliamentary privilege confers a freedom from arrest within the Commons, it appears this is confined to civil matters. In the case of **Bradlaugh v Gossett** (1884) 12 QBD 271 the courts asserted that there was no authority for the suggestion that criminal jurisdiction was excluded from the House of Commons. In 2012, a Labour MP was convicted and sentenced for

[9] This is a good example to include, demonstrating an ability to relate current events to the material you have studied.

common assault following a brawl in a bar in the Houses of Parliament.[9] It is highly unlikely that the fact the incident occurred in the Commons would protect Mrs Taylor from prosecution, as, if privilege were asserted, this would arguably damage the reputation of the House.[10]

[10] You will be rewarded for expressing an opinion here, as long as you can explain your reasons.

Mrs Taylor may also face difficulties if the allegations are investigated by the Commissioner for Parliamentary Standards and found to be correct. The role of the Commissioner was created in response to the report of the Nolan Committee in the wake of the 'cash for questions' scandal during the 1990s. The Commissioner is tasked with maintaining the Register of Members' Interests, and investigating allegations of breaches. The Commissioner reports findings to the Committee on Standards in Public Life, who can impose sanctions. Mrs Taylor should declare, on the Register of Members' Interests, a connection with an organisation providing her with a material benefit. Registration of the connection would not be sufficient in this case, however, as she has initiated proceedings in Parliament by introducing the legislation and should therefore have declared her connection at the introduction of the bill.[11] This would be considered an extremely serious breach of the rules regarding the registration of interests, and a clear contempt. Mrs Taylor should be advised that penalties for contempt can include an order to repay money. Following the 2009 scandal regarding MPs expenses, the Committee ordered a number of MPs to repay large sums of money. In addition, Members can be suspended from Parliament. George Galloway was suspended for 18 days by the Committee in 2006 for concealing matters on the register.[12] In extreme cases, an MP can be required to stand down at the next election. Since the creation of the office of the Commissioner, there has been doubt expressed about the willingness and ability of any parliamentary body to robustly ensure that Members comply with ethical standards. Loveland referred to the response to the Nolan Committee as 'a damp squib'. This issue arose in the wake of the expenses scandal, and resulted in the Parliamentary Standards Act 2009. This has also been criticised because, during the course of debate, clauses which would have resulted in paid advocacy (of the type alleged here) becoming an imprisonable offence were removed. However, given the public concern regarding the conduct of MPs, Mrs Taylor would certainly find herself under considerable pressure to resign irrespective of any action taken by the House.[13]

[11] This is a really important point to make, as it shows awareness of the different degrees of culpability that can arise in respect of the register.

[12] You will be rewarded for being able to demonstrate knowledge of examples of the application of law.

[13] Whilst it is important to use the answer to demonstrate a good knowledge of the topic, the information must be utilised to assist in giving an opinion about Mrs Taylor's predicament.

[14] As the answer has dealt with a number of individuals and issues, the conclusion should briefly summarise the advice to each party.

Mr Rafiq would be covered by absolute or qualified privileges in respect of all actions save for the casual conversation outside of the Commons chamber. Ms Clements would probably be able to rely on qualified privilege. Mrs Taylor may face criminal prosecution for the attack on Mr Rafiq. She may also face sanction from the Committee if the allegations are investigated and validated by the Commissioner on Parliamentary Standards.[14]

 Make your answer stand out

- Conduct of parliamentary business is extremely topical. You should ensure you keep up to date with developments that occur during your studies, as you may find illustrative examples to use that are not yet in the textbooks. This will demonstrate that you have a clear understanding of the legal principles, and can identify significant issues independently.
- By demonstrating an understanding of how Parliament operates in more detail, for example by explaining the role that the Speaker would play in each of the possible contempt situations.

! Don't be tempted to . . .

- Spend time explaining the origins of the privileges referred to. Most of the marks in this question will be given for being able to apply the law to the facts given. So, rather than explaining the constitutional justification for absolute privilege, you must instead concentrate on assessing whether Mr Rafiq can claim privilege.
- Explain the background to the cash for questions scandal in any detail. It is worth mentioning to be able to explain the origins of the office of the Commissioner, but you should avoid writing a long, descriptive account of what happened.

 Question 3

Membership of the European Union has ensured that parliamentary sovereignty is no longer a significant part of the United Kingdom constitution.

Discuss.

Answer plan

→ Outline the traditional doctrine of parliamentary sovereignty.

→ Consider the impact of the EU on the ability to legislate on any subject matter, or to be the supreme law-making body.

→ Consider the impact of the doctrine on implied repeal.

→ Discuss whether the 'enrolled bill' rule survives.

Diagram plan

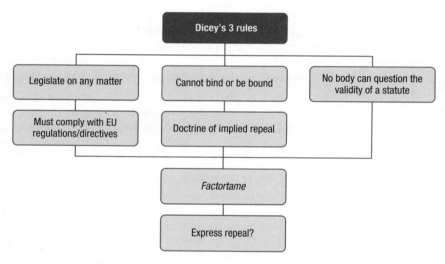

A printable version of this diagram plan is available from www.pearsoned.co.uk/lawexpressqa

Answer

[1] In order to do well with this question the focus must be on the impact of membership of the European Union on parliamentary supremacy. There is a need to explain the key tenets of the doctrine but this should be dealt with as succinctly as possible so that the answer can move on to address the central issue.

Dicey described the doctrine of parliamentary supremacy as the 'cornerstone' of the UK constitution. The doctrine consists of three elements. Parliament is the supreme law-making body, able to legislate on any subject matter of its choosing. No Parliament can bind its successors, or be bound by its predecessors. Once an Act of Parliament has received Royal Assent, no person or body can question the validity of the legislation.[1] It can be argued that membership of the European Union has diluted the principle of parliamentary supremacy. The United Kingdom became a member of the European Community in 1972, and the European Communities Act 1972 (ECA), section 2 allows Community law to take direct effect in domestic law. Section 2(4) states that domestic legislation should be construed subject to the rule in section 2(1); to give effect to EU rights.[2] It can be argued that these provisions lead to a position where it can neither be said that Parliament remains the supreme law-making body of the United Kingdom, nor that Parliament cannot be bound.

The institutions of the European Union can enact legislation which takes direct effect in the United Kingdom without the need for any further action by Parliament. In **Costa v ENEL** (Case 6/64) [1964] ECR 585 the European Court of Justice confirmed that community law prevails over the national law of member states.[3] This could suggest that supremacy was ceded to the European institutions. It should be noted, however, that this is limited to matters within the competence of the treaties. Further, although subsequent treaties have extended the scope of the European Union, the United Kingdom has retained the power to opt out of particular provisions.[4] For example, the United Kingdom has opted out of provisions giving the European Union powers in relation to immigration and asylum in the Lisbon Treaty (2009), and retains the power to opt in or out of any policies concerning justice and home affairs.[5]

Although it is clear that Parliament retains the theoretical power to legislate on any matter of its choosing, arguably membership of the European Union has limited this element of supremacy. Questions arise when domestic legislation conflicts with European Union law.[6] According to Dicey, Parliament cannot be bound by its predecessors, leading to the doctrine of implied repeal, illustrated by **Vauxhall Estates Ltd v Liverpool Corporation** [1932] 1 KB 733. The case concerned a dispute regarding the compensation scheme applicable in a compulsory purchase of land. The Acquisition of Land (Assessment of Compensation) Act 1919 laid down a scheme, and further stated that any inconsistent provision would be ineffective. The Housing Act 1925 created a different payment scheme, without expressly repealing the earlier Act. It was held that the later Act impliedly repealed the earlier provisions, and that any suggestion that an Act could prevent a future Parliament from making alterations was inconsistent with the constitution. Accordingly, it would seem clear that any legislation passed after 1972 which conflicts with

[2] It is important that you can explain section 2 of the Act, as it is this provision that, arguably, impacts on supremacy.

[3] When dealing with the relationship between the European Union and the United Kingdom, it will be important to note the effect of this case, even though it did not concern the United Kingdom; it creates a general principle applicable to all member states.

[4] It is helpful to include this information here, to give some balance and demonstrate an awareness that there is more than one way to view the significance of membership of the European Union.

[5] You will be rewarded for the ability to provide examples to support the points that you make.

[6] The relationship between Parliament and the European Union when there is conflict must be the central focus of the answer.

[7] It is important to not only explain the doctrine of implied repeal, but also to be very explicit about the issue that arises in relation to laws which conflict with EU law; evidence can now be considered to determine whether or not the doctrine applies to the European Communities Act.

[8] This is a good point to make, as it shows that instances of irresolvable conflict are relatively rare.

[9] Any question considering the effect of EU membership on supremacy will demand that you are able to explain the importance of the *Factortame* litigation, and the fact that it can be said to undermine the doctrine of implied repeal.

[10] The issue raised earlier regarding the doctrine of implied repeal and the ECA has now been examined, and a definitive answer can be given.

European Union law should take effect, as section 2(4) could not bind future Parliaments.[7]

In the majority of cases, conflicts have been resolved by the process of statutory interpretation, and have determined that, if there is any ambiguity, legislation should be read on the assumption that Parliament's intention would be to comply with EU law.[8] This was the 'purposive' approach adopted in *Pickstone v Freemans* [1988] AC 66 and *Lister v Forth Dry Dock Engineering* [1990] 1 AC 546. In both cases the courts declined to say that legislation was incompatible with EU law but in order to reach that position it was necessary to impose an interpretation which ignored the plain meaning of the words of the statute. These cases did not have to determine the correct approach arising if a legislative provision directly contradicted Community law and interpretation was not possible.

The issue fell to be determined in the series of cases concerning the Merchant Shipping Act 1988 (*R v Secretary of State for Transport ex parte Factortame Ltd* (No. 2) [1991] 1 AC 603).[9] The legislation, which sought to impose a registration requirement on foreign fishermen, contravened Community rights concerning discrimination, trade, and the free movements of workers. The company sought an interim injunction suspending the incompatible parts of the legislation pending a ruling from the European Court of Justice (ECJ). This left the House of Lords in a position where they had to determine whether or not to apply an Act of Parliament, or to apply Community law. The House of Lords referred the matter to the ECJ for a ruling, and accepted the decision that interim relief should be granted. The matter was ultimately resolved by amending legislation. However, the constitutional effect was an acceptance that Community law took precedence and, therefore, that section 2(4) appeared to be entrenched, and protected from the doctrine of implied repeal.[10]

To this extent then it appears that the 1972 Parliament was able to effectively bind its successors, undermining a key element of the doctrine of parliamentary supremacy. However, Laws LJ, in the case *Thoburn v Sunderland City Council* [2002] EWHC 195 (Admin), sought to draw a distinction between 'ordinary' statutes and statutes of 'constitutional significance'. In his view, the latter include all statutes which alter constitutional arrangements. Such Acts, according to this view, are not subject to implied repeal. He argued this is not a position created by, or unique to, the ECA but 'purely from the law of England'. Such statutes can be altered, but only by express repeal. If this is accepted, then the ECA alone has not altered the constitutional position of Parliament.[11] It is clear that, in theory, it would be open to any Parliament to expressly repeal section 2(4) or indeed any other part of the Act. In **McCarthys Ltd v Smith** [1979] ICR 785, Lord Denning expressed the clear view that the courts would apply an inconsistent legislative provision if it was made expressly. Such a decision would inevitably lead to conflict between the United Kingdom and the European Union, but this would be a matter for the legislature who can still choose to withdraw from the European Union.

[11] Recognition of the possibility of express repeal is important, as this shows that even though some supremacy can be said to have passed to the European Union, Parliament could reverse that decision.

Membership of the European Union has undoubtedly altered the constitutional landscape and has led to a situation where the domestic courts will not always obey a Parliamentary provision. It should always be remembered, though, that continued membership is a choice, and that any future Parliament could choose to withdraw. Although there may be political, economic and social constraints rendering this proposition purely hypothetical, it would appear that the constitutional position is clear. Any decision to cede supremacy to the European Union has been voluntary, and accordingly, supremacy can theoretically be reclaimed.[12]

[12] The conclusion should refer directly to the question and provide an answer. No new material is introduced here, but the conclusions refer to matters addressed in the body of the essay.

 Make your answer stand out

- By recognising that parliamentary supremacy is undermined by numerous factors, not just the EU. The focus needs to be on Community law, but you would be rewarded for stating that the growth in the power of the executive, devolution, and the Human Rights Act have also contributed.

- By exploring in more detail the suggestion that express repeal would be possible; though this may only be hypothetical as economic and diplomatic concerns would prevent this.

- By considering the effect of the Eurozone crisis upon the relationship between the UK Parliament and the European Union. You could, for example, look at the difficulties experienced by the Coalition in November 2012 following a Commons debate regarding the EU budget. This kind of example would allow you to explore the limits of parliamentary influence over negotiations with the EU.

Don't be tempted to . . .

- Focus on exploring Dicey's explanation of parliamentary sovereignty in detail. Students sometimes make the mistake of answering any question on parliamentary supremacy by explaining each of the rules in detail. You need to be able to recognise that the examiner wants you to focus on the effect of the legislative power of the European institutions.

- Ignore the fact that the United Kingdom is able to negotiate with Europe and opt out of certain provisions. Students sometimes overstate the extent of European powers, which leads to a rather simplistic argument.

📝 Question 4

Since the Human Rights Act 1998, the balance of power has shifted so that it is the judges who are sovereign, rather than Westminster.

Discuss.

Answer plan

→ Outline Dicey's traditional analysis of parliamentary sovereignty and the role of the courts.
→ Assess the effect of section 3 on the powers of the judiciary.
→ Assess the effect of section 4 on the powers of the judiciary.
→ Consider whether the HRA has significantly altered the relationship between the two institutions of state.

Diagram plan

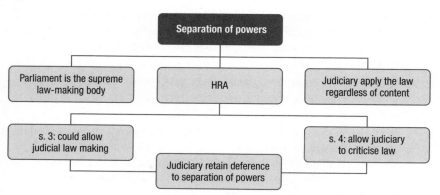

A printable version of this diagram plan is available from www.pearsoned.co.uk/lawexpressqa

Answer

It is commonly understood that Parliament occupies a position of supremacy within the United Kingdom. Dicey described parliamentary supremacy as a 'cornerstone' of the constitution. Under the doctrine of the separation of powers, Parliament has the authority to legislate, and the judiciary apply the law in accordance with Parliament's wishes.[1] The Human Rights Act 1998 imposed new obligations on Parliament when creating legislation, and granted the judiciary new powers to interpret and challenge legislation. It is sometimes suggested that this has led to a shift in the constitutional balance; however, it will be argued that the Act has not signalled any significant change.[2]

In considering Parliament's role in the wake of the Human Rights Act, it is helpful to begin by considering the traditional doctrine of parliamentary supremacy. Dicey described three constituent elements. First, Parliament is the supreme law-making body, free to make or unmake legislation on any subject matter. Secondly, each successive Parliament is sovereign; no Parliament can be bound by its predecessors, or bind its successors. Lastly, no person or body, including the courts, can question the validity of an Act of Parliament.[3] To address the question, it is necessary to consider Parliament's role as the supreme law-making body in the United Kingdom.

The United Kingdom signed the European Convention on Human Rights (ECHR) in 1950, and it has been possible for an individual to petition the European Court of Human Rights (ECtHR) since 1966, allowing a citizen to claim that legislation infringed one or more of their rights under the Convention and seek redress in Strasbourg. Although the Human Rights Act 1998 incorporated the Convention into domestic law, it did not confer any new rights upon citizens, but rather created a new 'procedural mechanism' for enforcing those rights[4] (**R v Lambert** [2001] UKHL 37). The question is whether the procedures established by the Act have impacted upon the constitutional relationship between Parliament and the judiciary.

In deference to the sovereignty of Parliament, the role of the courts is to interpret and apply legislation regardless of its content. Hence, in **R v IRC ex parte Rossminster** [1980] AC 952, the Lords considered powers conferred by the Taxes Management Act 1970 to be

[1] The respective constitutional roles of the legislature and the judiciary is central to the answer, and so the introduction should briefly set out the traditional position.

[2] Setting out the central argument about the effect of the HRA in the introduction will give the essay some shape, as the major points can refer back to this statement.

[3] This question requires demonstration of an understanding of the doctrine, but it is not the main focus. Therefore, the definition should be set out as succinctly as possible.

[4] It is important to recognise that the HRA has not granted new rights; citizens were able to enforce Article rights prior to 2000, although this would involve the laborious process of taking a claim to the ECtHR in Strasbourg.

a 'breath-taking' inroad upon rights of privacy and property, but nonetheless felt bound to apply the provisions.[5] The Human Rights Act gives the courts new powers. Section 3 requires the courts to interpret statutes in a manner compatible with Convention rights 'in so far as it is possible to do so'. If this is not possible, then section 4 gives the courts discretion to make a declaration of incompatibility. Amending legislation can then be laid before Parliament although this is not mandatory (s. 4).[6]

It is the operation of these sections of the Human Rights Act which raises questions about the continued supremacy of parliamentary legislation.[7] Shortly after the Act came into force, the courts had occasion to consider the extent of the power conferred by section 3 in the case of *R v A* [2001] UKHL 25. The courts found that provisions in the Youth Justice and Criminal Evidence Act 1999 conflicted with the rights of defendants under Art. 6, and it was held that the statute should be interpreted to give effect to those rights, despite the fact that this conflicted with the clear words of the offending legislation. Lord Steyn felt this was acceptable as section 3 of the Human Rights Act allowed for an interpretation that was 'linguistically strained'. In the dissenting judgment, Lord Hope expressed concern that such utilisation of section 3 ran the risk of the judiciary usurping the role of Parliament. If the Human Rights Act allows the courts to effectively rewrite legislation, then it is no longer correct to view Parliament as the sole and supreme legislative authority within the constitution.[8]

However, the decisions in cases such as *R v A*, and *Ghaidan v Godin-Mendoza* [2004] UKHL 30 should be viewed in the context of the general development of jurisprudence in the wake of the Human Rights Act. Lord Steyn felt that section 4 should be used as a 'last resort', but the courts have tended to resile from using section 3 to make radical alterations to statute. In *Re S* [2002] UKHL 10, whilst not directly criticising the decision in *R v A*, the judgment cautioned the judiciary against use of interpretative powers being used 'inadvertently' to stray from their constitutional role into making legislation. In *Wilson v First County Trust Ltd* [2003] UKHL 40 the Court of Appeal refused to impose upon the words of statute a 'meaning which they cannot bear', preferring to make a declaration of incompatibility under section 4. Indeed, despite Lord Steyn's view, it seems the courts have tended to defer to Parliament where there is conflict, and to invoke section 4 more frequently than he envisaged.

[5] This case provides a clear illustration of the traditional position, in which the judiciary enforced a law they plainly felt should be changed.

[6] You need to explain sections 3 and 4 because these are the critical sections of the HRA here, as they confer power and responsibilities on the judiciary.

[7] It is necessary to display a clear understanding of the mechanics of the Act, and how the particular sections have created powers which could be said to undermine supremacy.

[8] This point refers back to the question by directly addressing the effect of the HRA on parliamentary supremacy.

[9] Section 4 can be viewed as undermining supremacy by allowing the courts to declare an Act of Parliament incompatible but you should recognise that this is less radical than it may at first appear, as the courts cannot disregard legislation.

A declaration of incompatibility does not undermine the legislative authority of Parliament. Section 4 makes it clear that making a declaration has no effect on the parties in the case, as the legislation remains in force unless and until Parliament chooses to amend or revoke it.[9] In **A v Secretary of State for the Home Department** [2004] UKHL 56, a declaration was made in respect of the provisions in the Anti-Terrorism, Crime and Security Act 2001 allowing for the indefinite detention without trial of foreign nationals. Nonetheless, the individuals concerned remained in custody until the Act was repealed by the Prevention of Terrorism Act 2005.[10]

[10] The case of *A* v *UK* is generally used to highlight the increasing power of the judiciary to challenge Parliament; here, you show a detailed knowledge of the authority and should be rewarded for using the case to make a different point.

If it is accepted that, where the wording of statute is unambiguous, the courts prefer to use section 4 rather than to attempt an interpretation using section 3, then it is difficult to maintain that the Human Rights Act has resulted in a seismic shift in the constitutional balance of power.[11] It seems that the judiciary maintain a position of deference to the sovereign power of Parliament.

[11] This is reiterating the point made in the introduction, giving coherence to the answer.

 Make your answer stand out

- By addressing the argument that the Human Rights Act is a 'statute of constitutional significance' which arguably leads to partial entrenchment. This could be used to suggest that the effect has been to entrench the increased powers of the judiciary, therefore undermining the role of Parliament.

- By referring to the number of cases which still fall to be resolved at Strasbourg, which suggests that the domestic judiciary still defer to Parliament to a large extent. A fairly recent example would be *Gillan and Quinton* v *United Kingdom* [2009] ECHR 28, in which the ECtHR held that section 44 of the Terrorism Act 2000 breached Convention rights, overturning the decision of the House of Lords.

- By discussing the efforts of the Coalition to encourage greater subsidiarity, with reference to the Brighton Declaration of 2012 (http://hub.coe.int/20120419-brighton-declaration).

- You could consider the issue of prisoner voting and the resulting conflict between the will of Parliament and the ECtHR.

! Don't be tempted to . . .

- Make general points about the Human Rights Act (HRA). The question requires you specifically to address the impact of the legislation on the judiciary, so you need to be clear about identifying that section 3 and section 4 are the most relevant.
- Fail to provide evidence of how the courts use their powers. To do well in this question, you will need to be able to use case law effectively to illustrate how the HRA has taken effect.
- Ignore the fact that there are different views that can be taken about the effect of the HRA. You should be able to provide examples of the courts appearing to use the HRA to challenge legislative authority (*R* v *A*) but you will be rewarded if you also provide instances of continuing judicial deference.

Question 5

The Parliamentary Expenses Scandal focused public attention on the House of Commons, prompting an unprecedented programme of reform which has resulted in a more representative and more accountable legislature.

Discuss.

Answer plan

→ Briefly explain the parliamentary expenses scandal.

→ Define what is meant by 'representativeness'.

→ Outline the reforms which resulted from the scandal.

→ Consider the effect of the Parliamentary Standards Act.

→ Assess the impact of the Wright report.

Diagram plan

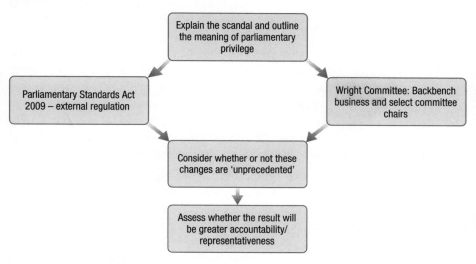

Explain the scandal and outline the meaning of parliamentary privilege

Parliamentary Standards Act 2009 – external regulation

Wright Committee: Backbench business and select committee chairs

Consider whether or not these changes are 'unprecedented'

Assess whether the result will be greater accountability/ representativeness

A printable version of this diagram plan is available from www.pearsoned.co.uk/lawexpressqa

Answer

In 2009, details of expenses claims made by MPs were leaked to the *Daily Telegraph*. The resulting public outcry led to cross party support for reform to the parliamentary system for dealing with expenses.[1] The Liberal Democrats and the Conservatives made much of the need to rebuild trust during the 2010 election campaign and the Coalition Agreement promised a series of reforms to both the Commons and the Lords. Although some key issues appear to have been removed from the agenda at least for the time being (reforms to the electoral system and the House of Lords), there have been significant alterations to the system regulating expenses and the conduct of parliamentary business. It will be argued that these reforms are far from unprecedented and that far greater change would be required before it can be claimed that the legislature is either representative, or accountable.[2]

The expenses scandal originated in a Freedom of Information Act request initially resisted by the Commons and, in particular, the then Speaker on the basis of claimed privilege. Parliamentary privilege

[1] There is no need to describe the facts exposed by the scandal in any detail: the focus here must be on the political response.

[2] A confident answer will often explain at the outset the direction the argument will take.

refers to the special protections enjoyed by members of both houses, both individually and collectively, enshrined by Article 9 of the Bill of Rights 1689 to ensure that the legislature can act without fear of arbitrary interference by the Crown.[3] Parliamentary privilege protects freedom of speech by granting members immunity from legal action taken in respect of 'parliamentary business', and grants exclusive cognisance to MPs and peers to regulate their own affairs without judicial interference. In the wake of the scandal there was an acknowledgement that trust needed to be rebuilt (see, *inter alia*, Fox (2009), and some argued that privilege (exclusive cognisance in particular) had contributed to a lack of accountability.[4]

Any view regarding the representativeness of the legislature will depend upon how the term is defined. If 'representation' requires members to accurately reflect the socio-economic, race and gender balance of the electorate, then Parliament (with its concentration of public-school-educated, white males) could not be described in these terms. For the purpose of this discussion, 'representation' will be used to refer to the ability of ministers to act in accordance with the views and opinions of their constituents.[5]

The first legislative response to the scandal was the Parliamentary Standards Act of 2009 which established an external body to regulate MPs' expenses: the Independent Parliamentary Standards Authority (IPSA). It also established the post of Commissioner for Parliamentary Investigations and a new criminal offence at section 10. On the face of it these measures have the potential to increase accountability and significantly erode the privilege of self-regulation by introducing external oversight of expenses. Some commentators have argued, however, that the changes are largely symbolic. Parpworth (2010)[6] has pointed out that despite the creation of a regulatory body, decisions of the Commissioner are likely to be immune from judicial scrutiny, given that in *R* v *Parliamentary Commissioner for Standards ex parte Al-Fayed* [1998] 1 WLR 669, it was held that 'the activities of Parliament are not the basic fare of judicial review'.[7]

In any event, IPSA will only deal with matters relating to expenses claims; all other forms of parliamentary misconduct still fall to be dealt with using systems of internal regulation, and this system depends upon a willingness within the House of Commons to apply enforcement measures. Referral to the Commissioner for

[3] Here, the answer explains clearly why the two issues are interrelated.

[4] It is important to link the expenses scandal to parliamentary privilege because you need to consider the events from the perspective of a constitutional lawyer.

[5] Where there is more than one way of interpreting a particular term it is important to demonstrate that this is understood. However, it is acceptable to discuss only one meaning as long as this is explained.

[6] Whenever you say there are 'some' or 'many' sources of support for a particular point you should provide at least one example in support of your claim.

[7] Here it can be seen that reading around the subject can be really beneficial, providing you with material to support a more complex analysis.

Parliamentary Standards for a breach of the Ministerial Code is, currently, a matter for the Prime Minister, a position that has been criticised following the decision not to refer Liam Fox and, later, Jeremy Hunt. The case of Hunt is particularly interesting, as the rationale for declining a referral was the ongoing judicial inquiry headed by Lord Leveson. Lord Leveson publicly stated that he would not rule upon whether Hunt had breached the code or not, as this fell outside the terms of reference of the inquiry. This situation demonstrates a difficulty with the coexistence of internal regulatory bodies with external tribunals – whilst the latter may appear to promise greater transparency, here it appears to have created an 'accountability gap'.[8]

Despite all the publicity surrounding the response to the scandal, the MPs in question were dealt with under the pre-existing law.[9] In **R v Chaytor and others** [2010] UKSC 52 the courts held that privilege did not, and had never, indemnified MPs from criminal prosecution.

The events of 2009 did not lead to 'unprecedented' reform. Attempts to restore confidence following a scandal are familiar: reforms implemented after the Nolan report are an obvious example. It is also doubtful that the changes introduced will truly result in increased accountability. It is notable that the most dramatic proposals made prior to the 2010 election are no longer on the political agenda. Electoral reform was abandoned following a referendum notable for its extremely low turnout, demonstrating the public's lack of interest in the issue. House of Lords reform has fallen foul of a rift within the Coalition.

It may be, however, that some measures which followed will be more effective in reforming the Lords to create a more representative legislature. As Russell (2011) has argued, the Wright Committee Report resulted in a number of significant changes. Select Committee chairs are now elected using an alternative vote system, which arguably opens the door for more robust scrutiny of government. Importantly, parliamentary time is now set aside to deal with issues raised by backbenchers. It can be argued that this will allow MPs to more effectively represent their constituents, by ensuring their concerns are aired. As Russell points out, these reforms are not concerned with expenses, but the scandal acted as the catalyst enabling reform.[10]

The expenses scandal marked a low point in public confidence in the parliamentary process, but it cannot be said that this was

[8] Similarly, here the answer is assisted by a knowledge of current affairs, allowing for the inclusion of more discursive examples.

[9] This is a small point but crucial for the argument being developed.

[10] This point relies on the definition of 'representative' that was set out earlier.

[11] It is acceptable, here, to set out a strong opinion in the conclusion because it is supported by the evidence from academic sources and examples drawn from current affairs.

unprecedented. Legislation rushed through Parliament may have been intended to restore trust, but it did not confront the issue of exclusive cognisance. If there is to be real accountability, there must be truly independent external regulation of all aspects of members' conduct. Although changes in response to the Wright Report garnered less publicity than other responses to the scandal, they will arguably have a greater impact in allowing Parliament to hold government to account and better represent the electorate.[11]

✓ Make your answer stand out

- By expanding the explanation of accountability of government, and considering whether or not the Wright reforms will reinforce the separation of powers. Arguably a stronger backbench presence in Parliament will lead to a more democratic legislature.
- By ensuring you are abreast of developments in this highly topical area of law. At the time of writing, for example, reports have appeared in the press detailing a practice of MPs renting out accommodation in an alleged attempt to claim additional expenses.
- By incorporating reference to earlier calls for reform of privilege. You could consider, for example, P.M. Leopold's (1999) discussion, in Report of the Joint Committee on Parliamentary Privilege *Public Law* 604. This would allow you to develop the argument that contemporary concerns have, in fact, been part of the political landscape for some considerable time.

! Don't be tempted to . . .

- Give too much factual detail about the allegations made during the scandal as this will lead to a descriptive, historical, account rather than a critical analysis of the response.
- Be distracted by discussion of the debate about the extent of privilege: students sometimes spend a long time on this aspect of the topic, using cases such as *Hansard* v *Stockdale*, or *Strauss's case*. Unfortunately, marks will not be awarded for demonstrating awareness of the issue of the limits of privilege. The question has a specific focus on criticisms of privilege raised by the expenses scandal.
- Read the question as a request to discuss the role of Parliament within the constitution, or the supremacy of Parliament. Students sometimes make the mistake of providing generalised information about the composition of Parliament, or of Dicey's account of supremacy but this will not gather marks. The answer must focus on the issues raised.

Question 6

'In a modern democracy it is important that those who make the laws of the land should be elected by those to whom those laws apply.' David Cameron and Nick Clegg, Foreword to the Draft House of Lords Reform Bill, May 2011 available at **http://www.official-documents. gov.uk/document/cm80/8077/8077.pdf** p. 5

Discuss the need for reform of the House of Lords.

Answer plan

➜ Explain the passage of the House of Lords Reform Bill.

➜ Outline the constitutional role of the House of Lords.

➜ Identify key criticisms of the unelected chamber.

➜ Assess the merits of various proposals for reform.

➜ Consider whether an elected chamber is an essential component of democracy.

Diagram plan

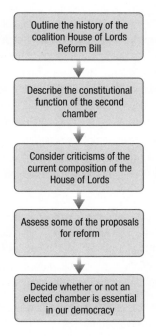

Outline the history of the coalition House of Lords Reform Bill

↓

Describe the constitutional function of the second chamber

↓

Consider criticisms of the current composition of the House of Lords

↓

Assess some of the proposals for reform

↓

Decide whether or not an elected chamber is essential in our democracy

A printable version of this diagram plan is available from www.pearsoned.co.uk/lawexpressqa

Answer

A bicameral legislature is a common feature of Western democracies, but the United Kingdom is unique in retaining an unelected second chamber. Proposals to reform the composition and constitutional position of the House of Lords have been on the political agenda for a century but, despite much debate, no consensus has been achieved. The arguments for and against reform of the House must be considered in the context of the constitutional role played by the Lords.[1]

The upper house acts as a constitutional brake on the powers exercised by the Commons, with the power to scrutinise, amend and, in some circumstances delay legislation.[2] No recent proposals for amendment have suggested any substantive alteration to the role of the second chamber: the foreword to the draft bill confirmed that these functions should remain unchanged.

The relationship between the two Houses of Parliament has, on occasion, been somewhat fraught. The first Parliament Act of 1911 was a response to a protracted refusal by the Lords to accept a budget endorsed by the Commons. The combined effect of both Parliament Acts was to remove the power of veto from the Lords;[3] effectively it was a 'statutory confirmation of the Lords' subordinate legislative role' (Lords Reform: The Legislative Role of the House of Lords, House of Commons Research Paper 98/103). Aspects of the relationship between the Houses are still governed by convention, the most important being the Salisbury Convention that the Lords will not oppose a bill that formed part of the government's manifesto pledge. The Coalition government's proposal argued that these conventions should remain, a view endorsed by the Joint Committee on House of Lords Reform.

The need for a second chamber as a scrutinising body in a democratic system, then, appears to be accepted as political and constitutional fact. Although there have been unsuccessful attempts since 1949 to further restrict the powers of the Lords in respect of legislation (during the Labour government in the 1960s),[4] the focus in recent times has been the composition of the upper house.[5]

When the Labour government was elected in 1997, the House of Lords had over 1,200 members, 750 of whom were hereditary peers. The House of Lords Reform Act 1999 reduced this number to 92 and

[1] Your introduction should make it clear that you are not going to make the mistake of only considering the reasons for the failure of the Coalition bill: a common mistake.

[2] Here, the answer describes the constitutional role of the Lords as succinctly as possible. There is no need to give more detail about the functions of the house as you need to focus on the areas that people have attempted to reform.

[3] There is no need to provide a full account of the passage of the Parliament Acts, as long as the answer makes it clear that you understand the effect of these important statutes.

[4] If you were to go into detail about these attempts, you would be straying too far away from the topic of democratic legitimacy, but by demonstrating that you are familiar with the history of attempted reform you demonstrate breadth of knowledge.

[5] Given that the role of the second chamber appears to be settled, it is important to make clear that the main issue is composition.

[6] Do not spend too much time setting out the detail of these reforms: the key point is that they were intended to be the start of a process.

[7] When discussing the issue of reform, it is really helpful to refer to the specific proposals that have been made rather than simply discussing the issues in the abstract.

[8] You do need to take care that, when dealing with the failed Coalition reforms, you do not spend too much time dealing with the political reasons for failure as this would take you too far away from the constitutional issues.

[9] Do not fall into the trap of vaguely citing 'some' or 'many' sources: you must show your examiner that you can refer to specific examples.

[10] This is a useful point to make and, in addition, demonstrates knowledge of the provisions of the bill, rather than simply the headlines about it.

established the House of Lords Appointments Commission, which now has responsibility for selecting cross-bench life peers.[6] The Labour administration saw this move as the first in an extensive programme of reform. Although the Constitutional Reform Act 2005 removed the Law Lords from the legislature, further progress stalled in the absence of political consensus. The Commission on Reform of the House of Lords, chaired by Lord Wakeham, proposed that the chamber should remain largely appointed, with a minority of elected members (Wakeham (2000)). The Public Administration Select Committee (2002), on the other hand, proposed that at least 60% of the chamber should be elected.[7] Despite opinion polls showing support for a move to a largely elected Chamber, votes within the Commons and the Lords failed to find an agreed balance between elected and appointed members. In 2008, the government published a White Paper proposing that 80% of peers should be elected for substantial terms of office, but the Bill that followed was far less radical, containing only a provision to abolish the remaining hereditary peers.

Reform was a manifesto commitment for the Liberal Democrats and became part of the Coalition Agreement. The draft bill published in 2012 contained proposals broadly in line with those set out in the 2008 White Paper. Following a rebellion by Conservative MPs and opposition from the Labour Party, the reform movement has ground to a halt. This is perhaps surprising given that, once the Coalition Agreement was drafted, there did at last seem to be cross-party support for the need for a largely elected chamber.[8]

Cameron and Clegg appear to endorse the view of the last Labour administration that democratic legitimacy requires at least a degree of electoral approval. Some constitutional observers would dispute this point.[9] For example, McKeown and Thomson (2010) argue that a distinction should be drawn between democratic and electoral legitimacy. If the constitutional role of the Lords is to scrutinise the Commons, they argue that this can be done more objectively and effectively by members who are not driven by party allegiance or the need for election. The Draft House of Lords Reform Bill did try to counter this kind of criticism by stipulating a single and lengthy term of office.[10] It did not, however, address the suggestion that a chamber consisting entirely of members appointed by an independent commission (on the basis of experience and expertise) may be better placed to examine legislation and more willing to challenge the Commons in

[11] Where academic opinion is divided on an issue, credit will be given to students who can acknowledge competing perspectives before reaching their own conclusion.

the absence of party allegiance. Phillipson (2004) rejects this suggestion, claiming that the comparison with other unelected bodies such as the judiciary is disingenuous.[11] He reminds us that no other unelected body is able to exercise such power over the elected House of Commons, pointing to the number of times proposals have been defeated in the Lords (Phillipson (2004)). He does, however, maintain that a partially appointed chamber could be a way to ensure both democratic (electoral) legitimacy and independent expertise. Notwithstanding comments made in the foreword to the draft bill set out in the question, it should be noted that the Coalition too supported the retention of some appointed peers, albeit in lesser numbers than Phillipson advocates.

It would appear that, following a century of discussion and disagreement, there is now a greater acceptance of the need to reform the composition of the House of Lords and an acceptance that this will require a move to some form of elected representation. The consensus within the proposals put forward since 1999 appears to be that some non-elected peers should remain to challenge executive hegemony in the Commons. It may well be that the move towards an elected chamber will be required in order to preserve the perception of democratic legitimacy, but the retention of at least some non-elected members would provide more substantive democratic benefit.[12]

[12] The conclusion must return to the issue of democratic legitimacy, as this is the key point made by the quotation used in the question.

✓ **Make your answer stand out**

- Having stated that the Lords will not defeat a bill which formed part of the government's manifesto, you could address the passage of the Hunting Act 2004. Here, the Parliament Act 1949 was invoked following rejection by the Lords. A report prepared for the Lords concluded that the manifesto commitment was to allow a free vote, not to secure a ban, and therefore there was no breach of the convention. This will be a good point to make because, not only does it give an example of the use of the Parliament Acts, but you have also demonstrated a more detailed understanding of the case and the issues it raised about the role of the Lords.

- Expanding the comment on the lack of political will to suggest abolition or radical reform. The relatively rare use of the Parliament Acts is worth exploring, as it does seem to suggest that there is an acceptance by the Commons that ignoring the views of the Lords may be seen as unconstitutional, or perhaps undemocratic.

> ## ! Don't be tempted to . . .
>
> ■ Spend time outlining the basic outline of the legislature; you are not required to address the role of the Commons at all in this question.
>
> ■ Describe reforms which have taken place in respect of the Lord Chancellor, or the establishment of the Supreme Court. You will not be given marks for knowing these details because they do not relate to the specific point of the question, which concerns the relationship of the legislative function of the Lords and ideas of democracy.
>
> ■ Make general statements about the Lords without providing examples to support what you say. It is not enough to say that the Lords reject legislation that has been approved by the Commons: you need to provide an example.

Question 7

'If Parliament can do anything, there is no reason why Parliament should not decide to redesign itself, either in general or for a particular purpose.' Per Baroness Hale, *R (on the application of Jackson)* v *Attorney General* [2006] 1 AC 262 at 160.

To what extent do you accept the 'manner and form' theory of parliamentary sovereignty?

Answer plan

→ Briefly set out Dicey's view and explain the focus on implied repeal.

→ Outline Jennings's (1959a) argument regarding the rule of recognition.

→ Consider counter arguments of Wade (1955).

→ Discuss the effect of the *Jackson* case.

→ Assess whether or not sovereignty is now limited.

Diagram plan

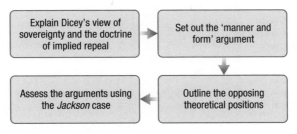

A printable version of this diagram plan is available from www.pearsoned.co.uk/lawexpressqa

Answer

¹ Even though Dicey is not mentioned in the question, his view is a good starting point for any assessment of parliamentary supremacy.

The traditional view of parliamentary sovereignty is drawn from the work of Dicey who saw a legislature able to operate without limits as the 'cornerstone' of the UK constitution.[1] According to his interpretation of sovereignty, courts will defer to the will of Parliament in applying its Acts, regardless of the subject matter. It is irrelevant if the application of a particular statute will result in injustice, as Parliament can amend or repeal it if it wishes. Crucially, he claimed that no Parliament can be bound by the acts of a predecessor, nor bind a successor, which gives rise to the doctrine of implied repeal.[2] No statute is entrenched, as any can be repealed without the need for specific procedure to protect Acts concerning the constitution. This, it is said, gives the UK constitution a unique flexibility.

² The 'manner and form' argument can be understood as a challenge to Dicey's view of supremacy but it is focused specifically upon the doctrine of implied repeal so it is helpful to make it clear that your answer will concentrate on this aspect of supremacy.

More than a century after Dicey's analysis, the legal supremacy of Parliament is far less certain. Devolution, membership of the European Union and the incorporation of the European Convention on Human Rights into domestic law can all be cited as evidence of other institutions encroaching upon the legislative freedom of parliament. The 'manner and form' theory suggests that in the modern constitution, Parliament can in fact be bound and a number of statutes are, at least partially, entrenched.[3]

³ The 'manner and form' argument is complex. You can demonstrate your understanding of this difficult area by making sure you can provide a short clear explanation.

There is an internal contradiction inherent in the doctrine of parliamentary sovereignty. If Parliament is supreme then, logically, any given Parliament should be able to bind a successor, to 'redesign' itself as Baroness Hale states.[4] By the same token, how can any single Parliament claim sovereignty if it is bound by the actions of a predecessor? Hart's suggestion for resolving this conflict was to acknowledge a distinction between 'self-embracing' and 'continuing' sovereignty.[5] Dicey described a form of continuing sovereignty: each time Parliament convenes it is a new, sovereign institution, free from any limitations, including those created by a previous Parliament. A 'self-embracing' concept of sovereignty, Hart explained, would mean that Parliament is seen as possessing a self-limiting power enabling it to pass laws to alter the way it would operate in the future (Hart (1994), p. 149). This theory sees 'Parliament' as one single entity, regardless of how many times it dissolves and reconvenes.

⁴ By referencing the quote in this way, you make it absolutely clear that you have understood the implication of the words Baroness Hale used for the doctrine of implied repeal.

⁵ One of the difficulties with this question is that, in order to understand the 'manner and form' argument, a number of issues must be explained. Make sure you know how to explain this view of sovereignty.

[6] Students are sometimes cautious about referencing the views of numerous academics in their work because they feel that it looks as if they are not able to think for themselves. When answering this kind of discursive question, this perception is completely wrong. Marks will be awarded to students who demonstrate familiarity with a number of academics and who are able to analyse a variety of arguments.

[7] You must refer to Jennings in your answer as the 'manner and form' argument is mainly drawn from his work.

[8] Again, these are complicated arguments, so make sure that before you enter the exam room you have considered how you are going to articulate them clearly.

[9] It is important to note the distinction between political and legal possibilities, as this is one of the strongest counter-arguments to the 'manner and form' argument.

[10] The facts of these cases are rather complicated but there is no need to give any details, as long as you show that you know why ex-colonies are in a peculiar position.

Loveland points out that there is little,[6] if any, academic support for the suggestion that there can be entrenchment of any substantive law. He argues that the position in respect of legislation affecting the parliamentary process can be distinguished and considerable support can be found for the 'manner and form' arguments here, with the work of Jennings being foremost (Loveland (2012), p. 35).[7] Jennings argues that whilst Dicey was correct to state that there are no limitations on the subject matter that can be addressed by legislation, the doctrine of implied repeal is open to challenge. He acknowledges that the courts will defer to Parliament, but states that as the rule of recognition is a common law concept and statute is legally superior, a statute must be able to change the rule of recognition and protect some acts from implied repeal.[8] There does seem to be great logical force to his suggestion that 'its power to change the law includes the power to change the law affecting itself' (Jennings (1959a), p. 149).

Adherents to the 'manner and form' argument, then, maintain that Parliament is able to entrench statutes which alter its own composition or the law-making process. Whilst we may point to examples such as the Reform Act of 1832, or the Acts of Union, these do not provide irrefutable support because, arguably, whilst there may be strong political constraints to consider, there is no legal reason[9] why the franchise could not be withdrawn or the union dissolved. Jennings pointed to three cases in support of his position: *A-G for New South Wales v Trethowan* (1931) 44 CLR 394, *Harris v Donges (Minister of the Interior)* (1952) 1 TLR 1245, and *Bribery Commissioner v Ranasinghe* [1965] AC 172. Each of these cases concerned countries which had previously been British colonies.[10] In each instance, a parliamentary attempt to alter an aspect of the constitution was overruled by the court. The problem with taking these as evidence that constitutional statutes enjoy special protection is that the constitution of each territory was created by the UK Parliament, which continued to exist as a source of 'higher' law.

Wade (1955) argues that the 'manner and form' argument was wrong and that the traditional position was more logical. He maintains that the supremacy of the legislature is self-evident: the rules setting out what constitutes an Act of Parliament are 'a political fact' which cannot be altered by any legal authority whether by Parliament itself or the courts. Wade does accept that change could be envisaged, but that this would require a revolution and could not be achieved by Parliament. In later years, faced with the reality of the European Communities Act 1972 and in the wake of the *Factortame* legislation, Wade (1996) suggests that there has been a 'technical revolution', which implies acceptance of the 'manner and form' argument.[11]

[11] Always remember the question you are being asked and ensure you show how the points you make help reach a conclusion. The main reason for discussing Wade is to show how academic theory appears to have shifted towards acceptance of the argument.

The most potent support for the 'manner and form' argument, arguably, is found in the judgment of **Jackson v Attorney General** [2005] UKHL 56, [2006] 1 AC 262.[12] The House of Lords considered the argument that the Hunting Act 2004 was invalid, as it was made using the procedure set out in the Parliament Act 1949. The contention was that the 1949 Act was itself invalid, as it was an ultra-vires use of the Parliament Act 1911. It was argued that the 1911 Act had only granted the Commons the power to make delegated legislation and certainly did not authorise the use of the Act to extend its legislative competence. The 1911 legislation did not alter the fact that an Act of Parliament requires the consent of the Commons, the Lords and the Queen, and so the 1949 Act could not be lawful. The House of Lords rejected this claim and accepted that the 1911 Act had created a new procedure for making an Act of Parliament.

[12] As the question quotes from this case, you cannot avoid discussing the judgment. It was very complicated so, again, make sure you are able to set out the key issue succinctly.

The judgments in Jackson demonstrate a degree of judicial acceptance of the 'manner and form' argument, although it was only directly referenced by Lords Steyn and Hope. Parliament may have always been constrained by political reality, but the case seems to demonstrate that Jennings's analysis was correct and the constitution has evolved to include some legal limitations on sovereignty.[13]

[13] Do not forget to return to the question and provide a direct answer in your conclusion.

 Make your answer stand out

- By including reference to a wider range of academic theorists. This is a topic that has engendered an enormous amount of debate, so you should read as widely as possible. Additional sources could include: Bradley, A. (2011) 'The sovereignty of parliament – form or substance?' in Jowell and Oliver (eds): *The Changing Constitution* (7th edn), Oxford: Oxford University Press; Elliot, M. Bicameralism, Sovereignty and the Unwritten Constitution *Int'l J Const*, 5: 370.

- Consider the judgments in *Jackson* in more detail. The Lords were not in complete agreement in this case, and it would be useful to explore the different approaches adopted in detail.

> **! Don't be tempted to . . .**
>
> ■ Spend time discussing each of Dicey's three propositions. Students who revise
>   parliamentary supremacy often do so assuming that any question will require
>   consideration of the orthodox view, and attempt an answer following that structure.
>
> ■ Attempt this question without knowing the arguments set out by a reasonable number
>   of academic theorists. Failure to engage with the academic debate will make it
>   impossible for you to obtain high marks.

? Question 8

Megan is a Member of Parliament belonging to the main opposition party. She is very unhappy about government plans to require council tenants to vacate their properties if their household income rises above the national average. The minister for housing has stated that this would allow waiting lists to be reduced by two thirds and reduce overall expenditure on social housing by six million pounds per annum. During a debate about the proposals, she attempts to voice her criticism but is shouted down by MPs from the government benches. One backbench MP yells at her to be quiet, calling her 'a stupid woman' with 'the brains of a drunken flea', and accuses her of being a liar. The Speaker does nothing to intervene.

Later on, she is approached by a senior civil servant who gives her a copy of an impact statement prepared for the housing minister. The document estimates that overall savings would be less than one million pounds per year. Megan leaks the document to a journalist from the *Daily Standard* newspaper.

Figures from the impact statement appear in an article in the *Daily Standard* which is very critical of the government. A week later, Megan is in her office at the House of Commons when police officers arrive and demand to search the room. She is horrified by this and asks why. She is told that she is suspected of a criminal offence of aiding and abetting misfeasance in public office. She asks to see a warrant and is told that none is required as the Speaker has agreed the search can take place. Megan is then arrested in respect of the offence.

Advise Megan of the implications arising from these facts.

Answer plan

➜ Outline the meaning of parliamentary privilege.

➜ Explain that there is no legal recompense for comments made in debate.

➜ Consider whether or not the Speaker has acted appropriately.

➜ Discuss the applicability of privilege to criminal investigations.

➜ Assess the legality of the police search.

Diagram plan

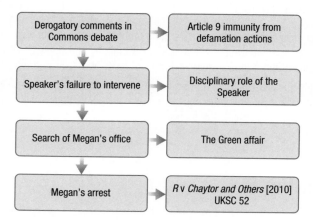

Derogatory comments in Commons debate	→ Article 9 immunity from defamation actions
↓	
Speaker's failure to intervene	→ Disciplinary role of the Speaker
↓	
Search of Megan's office	→ The Green affair
↓	
Megan's arrest	→ *R* v *Chaytor and Others* [2010] UKSC 52

A printable version of this diagram plan is available from www.pearsoned.co.uk/lawexpressqa

Answer

Parliamentary privilege refers to the constitutional protection given to both Houses of Parliament to protect Parliament from outside interference and therefore to protect the independence of democratic debate. Privilege protects individual members of either House, as well as applying collectively to each chamber as a whole. Parliamentary privilege can be divided into two main areas: immunity from civil action in respect of parliamentary proceedings; and the privilege of self-regulation. The facts of this scenario raise issues concerning both aspects of parliamentary privilege.[1]

Megan may well feel aggrieved about the personal nature of the abuse suffered during the House of Commons debate. However, there is no legal action that she can take. Article 9 of the Bill of Rights 1689 stated that 'freedom of speech, debates or proceedings in Parliament ought not to be impeached or questioned in any court or place out of Parliament'.[2] The intention was to protect parliamentarians from vexatious legal proceedings designed to stifle democratic debate, but extends in the modern age to confer immunity from any civil action for defamation. It is clear that this protection is absolute in respect of 'parliamentary proceedings', even in circumstances where the person making the statement knows it is false (***Wason v***

[1] There is no need to provide an account of the historical development of privilege or its constitutional significance in detail. It is important to concentrate on the facts given.

[2] It is always a good idea to refer to Article 9 as this remains the key authority providing the scope of parliamentary privilege.

[3] As this part of the problem is very clear, there are no marks for a broader discussion about activities which may be difficult to classify as proceedings.

Walter (1868) LR 4QB). Whilst there has been some debate about what business will be considered to be part of 'proceedings' there is no question that the debate about the proposals will be covered by privilege.[3]

The protection given to freedom of speech does not mean that there are no consequences for defamatory or abusive language in parliaments, only that these must be administered internally rather than through the court system.[4] The parliamentary privilege of self-regulation has been the focus of controversy on a number of occasions where it has appeared that the legislature has not had robust systems to prevent wrongdoing by its members, one of the most recent cases being the MPs' expenses scandal of 2009. The establishment of an independent body to regulate expenses (Independent Parliamentary Standards Authority) can perhaps be seen as the beginning of a shift towards external accountability.[5] In this instance, however, it is clear that the Speaker in his role as chair of Commons debates has the power to enforce discipline on the floor of the house. *Erskine May's Parliamentary Practice* (Millar (2011)) reminds MPs that 'good temper and moderation are the characteristics of parliamentary language'.[6] The Speaker should have intervened during this debate and asked the member to withdraw the abusive remarks and the accusation that Megan is a liar. Failure to comply would leave open the possibility of the Speaker 'naming' the MP and asking for their suspension from the house for five days (for a first offence).[7] It is clear, then, that the Speaker has acted improperly by failing to censure the remarks. There does not appear to be any way for Megan to seek recompense from the Speaker, as there is no clear system to enforce the requirements of the role. In 2009, Michael Martin resigned the position following unprecedented political pressure arising from his handling of the expenses scandal but this situation is highly unlikely to have a similar impact.

The facts surrounding the leaked memorandum are similar to those that led to the arrest of Damian Green MP in 2008 and, crucially, the subsequent search of his office in the Houses of Parliament.[8] It is now settled that privilege does not protect Members of Parliament from criminal prosecution (**R v Chaytor and others** [2010] UKSC 52), and therefore Megan cannot make a complaint about the fact of her arrest.[9] The unauthorised disclosure of material by the civil servant can amount to misfeasance in a public office. As with the Green

[4] Many scenarios only require a discussion of the protection from actions in defamation in respect of remarks in the chamber. The problem here, however, clearly demands consideration of the Speaker's disciplinary role.

[5] This is a valid point but you must not spend too long on a general discussion about exclusive cognisance as your focus should be on the Speaker's role as chair.

[6] You may not be able to remember quotes in your examination but it is a good idea to refer to *Erskine May* as this demonstrates that you can provide the authority for your assertions about the Speaker's role.

[7] There is no need to outline the various sanctions available for different forms of contempt, but you will be rewarded for knowing the specific consequences that could arise here.

[8] Because the problem scenario mirrors the Green affair so precisely, it would be really difficult to gain high marks if you are not familiar with both the facts, and the consequences that followed his arrest.

[9] This is quite an important point to note. Concern about the motivation for the arrest does not affect its legality.

affair, however, there could be concerns here that a report to the police and subsequent arrest are a disproportionate political reaction to the publication of material which caused difficulties for the government but fell short of a breach of the Official Secrets Act (Bradley (2012)). The parallels with this scenario are so strong it seems safe to advise Megan that the arrest is highly unlikely to result in charges. The CPS would be unable to determine that there was a realistic prospect of conviction on these facts.

A second issue arises about the search that has taken place with the consent of the Speaker. This should not have occurred.[10] Following the Green affair, the House of Commons Committee on the Issue of Privilege produced a report chaired by Sir Menzies Campbell which criticised not only the decision to arrest the MP, but also the conduct of the search of his office. The report reiterated the need for a warrant to search any part of the precincts of Parliament. Any materials concerning parliamentary proceedings will be covered by privilege and must not be examined by the police (it is usual for the police to instruct independent legal advisors to consider the material and withhold any items deemed subject to privilege).[11] As with the Green case, the actions of the police here should be the source of considerable concern as they appear to undermine the purpose of Article 9 in ensuring Members of Parliament can operate without fear of executive interference.

Again, any action that Megan may wish to take is circumscribed by the fact that privilege not only protects her, it also protects the Speaker and their assistants in the House. Therefore, whilst she may be able to make a complaint to the police, she has no obvious means of seeking recompense from the Speaker. This situation is considerably more serious than the first in light of the Green affair, which resulted in not only the report referred to above but also a declaration of protocol by the Speaker in 2008, confirming that no consent can be given to any search without warrant. Michael Martin was the first Speaker to be forced from office for 300 years and his resignation was described as being unprecedented. Arguably, however, it does now provide a precedent to show that serious criticism may create unbearable political pressure to relinquish the office. It may well be that this would be such a case.[12]

Parliamentary privilege is often discussed because of the benefits it provides to MPs. Here it can be seen that operating outside of the

[10] Where you are absolutely certain of the position, do not be afraid to set it out unequivocally. This demonstrates considerable confidence in your ability to assess the facts given.

[11] The scenario does not mention whether or not any items were seized, but it is worth noting to show the examiner that you understand the procedures that apply.

[12] You will be rewarded for offering this kind of analysis as it shows you are able to draw conclusions from the materials you have studied, but do take care not to overstate the likelihood of this as you are only able to speculate.

ordinary law may, in rare instances, result in an MP having less protection than the average citizen.[13] Megan has no legal mechanism available to her to obtain redress from the Speaker and will therefore be forced to rely upon the far less certain effects of public and political opinion.

[13] This is an unusual but a fair conclusion to make as the answer has carefully set out the arguments that support it.

 Make your answer stand out

- By explaining a little more why the Official Secrets Act could not be invoked here. It could be said that the provisions are broad enough to criminalise an extremely wide range of conduct. This could be used to lend more weight to the suggestion that the police action in this case was wholly disproportionate.

- By considering the issue of the extent to which documents in an MP's office should be covered by privilege. It has been suggested that correspondence between an MP and their constituents should be treated as privileged in the same way as communication between a solicitor and their clients.

- By setting the discussion about the need for a warrant in a wider constitutional context. You could draw parallels between this situation and the judgment in *Entick* v *Carrington* (1765) 19 St Tr 1029.

- By considering the constitutional role of the Speaker and considering whether or not the introduction of external bodies to regulate expenses, and the Martin resignation has significantly diminished the importance of the role.

! Don't be tempted to . . .

- Assume that the question is primarily concerned with freedom of expression. The inclusion of information about the leaked report could lead students into a fruitless discussion about Article 10 of the European Convention on Human Rights and press freedom.

- Spend too long explaining the case law concerning privilege and defamation. There is no need, for example, to consider the Hamilton affair or the Defamation Act 1996. In this case you are being invited to assess the Speaker's role, rather than the fact of the comments made.

www.pearsoned.co.uk/lawexpressqa

 Go online to access more revision support including additional essay and problem questions with diagram plans, You be the marker questions, and download all diagrams from the book.

Prerogative powers and constitutional conventions

3

How this topic may come up in exams

Essay questions are more common in this area. Problems may require you to recognise situations in which particular conventions could apply. There is little case law concerning conventions, and therefore you will need to have a number of illustrative examples to draw on. It is important to be able to discuss a range of academic opinions. You should be able to discuss the relationship between prerogative powers and constitutional conventions. This area of the syllabus overlaps with consideration of the separation of powers.

■ Attack the question

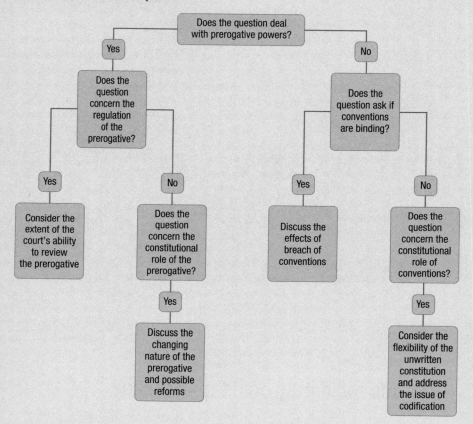

A printable version of this diagram is available from www.pearsoned.co.uk/lawexpressqa

 # Question 1

'Is it not true that we have found that constitutional conventions that are universally accepted can, arguably, have greater force and staying power than legislation? But surely those conventions, by definition, can apply only if they are universally accepted.' (Viscount Cranbourne: *Hansard* text for 22 February 2000: http://www.parliament.the-stationery-office.co.uk/pa/ld199900/ldhansrd/vo000222/text/00222-08.htm.)

To what extent do constitutional conventions remain an important part of the constitution of the United Kingdom?

Answer plan

→ Outline the definitions of conventions given by Dicey and Jennings.

→ Consider particular conventions and the consequences of breach.

→ Analyse how particular conventions could be said to lose their force.

→ Consider whether or not some conventions could be codified.

→ Draw some conclusions about the extent to which conventions are binding.

Diagram plan

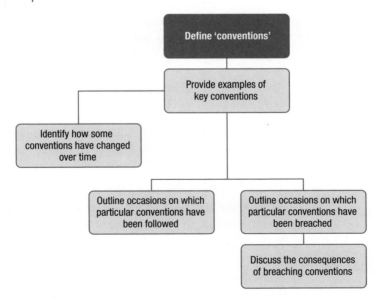

A printable version of this diagram plan is available from www.pearsoned.co.uk/lawexpressqa

Answer

The constitution of the United Kingdom is generally described as 'unwritten'. Whilst it is true to say that it is not codified within a single document, much of the constitution can be found in formal, written sources. Conventions are an informal unwritten source of the constitution.[1] The origins and enforceability of conventions are uncertain, and whilst some may appear to have great force, others will fall away over time. Some would argue that the possibility of evolution and change gives the unwritten constitution the benefit of flexibility and responsiveness. Alternatively, it could be suggested that it is inappropriate for rules governing important areas of conduct in public office to be so poorly defined, and without legal sanction.[2]

Dicey defined conventions as habits, understanding and practices which are not enforceable by the courts.[3] Constitutional conventions are perhaps more than simply 'habits', however; as Waldron (1990) points out, they are accepted as rules by those who are bound by them despite the lack of legal enforceability (p. 62). Loveland (2012) suggests that the function of a convention is to 'fill in the gaps' in the constitution (p. 271). It can be hard to determine when a form of conduct is simply an accepted practice, and when it should be considered to be a convention that forms part of the constitution. Jennings (1959a) argued that a convention requires precedent, acceptance of the precedent by the individuals concerned, and a reason for the rule.[4] (p. 134). It is clear, then, that a constitutional convention emerges from tradition and practice, and can indeed carry great weight as a breach may have severe consequences.

Conventions regulate some of the key relationships between individuals working in the various organs of the state and can therefore be said to be of considerable constitutional importance,[5] and yet a cursory examination highlights how the rules are far from fixed.

By convention, the government of the day should be supported by a majority in the House of Commons, and should resign if it is unable to do so.[6] Whilst for many years it was assumed that this meant defeat on any major policy issue would lead to resignation, as Loveland points out, this was consistently ignored from the 1970s onwards; so the rule now appears to be that resignation need only follow the loss of an explicit motion of no confidence.

[1] In order to deal with the issue of conventions, you do need to explain that the constitution is 'unwritten', but you should be as brief as possible.

[2] This question requires an examination of the pros and cons of conventions, so it is helpful to set out the main arguments in the introduction.

[3] Any discussion of conventions must include Dicey's definition as a starting point.

[4] It is a good idea to mention Jennings here as, in addition to Dicey, he is one of the most important theorists who have written about this subject.

[5] You need to be able to explain the function of conventions because the question is asking for an evaluation of their place in the constitution.

[6] A good answer will need to be able to examine how a number of conventions have developed over time. There are many conventions that you could focus on but, whichever you choose, make sure you can give some concrete examples to support the argument.

The conduct of ministers in office is largely governed by convention. There are different aspects to this: individual and collective responsibility. The convention of collective responsibility requires all Cabinet Ministers to support government policy once it has been determined, irrespective of their personal views.[7] Numerous examples can be found which demonstrate compliance with the convention, including the resignation of Michael Heseltine over the Westland affair and, more recently, the resignation of Robin Cook who was unable to support the Iraq war. Collective responsibility can also be used to illustrate the lack of clarity that surrounds the definition and application of conventions. The rule was suspended by the Labour government in the 1970s, allowing ministers to air their views regarding membership of the European Community, to encourage a public debate. The suspension was temporary, voluntary, and limited to a single issue. This perhaps demonstrates the utility of conventions, which allow flexibility in government. It may be acceptable to envisage a rule that can, with agreement from all parties, be lifted. The convention was flouted, seemingly without agreement, by Clare Short who, like Robin Cook, was opposed to the Iraq war. She spoke out publicly against the war but remained in Cabinet for another two months, which demonstrates that the operation, or otherwise, of the convention appears to depend upon the discretion and preference of the Prime Minister of the day rather than any legal principle.[8]

The convention of individual responsibility holds a minister accountable for conduct whilst in office, but the requirements of the rule have shifted over time. It no longer appears to be the case that personal 'scandal' will inevitably result in resignation. In the 1990s, newspaper accounts of an affair led to the resignation of Cecil Parkinson, whereas John Prescott remained in office following similar revelations. Perhaps this is indicative of the constitution responding to reflect the shift in attitude of the public at large.[9] However, as numerous commentators have pointed out, the rule has rarely been fixed, and sexual scandal generally only leads to resignation if there are other implications.[10] Parkinson was a member of a government that stressed moral values, but had fathered an illegitimate child; it could be argued that it was this hypocrisy that led to the view he was unfit for office.[11]

It appears that a minister is still accountable for failings within their department, but this convention is also subject to a variety of

[7] Collective responsibility is a good convention to focus on, as there are so many examples that help illustrate instances where convention is followed, and instances where it appears to have been ignored.

[8] This is a good point to make, as it helps develop an argument that conventions are governed by political pressure rather than legal principle.

[9] Here, you acknowledge the argument that flexibility of the unwritten constitution is its greatest strength. As this is one of the key points that is made in favour of conventions, it should certainly be mentioned.

[10] The answer is referring again to the argument that political issues are the main issue that determines how a convention will operate in any given circumstance. This is going to be a key part of the conclusions, so it is helpful to keep showing how the examples you choose support this opinion.

[11] You do need to be familiar with the facts of the examples that you choose, so that they can be used to support your argument. Remember, though, that you are using the facts to make a point, so keep it as brief as you can.

interpretations. Hence, although the Prime Minister refused to accept it, William Whitelaw felt compelled to offer his resignation following the discovery of an intruder in Buckingham Palace. Thereafter, ministers appeared to draw a distinction between matters of policy and matters of administration. James Prior refused to resign following a prison escape, on the grounds it did not result from any decisions he had made.

The precise obligation imposed by a particular convention can be hard to define, and may alter over time and in differing circumstances. The relevance of conventions to the constitution is clear. The Cabinet Office has published guidance on the operation of ministerial responsibility, and the appointment of government. Conventions may not be enforceable in the courts,[12] but they are recognised as an aid to interpretation (see, for example **A-G v Blake (Jonathan Cape, third party)** [1998] 1 All ER 833). Jaconelli suggested that whilst there may be no legal consequence, loss of office occurs so regularly as a result of a breach of convention that it can be considered to be a sanction (Jaconelli (2005)). However, Loveland highlights that it is common for a minister to resign, only to be reinstated a short while later (Parkinson, Blunkett and Mandelson to name but a few). Dewan and Dowding (2005)[13] suggest that ministerial resignation is triggered less by convention than political expediency, and occurs when it is required to improve public perceptions of government.[14]

It appears that conventions can fall out of use if public, or political opinion allows. Whilst this demonstrates the ability of the constitution to adapt to changing times, it is perhaps a concern that these 'vital pillars' (Loveland (2012), p. 261) of the constitution have no legal basis.

[12] Rather than simply stating that conventions are important, the answer points to evidence of this by outlining how both government and the judiciary have acknowledged their role.

[13] A good answer will be familiar with a range of academic opinion, and be able to analyse a number of differing academic views.

[14] This is a key point and one which is supported by the examples explored earlier on in the answer.

Make your answer stand out

- By exploring the argument that conventions should be codified in more detail. You could note that the Constitutional Reform and Governance Act 2010 has placed the Ponsonby convention on a statutory footing, and consider whether this signifies a move towards codification.

- By utilising academic opinion about the possibility of codification. There is a great deal of academic writing on the subject of conventions. An authoritative discussion regarding the benefits and perils of codification can be found in de Smith, S. and Brazier, R. (2008) *Constitutional and Administrative Law* (8th edn). London: Penguin.

- By noting occasions when conventions have been supported during the process of constitutional reform. You could point to the Sewel convention established during the process of devolving powers to Scotland, or the introduction to the Draft House of Lords Reform Bill 2012 in which the Coalition endorsed the preservation of conventions in the second chamber.

- By considering the relationship between conventions and the prerogative and emphasising the role that they play in regulating the use of discretionary power. This would demonstrate an ability to consider constitutional law as a whole, rather than in discrete topic areas.

! Don't be tempted to . . .

- List all the conventions that you can remember. It is far better to concentrate on two or three examples, and spend time exploring how they operate in some detail. Remember, marks are awarded for the ability to analyse the question, rather than simply remembering the law.

- Ignore the need to be able to provide examples to support your argument. This topic can pose difficulties because there is a lack of case law authorities (due to the nature of conventions) and therefore your revision will need to include remembering illustrations from recent political history.

Question 2

The United Kingdom is typical of states which permit ministers to use certain powers without parliamentary approval, but it is highly unusual among democracies in having neither a codified constitution nor having been made such express grants of power by the legislature. (Select Committee of Public Administration, 4th Report Session 2003–2004).

Discuss the adequacy of the regulation of the exercise of prerogative powers.

Answer plan

→ Provide a definition of prerogative powers, and identify key powers exercised by ministers.

→ Explain the role of the court in regulating use of the prerogative.

→ Consider the relationship between Parliament and the prerogative.

→ Highlight some criticisms of the use of the prerogative and proposals for reform.

Diagram plan

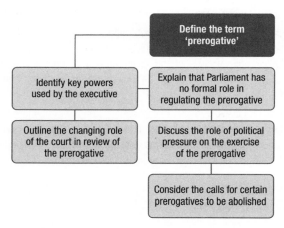

A printable version of this diagram plan is available from www.pearsoned.co.uk/lawexpressqa

[1] Although it is not essential to remember quotes, you do need to provide Blackstone's definition of the prerogative. It would be acceptable to paraphrase the definition, but it should be the starting point for an explanation of prerogative power.

[2] The question asks you to consider the regulation of the prerogative, and it is helpful to highlight in the introduction that you recognise that the issue is control of executive power by the other constitutional bodies.

Answer

Blackstone described the royal prerogative as 'that special pre-eminence which the King has, over and above all other persons, and out of the ordinary course of the common law, in right of his royal dignity'.[1] Prerogative powers are those exercisable by the Crown without statutory authority. Although, historically, the prerogative was exercised by the monarch, the majority of powers are now used by ministers of state, and very few remain the personal preserve of the sovereign. The extent to which the judiciary and the legislature are able to regulate the exercise of prerogative powers by the executive has increased;[2] however, there are still some people who are concerned by the lack of control that can be exerted by the other constitutional bodies.

The prerogative encompasses a number of important matters of state, including the regulation of the civil service, making treaties, control of the armed forces and the appointment of ministers.[3] The powers that fall within its scope are often of crucial importance to government, and it is perhaps peculiar that the limitations and controls upon the prerogative have not yet been formalised.

Traditionally, the judiciary would not interfere with the exercise of a prerogative power beyond assessing whether or not an action by the executive fell within its scope. The courts refused to countenance any extension of prerogative: Lord Diplock stated in **BBC v Johns** [1965] Ch 32: 'it is 350 years and a civil war too late'[4] for the executive to claim new powers. This position appeared to be contradicted by the controversial judgment in **R v Secretary of State for the Home Department ex parte Northumbria Police Authority** [1989] QB 26, in which it was accepted that a prerogative power to keep the peace existed. Despite the absence of previous authority confirming, it was held that the absence of authority might, in fact, point to 'an unspoken assumption' that it existed.

In more recent times, the courts have adopted a less deferential approach to executive actions following the **'GCHQ' case (Council of Civil Service Unions v Minister for the Civil Service** [1985] AC 374), in which it was held that a decision was not exempt from review simply because it fell within the scope of the prerogative.[5] There remained, however, 'non-justiciable' areas of decision-making; matters of policy that were considered to be appropriately within the discretion of the executive. These included the disposal of armed forces, matters of national security, the dissolution of Parliament and appointment of ministers, the prerogative of mercy and the making of treaties. Since the **GCHQ case**, it can be seen that the courts are increasingly willing to review a broad range of matters, including some that the judgment sought to exclude. In **R v Secretary of State for the Home Department ex parte Bentley** [1994] QB 349, the prerogative of mercy was subject to review. The treatment of homosexuals in the military was considered in **R v Ministry of Defence ex parte Smith** [1996] QB 517, despite the fact that the matter concerned the disposal of the armed forces.[6] There is, then, an increased degree of regulation of the exercise of the prerogative. Matters which directly concern national security or diplomatic relations, however, appear to remain exempt from judicial interference.[7]

[5] This is probably the single most important authority regarding the prerogative and must be discussed. It is essential to consider it in a question dealing with regulation of the use of the power.

[6] There are a number of cases that could be used here, and there is no need to include a comprehensive list. It is perfectly acceptable to use one or two, but it is necessary to provide an explanation of the area of the prerogative that your authorities deal with. This shows the examiner that you know how the cases illustrate a change in judicial attitudes.

[7] This point helps to make a balanced argument by acknowledging that in some areas the judiciary remain deferential.

R (Abbasi) v *Secretary of State for Foreign and Commonwealth Affairs and Secretary of State for the Home Department* [2002] All ER (D) 70, and *R (Al Rawi)* v *Foreign Secretary* [2007] 2 WLR 1219). Further, in the case of *CND* v *Prime Minister of the United Kingdom* [2002] All ER 245 the courts refused to interfere with the government's determination of the legal effect of the UN resolution regarding Iraq.

The power to declare war has been the focus of debate about the role of Parliament in regulating the use of the prerogative.[8] Under the doctrine of supremacy, it appears clear that an Act of Parliament can abolish a prerogative power, either expressly or by implied repeal (as confirmed in *Attorney General* v *De Keysers Royal Hotel* [1920] AC 508).[9] In addition, the exercise of prerogative powers can be put on a statutory footing; see for example the Security Service Act 1989. Many commentators have argued that there should be further legislative action to limit the extent of the prerogative. In 1994, whilst in opposition, the Labour frontbencher Jack Straw referred specifically to the power of ministers to ratify treaties and to declare war as a 'smokescreen' designed to 'obfuscate the use of power for which they are insufficiently accountable'[10] (1994, p. 129). Following election, the Labour administration made no move to abolish the prerogative to declare war, despite the recommendation of the Public Administration Select Committee in 2004, and four Private Members Bills on the subject. The Constitutional Reform and Governance Act 2010 has, however, placed the Ponsonby convention on a statutory footing; formalising the requirement for treaties to be laid before Parliament prior to ratification.

Those who argue that the legislature should have a greater role in the exercise of key prerogative powers claim that this would ensure greater legitimacy, and increased accountability.[11] A number of witnesses to the House of Lords Constitution Committee made the point that the decision to send troops to war required democratic authorisation (Fifteenth report, 2006). It is perhaps for this reason that Tony Blair, when giving evidence to the liaison committee, declared it 'unthinkable' that the decision would occur without consulting Parliament. It may be politically expedient, but the fact remains that there is no legal requirement to consult the legislature on the matter and, as has been shown, no judicial regulation of such a decision after the fact.[12]

[8] A good answer will recognise that the question is not limited to the role of the judiciary; you should address the position of Parliament as well.

[9] Reference to the doctrine of parliamentary supremacy and implied repeal demonstrates an ability to place the topic in context and draw links between different areas of the syllabus.

[10] The prerogative to declare war is an excellent issue to focus on as it has been subject to much recent debate and there are numerous sources of political and academic opinion for you to draw on.

[11] This is a key point to make, as you must address the reasons why codification has been called for. This is the central argument.

[12] It is useful to be able to draw a distinction between political and legal restraints on the exercise of prerogative power.

Since the **GCHQ case**, there is no doubt that the use of prerogative powers is subject to greater regulation and control across a range of areas. Successive administrations have, however, resisted pressure to place key decisions in the hands of the legislature. It is undoubtedly true that the exercise of the prerogatives pertaining to issues of defence and diplomatic relations is subject to political scrutiny, and a degree of democratic accountability at the ballot box. Nevertheless, in the absence of judicial sanction or legislative approval, it can be argued that there is still a lack of constitutional control of the prerogative.[13]

[13] You must attempt to address the question directly in your conclusion.

✓ Make your answer stand out

- When considering the *Northumbria* case, a parallel could be drawn with *Entick* v *Carrington* (1765) 19 St Tr 1029, considered to be a key constitutional case, in which it was said that no power existed without a lawful authority. There appears to be a direct contrast between the two decisions, which could be highlighted. This would show the examiner that you are aware of the fact that there are competing interpretations of the constitutional position.

- By exploring the reasons behind government reluctance to abolish key prerogative powers. This answer has touched on the difference between the views of Jack Straw in opposition and the actions of the Labour administration. You could consider the utility of discretionary powers to government and argue that these are necessary to enable swift and efficient decision-making.

- By referring to additional academic and political comment. The reports of the Constitution Committee of the House of Lords regarding the prerogative to declare war are a good starting point: *Waging War: Parliament's Role and Responsibility* (2005-06 HL Paper 236-I and II), and the follow-up report (2006-07 HL Paper 51).

- By including a discussion of so-called 'Henry VIII clauses' in legislation, which grant power to executive bodies to amend or repeal statutory provisions without reference to Parliament. Care would have to be taken to ensure that the material remains relevant to the question. Such powers are created with parliamentary approval but you could note that they confer an extremely broad discretion, which gives rise to an argument that the legislature should maintain oversight.

> **! Don't be tempted to . . .**
>
> - List all the prerogative powers. Focus on a few that have been the subject of judicial or parliamentary consideration.
> - Discuss the personal prerogatives of the monarch. The quote used in the question refers to the power used by ministers; this is an indication that the examiner is looking for a discussion about the regulation of the executive.
> - Write an answer that concentrates on whether or not there should be codification. Whilst this should be touched upon, it is important not to lose sight of the specific question posed which is whether or not the regulation of existing powers is adequate.

❓ Question 3

The (fictional) government is planning to develop green field sites across the north of England in order to manage a housing crisis and stimulate growth in the economy. The matter is included in the Queen's Speech. The Cabinet is torn by a very public row about the plans. In a radio interview the Minister for the Environment, Gulfraz Khan, declares that the plans are 'ludicrous' and states that his colleagues are making a grave mistake.

He is placed under considerable pressure from colleagues to resign, but he refuses to do so.

A few days later, a scandal erupts when an interview is published with a young woman who claims she had an affair with Mr Khan whilst she was a student on a work placement in his constituency office. The media call for his resignation, but he refuses.

The plans for development go ahead, but within weeks it is clear that the cost will be several million pounds more than originally thought. The plans drawn up by the Department for Housing contain serious anomalies. During Question Time, the opposition call for the resignation of the Minister for Housing. He refuses.

A political storm follows over the next few weeks, and numerous MPs demand a vote of confidence. The vote takes place and the government loses by three votes. The Prime Minister declares that there will be no election.

Discuss.

Answer plan

➜ Outline the role of conventions in the constitution.

➜ Discuss the effect of a breach of the convention of collective Cabinet responsibility.

➜ Consider the differing approaches to ministerial responsibility that may apply in relation to personal, and political, scandal.

➜ Explore the ramifications of failing to comply with the convention regarding a vote of no confidence.

Diagram plan

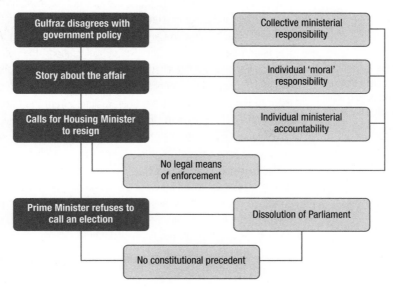

A printable version of this diagram plan is available from www.pearsoned.co.uk/lawexpressqa

Answer

[1] Before addressing the facts of the scenario, the answer should identify conventions as the subject matter. A brief explanation of constitutional conventions is necessary: Dicey and Jennings are a useful starting point.

[2] You should make reference to the facts of the scenario in your introduction; this reassures the examiner that you are going to be focused on addressing the problem rather than a generalised discussion about conventions. However, don't fall into the trap of writing out all the facts in place of an introduction.

The United Kingdom is often said to have an unwritten constitution, and there is no single documentary source setting out the roles and responsibilities of the different organs of government. Much of the constitution is now codified, but some of the business of state is regulated by the operation of unwritten conventions. Dicey defined conventions as understandings, habits and practices, which are not enforceable by the courts. Jennings (1959a) identified that a key characteristic of a convention is that individuals feel themselves to be bound by it.[1] Arguably, the unwritten nature of this element of the constitution leads to difficulty in identifying the precise requirements of a convention. Further, conventions may change over time. The events which occur in relation to the development plans are governed by various constitutional conventions.[2] The requirements of each will be considered, and the ramifications of breaching the conventions will be assessed.

The relationship between Cabinet Ministers is not prescribed by law, but instead is regulated by conventions. These have, to a degree, now been formalised in the Ministerial Code of Conduct published by the Cabinet Office. By convention, the Cabinet exercises collective responsibility and presents a unified approach to policy. Any differences of opinion can be aired in Cabinet discussions but, once agreement has been reached, all ministers will publicly support the policy and will not speak or vote against it.[3] Jennings (1959b) stated that, if a minister cannot express public support, then the convention obliges them to resign. In 2003, Robin Cook resigned from the Cabinet as he felt unable to support the Iraq war. According to convention, then, Mr Khan should not criticise the policy and, if he cannot support it, he should resign his position. There is, of course, no legal requirement to do so, which raises the question of how conventional obligations can be enforced.[4] Whilst Mr Cook did resign his position, his Cabinet colleague Clare Short remained in post for two months after publicly denouncing the war in Iraq. The Prime Minister is entitled to dismiss Khan, but cannot legally require resignation.[5]

In addition to collective responsibility, by convention, a minister takes individual responsibility for the conduct of all those employed by the department. There has been some suggestion that convention requires a minister to take responsibility for private conduct, and to resign if there is a scandal. Jaconelli (2005) argues this is not a 'true' convention, as it does not regulate the business of office. If resignations on such grounds did result from the operation of convention rather than political expediency then, arguably, the principle has become less rigid as the moral boundaries of wider society have relaxed. Hence, while David Mellor resigned in the wake of a sex scandal in 1992, 14 years later John Prescott remained in office despite revelations that he had had an affair. It is, therefore, doubtful that convention requires Mr Khan to resign due to the scandal regarding the student.[6]

It is clear that a convention exists which requires a minister to be accountable for the actions of the department that they head. A House of Commons research paper lists the options available to a minister who is subject to the convention as: inform and explain; apologise; take remedial steps and, lastly, to resign. There are many examples of ministerial resignation due to failings in their department including, famously, Sir Thomas Dugdale as a result of the 'Crichel Down Affair',[7] despite the fact he had had no personal involvement in the matter. More recently, Estelle Morris resigned as Education Secretary following delays in marking A-level exams.[8] It is also possible to find examples

[3] It is helpful to adopt a simple structure in which the convention is briefly explained, and then applied to the facts of the scenario.

[4] The answer should identify the conventions that are engaged and recognise that a key issue is the difficulty when they are ignored.

[5] You must make sure that you keep relating the legal points to the facts of this problem scenario.

[6] You should ensure that you can provide contrasting examples of how conventions have operated in practice. This is because the answer will suggest that it is not possible to be certain how conventions will operate in the scenario, as the nature of, and enforcement of conventions depends on many factors.

[7] There are many examples that can be used, and few are essential, but the Crichel Down affair is usually cited when discussing ministerial accountability.

[8] Similarly, there are lots of examples to use but including something fairly recent will show that you can relate your studies to events in the current political world.

[9] The answer should recognise that there is no clear precedent that shows how a minister must behave.

[10] This is a key point, as it is often suggested that conventions are enforced by non-legal pressures.

[11] Although it is difficult to predict the outcome of any issue concerning conventions, you will receive credit for attempting to draw some conclusions based on the analysis of examples considered in the answer.

[12] This is such an important point, it is worth setting out explicitly.

[13] Marks will be given for including relevant, current examples to illustrate the argument as this shows real understanding of the material.

[14] Unlike the conventions considered in relation to ministers, there are no examples to draw on here. The examiner is asking for (informed) speculation.

[15] Bagehot's description of the role of the monarch is important and should be included in this discussion of the constitutional position of the Queen.

[16] The assessment of what could occur in this hypothetical situation should be supported by some academic opinion.

where a minister has resisted calls for resignation.[9] The Secretary of State for Northern Ireland, James Prior, refused to resign in 1983 after 38 convicts escaped from the Maze Prison, on the basis that policy decisions were not the cause of the escape. Michael Howard drew the same distinction between administration and policy when he too declined to resign as Home Secretary in the wake of prison escapes. Analysis of ministerial responses seems to suggest that resignation depends less on the existence of a conventional rule and more on the political support the individual can command from colleagues and the media.[10] Serious financial anomalies do appear to be issues relating to formulation of policy rather than administration, so the minister may well face sustained pressure to resign.[11]

In all of the examples concerning the conduct of ministers, it should be stressed that, as conventions are not enforceable by the courts, a refusal to comply carries no legal sanction.[12]

By convention, the Prime Minister should request the dissolution of Parliament and call a general election following a vote of no confidence. This last occurred in 1979 when James Callaghan was defeated by a majority of one. The current Coalition government proposed amending the rules to specify that a majority of 55% should be required to force dissolution, but rescinded from that position following considerable opposition.[13] The refusal to request the dissolution of Parliament is a serious breach of convention which has the potential to trigger a constitutional crisis.[14] The power to dissolve Parliament remains within the personal prerogative of the monarch, but conventionally, this is done at the request of the Prime Minister. The monarch has not interfered in political matters for centuries, since the refusal of Queen Anne to assent to a bill in the eighteenth century. Bagehot (1963) described the role of the monarch as the right to be consulted, to encourage, and to warn.[15] There was speculation that, in the event of a hung Parliament, the monarch may be called upon to take a more interventionist approach but in the event the Queen played no part in the political negotiations that followed the election in May 2010. Should the Prime Minister insist on remaining in office without a democratic mandate, this may demand that the monarch play a greater constitutional role. Marshall (2002) argued that the Crown should act as a 'genuine instrument of residual constitutional protection'.[16] The breach of convention by the ministers is not subject to legal sanction but will create considerable political pressure for the individuals concerned. The consequences of refusing to dissolve Parliament are far more serious and may demand unprecedented action by the monarch if political pressure fails.

[17] You must make sure that you return to the facts of the scenario and summarise your findings.

Whilst convention appears to suggest that Mr Khan should resign, precedents can be found to support his decision to decline to do so. No such precedent exists for the failure to call for the dissolution of Parliament.[17]

✓ Make your answer stand out

- By providing current examples of the operation of conventions. If you listen to the news, you will certainly be able to find relevant issues. Whilst writing this edition, there was some controversy over the conduct of a special advisor to the then culture secretary, Jeremy Hunt. Arguably, Hunt should have been accountable for any misconduct according to the convention of ministerial responsibility.
- You could refer to political research and guidance on the use of conventions. For example, a Commons research paper is available: Gay, O. and Powell, T. (2004) 'Individual Ministerial Responsibility – Issues and Examples', Research Paper 04/31. The Cabinet Office Manual, published in 2010, included draft guidance on how conventions would operate in the event of a hung Parliament. Use of these kind of sources can show real confidence, provided that they are related to the legal issues.
- By referring to academic commentary. There is a useful article considering the enforcement of conventions: Barber, N. (2009) Laws and constitutional conventions *LQR* 125 at 194.

! Don't be tempted to . . .

- Explain the relevant conventions without providing examples of how they operate. There is very little case law concerning conventions, but you still need to provide support for any propositions that you make.
- Write a generalised account of the operation of conventions in the constitution. Students who revise the topic assuming it will appear as an essay question can be wrong footed by a problem scenario. Ensure that you use the knowledge you have about conventions to draw conclusions about the events described here.
- Ignore the fact that, when dealing with this topic, there are no clear answers. As the answer shows, it is possible to find examples supporting contrasting outcomes here; you will be rewarded for acknowledging this fact.

 Question 4

'In a word, the Queen could by prerogative upset all the action of civil government within the government, could disgrace the nation by a bad war or peace, and could, by disbanding our forces, whether land or sea, leave us defenceless against foreign nations.' Walter Bagehot, *The English Constitution* (1963), London: Fontana.

Discuss the relevance of the prerogative powers held by the monarch to the modern constitution.

Answer plan

→ Define the prerogative, and briefly outline the historical development of the power within the constitution.

→ Outline the powers thought to be personal to the monarch.

→ Discuss the limitations upon those powers created by convention.

→ Analyse hypothetical situations in which it is said the monarch may play a decisive role.

Diagram plan

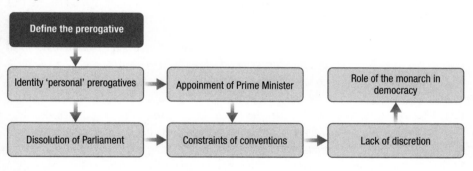

A printable version of this diagram plan is available from www.pearsoned.co.uk/lawexpressqa

Answer

[1] Blackstone's definition is usually the starting point for a discussion of the prerogative. If you cannot remember the quote, you do need to make sure that you are able to paraphrase the definition. The key point is that the prerogative is a non-legal power.

The royal prerogative was defined by Blackstone (1787) as 'that special pre-eminence which the King has, over and above all other persons, and out of the ordinary course of the common law, in right of his royal dignity'.[1] Prerogative powers are still an important source of constitutional power, although few are considered to be within the personal discretion of the monarch. Powers that are personal to the

[2] This is an important point to make, as the relationship between the two 'non-legal' sources of the constitution needs to be explored.

Crown are often constrained by convention to such an extent that it is questionable whether any discretion really exists.[2] Constitutional theorists have hypothesised about situations in which the Queen may be called upon to play a more decisive role in the organisation of the state, but it will be suggested that recent events have demonstrated that the monarch's prerogative is effectively symbolic.[3]

[3] A strong introduction should signal the direction that the argument is going to take.

The Bill of Rights of 1689 can be seen as the historical origin of the supremacy of Parliament, and since that point many of the prerogative powers have been abolished or superseded by statute. Prerogative powers, then, can be described as the residual powers of the state that are not governed by legislation and do not require authorisation by Parliament.[4] They include important matters of governance: the disposition of the armed forces; regulation of the armed forces; the grant of honours; diplomatic relations and making treaties; the appointment of the Prime Minister and the dissolution of Parliament. The majority of powers are now exercisable by the government of the day acting in the name of the Crown. The Queen retains the personal power to grant certain honours, to assent to bills passed by Parliament, to appoint the Prime Minister and to dissolve Parliament.

[4] It is very important to note that the prerogative is exercised without parliamentary approval as this emphasises the special constitutional position of the power.

[5] This is an important point to make, as the fact the monarch does not have a democratic mandate supports the argument that the role is necessarily symbolic.

In a modern democratic state, it would be anachronistic if an unelected monarch were to enjoy free rein to choose the government or to determine the duration of Parliament.[5] The discretion of the monarch is constrained by the operation of constitutional conventions which determine how it will be exercised. The dissolution of Parliament results in a general election, but by convention the power is exercised at the request of the Prime Minister.[6] The Crown has not dissolved Parliament on its own initiative since 1835. Dicey (1885) maintained that the power remained and could be exercised in circumstances where the legislature no longer acted in accordance with the 'wishes of the nation' (p. 443). It is, however, almost impossible to imagine a situation in which the monarch could lay greater claim to represent the electorate than the House of Commons. Bagehot (1963) asserted that the possibility of a dissolution instigated by the Crown had 'dropped out of the reality of our constitution' (p. 230), and it is submitted this is the more tenable argument.[7]

[6] The relationship between the prerogative and conventions is central to the argument, and the answer should be able to provide illustration of how this operates in practice.

[7] A confident approach will be able to include opposing academic arguments, and to draw some conclusions about the merits of the different views.

Bagehot described the constitutional role as to consult, to encourage, and to warn. It would appear that the monarch plays no significant role in taking a political decision. Bradley and Ewing (2010) note that it is recorded that both George V and George VI often insisted on being given the advice of Cabinet in writing if it dealt with contentious issues, suggesting a more active, supervisory, interest in the matters of state (p. 237). More recently, the Queen's private secretary clarified his view that, whilst the monarch may express opinions to the Prime Minister, ultimately she is bound to act on government advice[8] (*The Times*, 29 July 1986, quoted in Bradley and Ewing 2010). The monarch has the power to refuse to grant Royal Assent to a bill, but in practice this has not taken place since 1704. Jennings maintained that George V believed he had both the legal and constitutional right to refuse assent but recognised that, were this to occur, this would inevitably result in the dissolution of Parliament and an election contested largely on the issue of the extent of royal power.

The monarch is also empowered to appoint a Prime Minister. Again, this should not be misconstrued as conferring freedom of choice upon the Queen. By convention, the monarch will always appoint the person most able to command a majority in the House of Commons.[9] In the 'first past the post' electoral system, this is generally straightforward and requires the appointment of the leader of the political party who obtains the most seats at a general election. There has been considerable academic debate about the appropriate course of action that should occur in circumstances where an election does not produce a clear majority for any party, as, in the absence of a written constitution, it could be suggested that the rules are unclear.[10] Bogdanor suggested in 1986 that the situation would raise 'major constitutional questions', although by 2008, he had resiled from that view and considered the matter to be a purely political issue[11] (cited in House of Commons paper (2010) 'Hung Parliament':). Brazier (1999) felt that the Queen should, in all but the most extreme of circumstances, refrain from involvement in the decision-making process, but did seem prepared to countenance the (albeit remote) possibility that the monarch may need to take action if no political solution could be found. Blackburn (2004) argued that any suggestion that the monarch would have a role to play in the event of a hung Parliament was erroneous and anachronistic.

Prior to the election of 2010, the Cabinet Office published draft guidelines seeking to clarify the position, as the polls suggested that

[8] As there is little case law in this area, the use of examples to illustrate the points made shows a good grasp of the material.

[9] Here, the answer returns to the central argument, that conventions mean the personal prerogative of the monarch has little real effect.

[10] It is important to recognise the range of opinion in this area, and you will need to ensure that you are familiar with the views of at least two academics.

[11] Professor Bogdanor is one of the leading constitutional lawyers and this is a good point to include, as it demonstrates familiarity with his work.

[12] Reference to these
guidelines shows familiarity
with the current constitutional
position.

a hung Parliament was likely.[12] It was acknowledged that the monarch would invite the person most likely to be able to command the confidence of the Commons to form a government. It was, however, for the political parties to determine and to clearly communicate to the monarch who that person should be. The guidelines went on to stress that, where a range of possible administrations existed, it would be for the political parties to reach agreement and the monarch would 'not expect' to play a part in deliberations.

In the event, none of the main political parties achieved an overall majority, and negotiations did have to take place to see how a government could be formed. The monarch played no part in negotiations, and appointed the leader of the Coalition government, David Cameron, when asked to do so. This would appear to confirm that, despite academic hypothesising, the exercise of the prerogative power to appoint the Prime Minister is a purely symbolic event.[13] It could conceivably be argued that the extreme position posited by Brazier did not, in fact, arise because the political parties were able to negotiate to form an administration in a relatively short period of time. It is submitted, however, that the matter is now settled, and the guidelines set out in draft will become constitutional practice.[14]

Perhaps Blackburn (2004) is correct to criticise continued usage of the term 'personal prerogative', as it appears clear that the monarch does not retain any residual powers involving the exercise of discretion. The constitutional relevance of the monarch is now minimal, as the Queen is simply a figurehead of state.[15]

[13] It is a fairly commonplace assertion to state that the monarch's constitutional role is symbolic, but can be made more convincing by providing an example.

[14] You will be rewarded for being able to make this kind of assertion as it shows that you are confident enough with the subject matter to draw your own conclusions.

[15] Here, the answer returns to the suggestion made in the introduction but, having set out the arguments, a clear and certain conclusion can be articulated.

Make your answer stand out

- Arguably, the publication of Cabinet Office guidance represents a move towards codification of conventions. You could consider whether or not this can be seen as a signal that the 'flexibility' of the constitution is diminishing and the extent of the personal prerogative will become more certain. This would link your answer into broader issues concerning constitutional reform and demonstrate the ability to draw links between different areas of the syllabus.

- By considering some constitutional justifications for reserving the personal prerogative in more detail. You could link this to consideration of the rule of law, and the suggestion that, in the final analysis, the monarch may provide protection against arbitrary government. Again, this shows the confidence to place the discussion into a broader context.

- You could touch upon a more general discussion of royal involvement in the political process and discuss whether or not the exercise of personal prerogatives could be compatible with political neutrality. This would allow you to mention controversy in 2012 that arose in relation to a journalist's request to see letters sent by Prince Charles to government ministers. The Attorney-General blocked the release on the grounds that neutrality would be undermined. As long as you can ensure the discussion is relevant to the question, you will be rewarded for being able to draw upon current examples to illustrate your arguments.

! Don't be tempted to . . .

- Make unsupported statements of opinion. This question requires you to use academic viewpoints to support the points that are made. There are, as this answer shows, numerous sources that you can refer to. You must make sure that you are able to refer to a number, and it is advisable to try to reference academics with contrasting views (such as Brazier and Blackburn) because this means you can provide support for both sides of the argument.

- Discuss the prerogative in general terms. It is crucial that the answer focuses exclusively on the issue of the powers that are said to be personal to the monarch. It is more usual to be asked to consider the use of prerogative powers by the executive. You must make sure that you address the question asked here.

🔖 Question 5

Discuss the constitutional implications of the following scenarios.

(a) Grierson Blake has recently been appointed as Secretary of State for Education. The government has proposed new legislation, currently before the House of Commons, which (if enacted) will authorise local authorities to refuse to give free school meals to children whose parents have criminal convictions for fraud. Mr Blake appeared on a political discussion programme on the radio in which he condemned the proposals as 'discriminatory and absurd'.

(b) Over the Easter Bank Holiday Weekend, a British naval vessel is the target of a missile attack launched from Brazil. Several hours after the attack, the Prime Minister declares war upon Brazil.

(c) Simeon Davies is a student who firmly believes that militaristic interventions are wrong and he wishes to lodge a claim for judicial review of the decision to go to war.

Answer plan

→ Explain that each scenario deals with the unwritten parts of the constitution.

→ Outline the convention of collective Cabinet responsibility and consider the consequences of Blake's comments.

→ Briefly explain the meaning of a 'prerogative power' and identify the prerogative used by the Prime Minister.

→ Consider whether Simeon has standing to seek judicial review and whether the court will review the exercise of the prerogative.

Diagram plan

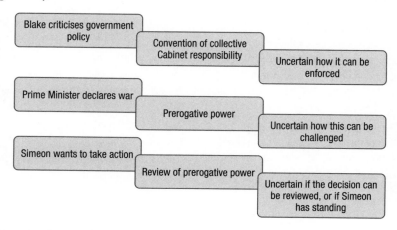

A printable version of this diagram plan is available from www.pearsoned.co.uk/lawexpressqa

Answer

The United Kingdom constitution is often described as 'unwritten'. This is misleading as much of it is documented. Despite an increase in codification more recently, some executive powers are still derived from the unwritten royal prerogative and aspects of executive conduct rest upon unwritten constitutional conventions. Each of the scenarios outlined concerns the operation of unwritten parts of the constitution and requires consideration of the consequences that may result from failure to comply with conventional 'rules'.[1]

Constitutional conventions were described by Dicey as 'understandings, habits and practices' which are not legally enforceable. Conventions regulate the use of prerogative powers, the conduct of ministers, and the relationships between different parts of the government. Conventions concerning ministerial conduct can no longer be described as 'unwritten'; the Ministerial Code of Conduct was codified during the Blair administration and is updated after each election.[2] Matters set out in the Code can still be described as 'conventions' as they are still immune from judicial regulation or legal enforcement. As a minister, Mr Blake should consider himself bound by the conventions set out in the Code of Conduct, one of the most important being the principle of collective Cabinet responsibility. This is explained in the most recent edition of the Ministerial Code (at part 2) as the requirement for all members of the Cabinet to support government policy once it has been agreed. By convention, any minister who is unable to publicly endorse the collective decision should resign, as Robin Cooke did in 2003 due to his opposition to the declaration of war against Iraq. The interview given by Blake, then, is a clear breach of convention.[3] He will not be able to argue that the position is different in a coalition government: the Coalition Agreement makes it clear that the convention applies unless it is expressly waived for a specific issue[4] (such as the renewal of Trident or university tuition fees). There is no suggestion here that the convention has been waived in respect of free school meals.

Although it is clear that Blake has breached the convention, the consequence of doing so is not so certain.[5] There are no legal consequences, as conventions are not legally enforceable. The Prime Minister can, however, sack a minister at will as the appointment and

---

[1] This question can be misinterpreted by students and is often answered as a problem about the procedure and grounds for judicial review. You should, therefore, reassure the examiner that you understand what you are being asked to address.

[2] It is a good idea to demonstrate familiarity with the Code of Conduct as it is more accurate than referring to 'unwritten' conventions of ministerial behaviour. Having done so, you do need to show why codification has not changed the constitutional definition of these issues as conventions.

[3] It is imperative that the answer keeps returning to the facts set out in the scenario. Even if every legal point is clearly explained, a failure to apply the law will lead to a substantial loss of marks. You should do this throughout the answer.

[4] Reference to the Coalition Agreement demonstrates a degree of current awareness.

[5] The question asks you to discuss the implications of each scenario: some students describe the requirements of the relevant convention here, but then forget to consider the implications of the minister's actions.

dismissal of ministers is a prerogative power. The example of Clare Short can be cited in support of the argument that conventions are only binding if they are observed, as she remained in post for some months after voicing public opposition to the declaration of war in Iraq (in stark contrast to Robin Cooke's resignation). Arguably, however, this resulted from the then Prime Minister's reluctance for political reasons to demand her resignation. In this scenario, then, it seems more likely that political pressure will be brought to bear on Blake to resign in accordance with the convention and, if he refuses, he risks being sacked.

[6] There is a lot of information to be dealt with in this scenario and, given the time constraints of an exam, you will need to be able to provide short explanations of constitutional terms.

[7] Wherever you can provide an authority to support your point, you should do so.

Prerogative powers of the crown are generally exercised by the executive and derive from the historical power of the monarch to govern.[6] Such powers are controversial, as some important matters of state are free from Parliamentary control. Prerogative powers can be abolished or restrained by statute; for example, the Constitutional Reform and Governance Act 2010 placed the regulation of the civil service under statutory control.[7] Despite numerous calls for reform, however, the prerogative power to declare war remains. Although Blair did seek parliamentary approval by allowing a debate and a vote on the matter, this was a political decision borne out of a desire for democratic legitimisation, and not a legal requirement. Here, then, it can be seen that the declaration of war against Brazil is an exercise of prerogative power.[8]

[8] This part of the scenario is fairly straightforward and you should not spend too much time on it. You are not being asked to debate whether or not this prerogative should be abolished. Careful reading of the problem should help you to see how much weight to give to each part of the question.

[9] It is always worth making this point when advising on judicial review, as the applicant may not be satisfied if the outcome cannot be a reversal of the decision.

Simeon should be advised that there are two main difficulties facing his proposed application for judicial review. Judicial review is a mechanism which allows the executive decision-making process to be scrutinised. Simeon should note that any review will not be concerned with the merits of the decision, only with how it was reached.[9] As judicial review is not an automatic right, leave of the court will need to be obtained in accordance with the requirements of the Senior Courts Act 1981. Simeon would have to demonstrate that he has 'sufficient interest in the matter complained of' (s. 31),[10] but as he is not directly affected by the decision, it is unlikely that he would succeed in doing so. An application as part of a pressure group may be more successful as the courts have, on occasion, adopted a liberal approach to the issue of standing, particularly where it could be argued that the decision complained of touches on a matter of great public interest. For example, in *R v Secretary of State for Foreign Affairs ex parte World Development Movement* [1995] 1 All ER

[10] Here, you will again need to be selective in deciding which aspects of the review process require explanation. Remember, this part of the question is primarily about prerogative powers not judicial review, so take care only to address procedural aspects that are directly pertinent to the issues raised. You do not, for example, need to deal with the time limits imposed by the CPR.

611, the pressure group was deemed to have 'sufficient interest' even though none of its members could be said to be affected by the decision.[11] Here, even if Simeon (or a pressure group) were considered to have sufficient interest, an application may still be declined if it is held that the exercise of the prerogative power to declare war is exempted from review.

[11] This is a good case to cite here, but do not spend too long detailing the various approaches to the standing of pressure groups. You would only need to do so if the facts you were given made it clear Simeon was a member of such a group.

The important decision in *Council of Civil Service Unions* v *Minister for the Civil Service* [1985] AC 374 allowed, for the first time, for judicial review of the exercise of prerogative powers. It was held, however, that some powers would not be reviewed, as they dealt with issues that should be a matter for executive discretion: this shows deference to the principle of the separation of powers.[12] Examples of excluded matters were listed in the judgment and included powers used to protect national security and powers relating to the conduct of foreign affairs. In the years that have followed, there has been an increasing willingness by the judiciary to review powers once deemed 'non-justiciable'. In this case, it is unlikely that the court would hear the application, as it touches on matters concerning foreign affairs and national security. The authorities suggest that such issues remain, for the time being, outside of the scope of review: for example, an attempt to challenge the legality of the decision to declare war on Iraq failed, on the basis that the court had no jurisdiction to consider international law (*R(CND)* v *Prime Minister and others* [2002] EWHC 2777).

[12] Mention of the separation of powers shows an awareness of the broader constitutional issues pertaining to judicial review, but, again, you do need to make sure that you do not stray too far from the core topic area.

The situations described demonstrate that constitutional behaviour still rests upon conventions, and the executive is still able to exercise prerogative powers which are, effectively, immune from parliamentary or judicial scrutiny and control.[13]

[13] It can be challenging to find a way to conclude an answer to a problem question. Here, as you were asked to comment on the constitutional implications raised, you can conclude by referring to the key constitutional topic areas addressed: the prerogative and conventions.

Make your answer stand out

- You could incorporate some academic commentary into your answer, in particular, as it relates to a potential judicial review challenge and the issue of standing. You could refer to Cane, P. (1995) Standing up for the Public *Public Law* 276.

- By referring to some additional case law to expand the discussion of whether or not this is the kind of decision that could be amenable to review. You could, for example, consider the ramifications of *R (Bancoult)* v *Secretary of State for Foreign and Commonwealth Affairs (No. 2)* [2008] UKHL 61.

- By spending more time considering the effect of a breach of the Ministerial Code, in particular the fact that enforcement depends upon a referral from the government, which arguably reinforces the point that these matters will ultimately be political decisions rather than matters of constitutional law.

! Don't be tempted to . . .

- Speculate about what you think the response to events may be without showing what precedents you have identified to support your view. It can be difficult dealing with questions regarding conventions because your examples will tend to come from political events rather than case law. Spending time reading reputable news websites will pay dividends when dealing with this part of the syllabus.

- Discuss conventions in general terms. In this question, no marks will be available for demonstrating that you can explain a number of different constitutional examples; you are only required to think about ministerial responsibility. Sometimes students make the mistake of thinking that the examiner simply wants to see how much knowledge they have retained. Far more credit will be given for selecting only those matters that are raised by the question.

www.pearsoned.co.uk/lawexpressqa

 Go online to access more revision support including additional essay and problem questions with diagram plans, You be the marker questions, and download all diagrams from the book.

Judicial review

4

How this topic may come up in exams

Judicial review is often examined by means of problem scenarios requiring you to provide advice to a hypothetical client, or clients. Most problem questions can be tackled in a similar way by employing a logically structured approach. Although the amount of case law can be intimidating, answers are improved by demonstrating a solid understanding of the procedures necessary to bring a claim. Essay questions will generally require an evaluation of the effectiveness of judicial review; this often overlaps with the topic of separation of powers and the ability of the judiciary to restrain the arbitrary use of executive power.

■ Attack the question

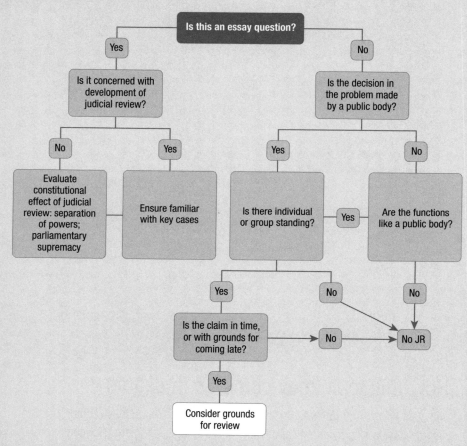

A printable version of this diagram is available from www.pearsoned.co.uk/lawexpressqa

❓ Question 1

Marie Chadwick seeks your advice. She has a degenerative illness, and is cared for by her husband. Twice a week, the local authority arranges transport to take her to a daycare facility two miles from her home, so that Mr Chadwick can have some respite. The Chadwicks do not have a car and Marie's disabilities make it impossible for her to use public transport.

Last week, she received a letter from the local authority, informing her that the facility has been selected for closure. A place has been provided for her at an alternative facility 25 miles from her home. Mr Chadwick telephoned the local authority to ask what time the transport would collect Marie and was told that the policy was not to provide transport for journeys over 20 miles long.

The (fictitious) Local Authority (Patient Care) Act 1987 states, at section 12:

The authority has a duty to provide adequate support for patients with longterm health needs, and their carers. Facilities should be available that are appropriate and accessible for patients and their carers. In determining the appropriate provision, the authority may consider such factors as appear relevant.

Marie tells you that she feels the decision to close the daycare facility is absurd and she wants to know if she can go to court to change the decision. She would like compensation for the price of the taxi fares to and from the new centre, as well as damages for her distress.

Advise Marie.

Answer plan

→ Explain the process of judicial review.

→ Analyse the possible available grounds against the local authority.

→ Discuss the availability of compensation or damages.

→ Mention other remedies that may be available.

→ Outline the effect of a remedy.

Diagram plan

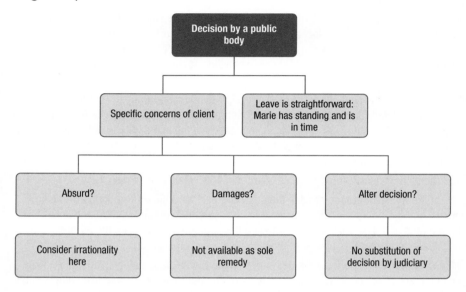

A printable version of this diagram plan is available from www.pearsoned.co.uk/lawexpressqa

Answer

Marie may be able to apply for a judicial review of the local authority's decision to close the respite facility and cease to provide transport. Judicial review is a mechanism which allows the courts to consider the process by which a public body exercising delegated powers has reached a decision. Marie should note that judicial review is a procedure concerned with ensuring that discretionary powers are exercised lawfully and fairly; it is not an appeal regarding the merits of the decision. Marie will need to be advised of the available remedies, as it may not be possible to claim compensation or damages.

The courts may review any decision made by a public body exercising delegated powers. This is not problematic, as the local authority is clearly a public body and therefore amenable to review. It should be noted that leave is required to bring an application. Dealing first with the application to review the local authority's decision: it appears that leave should be granted. Marie is an individual who has sufficient interest in the matter complained of (s. 31, Senior Courts Act 1981) so this is unproblematic. An application must be brought promptly and in any event, no later than three months after the decision complained of (Civil Procedure Rules 1998 (CPR), r. 54). As the letter was received last week, then it seems the application will be in time.[1]

Provided leave is granted, the courts will need to consider the grounds for the application. There are a number of potential grounds for review, listed in *Council of Civil Service Unions* v *Minister for the Civil Service* [1985] AC 374 as irrationality, illegality and procedural unfairness. Arguably, the Human Rights Act 1998 has allowed for the development of a fourth substantive ground of review: proportionality. Marie has stated that she believes the decision is absurd. She may wish, then, to consider whether it would be possible to argue that the decision was irrational.[2] The test to be applied is drawn from the case of *Associated Provincial Picture Houses Ltd* v *Wednesbury Corporation* [1948] 1 KB 223, in which it was held a decision would be irrational only if no reasonable decision-maker could have reached the same conclusion. Successive cases reinforce the point that the test for irrationality is stringently applied, and demonstrate that the judiciary are wary of stepping outside of constitutional boundaries by interfering with executive autonomy,[3] a point stressed in *R* v *Secretary of State for the Home Department ex parte Brind* [1991] 1 AC 696. Marie should note that an extremely high threshold has been set in respect of claims for irrationality. Judicial support for a claim in similar circumstances can be found in *R (B)* v *Worcestershire County Council* [2009] EWHC 2915. In that case, the failure to carry out proper assessment meant that the authority had been unable to arrive at a rational decision.[4] Further information would be required regarding the decision-making process, but this could be an arguable ground if it can be shown that the authority has not obtained the information needed to determine whether or not the closure was necessary. The lack of transport may suggest that the authority did not obtain all the material required. Whilst it is for the authority to determine 'relevant' factors, they should be mindful of the statutory duty to consider accessibility.[5]

It is probably worth challenging the decision not to provide transport for Marie as a separate ground of claim to ensure that, if the centre does close, the authority has to reconsider the issue. Where an authority has discretion, any policy which is a binding rule preventing proper consideration may be considered to be 'fettering discretion'

[2] It is important to take note of the wording used in the question. Here, because the word 'absurdity' is used, your examiner is inviting you to concentrate on the ground of irrationality.

[3] Although this is a problem scenario, you will be rewarded for this point which is more analytical and places the topic in the broader context of the study of the constitution.

[4] You do need to have at least one authority to illustrate the kinds of situations in which the court has held that a decision is bad for irrationality, as the answer will suggest Marie has an arguable case.

[5] You do need to draw some conclusions about the relative strengths of Marie's case but you should take care not to speculate too much. The advice needs to be qualified by making it clear that you would need further information.

[6] There are a number of cases you could use here, and there is no need to give any detail. You are simply showing the examiner that you are aware there are authorities that support the proposition that it is illegal to fetter discretion.

[7] The question specifically directs you to address this point and it will be hard to obtain good marks if you ignore the issue of damages.

[8] You need to include the statutory authority but you will be rewarded if you are able to refer to a relevant case law authority as well.

[9] You are only required to discuss the remedy of damages and that will be the focus of this part of the answer. If you are able to comment on appropriate additional remedies then this demonstrates comprehensive knowledge of the topic.

[10] Almost every judicial review answer should note the difference between review and an appeal. Again, close reading of the question shows that this is an issue you need to explore in more detail because of the client's specific request for advice about whether the court can change the decision.

[11] This is a good point to make as it shows that you not only know that the court will not consider the merits, but understand the constitutional reasons why.

[12] This kind of detailed knowledge of the rules, and relevant case law, will impress your examiner.

and this will be illegal (see, for example, **British Oxygen Co v Board of Trade** [1971] AC 610).[6] As the authority stated the refusal was on policy grounds, this may well be a point worth exploring.

Marie has instructed that she wishes to obtain damages. Damages may be awarded, and accordingly may be included in a claim (CPR 54.3(2)), but cannot be the sole remedy claimed.[7] Damages will only be payable if they would have been recoverable in a civil claim (s. 31(4), Senior Courts Act). **R (Kurdistan Workers Party) v Secretary of State for the Home Department** [2002] EWHC 644 confirmed that damages can be awarded but cannot be 'a good reason for permitting judicial review'.[8] The appropriate remedy to be claimed may be determined in part by the speed at which a claim can be lodged and whether or not the centre is still open at that time. If it is, then Marie should seek a prohibiting order, to prevent the closure, and a quashing order to void the decision.[9] Together, this would have the effect of ensuring the centre remained open whilst the authority reconsiders the decision.

Marie has indicated that she hopes the court will change the decision and must be advised that this is highly unlikely.[10] The effect and intention of judicial review remedies are, in the main, to make sure that those empowered to exercise discretion do so fairly and lawfully. It would be usurpation of the power conferred on the relevant body for the judiciary to substitute their discretion for that of the decision-maker.[11] A successful judicial review, then, will result in the matter being remitted to the local authority for reconsideration. The CPR and the Senior Courts Act do both state that the court may take the decision itself but only in circumstances where there is 'no purpose to be served in remitting the matter'[12] (CPR 54.19(3)). This will only be appropriate where the initial decision was taken by a court or tribunal and resulted from an error of law where, without the error, only one result would be possible. In other words, it is only appropriate as a time saving device as confirmed in **R (Dhadly) v London Borough of Greenwich** [2001] EWCA Civ 8122.

It seems that Marie has good grounds to seek judicial review of the local authority's actions. She may be awarded damages, but the primary remedy will result in reconsideration of the decision.

Make your answer stand out

■ By spending more time considering the grounds that could be relevant to both parts of the decision. You do need to focus on irrationality because the question demands this but, if space permits, you could open up the discussion to consider whether or not a decision made solely for financial reasons could be classified as for an improper purpose. This would be impressive, as this is quite a narrow point and beyond the scope of generalist text books. It would show real confidence in analysing the law.

■ By referring to the Law Commission report (No. 322) on the issue of damages published in May 2010, *Administrative Redress: Public Bodies and the Citizen* (available at: www.lawcom.gov.uk/docs/lc322.pdf). The Law Commission propose that damages should be available as a sole remedy in review proceedings. Although you must limit your advice to the current law, you could suggest that there is a perceptible shift in favour of the award of damages, which could assist Marie. This would show the examiner that you have read around the subject.

■ By explaining the available remedies in more detail. There are a number of useful texts you could consider, including: Sunkin, M. (2010) 'Remedies available in judicial review proceedings', in D. Feldman (ed.), *English Public Law* (2nd edn). Oxford: Oxford University Press.

! **Don't be tempted to . . .**

■ Ignore the wording of the question. Your examiner will provide clues that should help you find the issues that they really want you to talk about. Here, use of the word 'absurdity' should trigger you to consider irrationality. Students who fail to pay close attention to the wording can miss this kind of hint and lose out on valuable marks.

■ Not spend enough time discussing the effect of successful review here. The client has raised it and you need to show the examiner that you can point out the issues that matter to the client, and advise accordingly.

■ List all the grounds for review that you can remember. You will get more marks for being able to pick out a few that are applicable. It is always important to remember that marks are given for application of relevant law, but judicial review seems to be an area where students are particularly likely to tell the examiner everything they know. It can be daunting, because you don't want to miss a relevant ground. An answer that includes a discussion of two grounds that could be relevant but omits a third will get higher marks than an answer listing every possible ground without explaining how they are relevant.

❓ Question 2

Marcia, who lives in London, is a wildlife enthusiast and is particularly interested in otters. She is horrified, therefore, to read in the newspaper that Northumbria Council are planning to start a cull of otters, as they are blamed for the spread of a rare infectious disease affecting sheep in the area. The cull was authorised by the Minister of Agriculture five months ago after thousands of sheep had to be destroyed, threatening the livelihood of local farmers. She does some research and discovers that otters are a protected species under the Wildlife and Countryside Act (as amended) 1981, making it an offence to kill them unless it is necessary to prevent the spread of disease. The Animal Welfare Act 1981 confers a power on the Minister of Agriculture to order a cull if it is necessary to eliminate, or substantially reduce, disease (s. 21). She also finds a number of scientific journal articles claiming that although otters do carry the infection, it is unlikely that they are the primary source of infection in the sheep. She feels that the minister has not taken into account all of the scientific evidence.

Marcia has also found that the Otter Preservation Society (OPS) is campaigning against the cull and she decides to join. She receives her membership confirmation and is given a membership number: 10234.

Marcia would like to know if she can take action to stop the cull.

Answer plan

→ Explain the function and purpose of review.

→ Consider whether or not a review out of time would be permitted.

→ Consider whether or not the OPS could obtain standing.

→ Assess the strength of the possible grounds.

Diagram plan

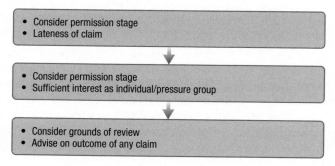

- Consider permission stage
- Lateness of claim

- Consider permission stage
- Sufficient interest as individual/pressure group

- Consider grounds of review
- Advise on outcome of any claim

A printable version of this diagram plan is available from www.pearsoned.co.uk/lawexpressqa

Answer

In this scenario, the only legal action that may be open to Marcia is a claim for judicial review. Judicial review is a process which allows a party to challenge decisions made by or on behalf of the executive. It is important to note that, unlike an appeal, judicial review is not concerned with the merits of the decision, only the manner in which it was made. There are a number of issues which may make it difficult for a claim to be brought in these circumstances.[1]

[1] It is quite common to assume that the examiner always presents a scenario containing a potentially strong claim, with arguable grounds. Here, the case is extremely weak. A good answer will realise this and advise accordingly. Setting this out in the introduction strikes a confident tone.

Judicial review is not an automatic right: leave of the court must be obtained. This is governed by the Senior Courts Act 1981 (SCA) and the Civil Procedure Rules (CPR). Leave will only be granted if the applicant has sufficient interest in the matter complained of and the claim is lodged promptly (s. 31, SCA) and no later than three months from the date of the decision (CPR r. 54).[2]

[2] There is no need to give detail setting out the courts' approach to the permission stage here; it is far better to do this with reference to the facts given in the problem as this shows an ability to apply the law.

In this case we are told that the Minister of Agriculture authorised the cull five months ago. Any claim, then, would be at least two months late. Even where the claim is within the three-month limit, the court can still refuse leave if, in the circumstances, the applicant has not been prompt. The court may exercise discretion to extend the time limits with 'good reason' (r. 53 (4)). In *R v Secretary of State for Trade and Industry ex parte Greenpeace Ltd* [1998] COD 59 it was held that when deciding whether or not to allow a late claim the court should consider whether there is an objective excuse for late application, the possible detriment to third party interests and the public interest in reviewing the decision. Here, it appears that Marcia can only offer the fact that she has only recently seen the media report.[3] It is doubtful that this would be considered a good enough excuse: in fact, it may simply reinforce the difficulties that she will face in establishing sufficient interest.[4] Conversely, the financial hardship faced by the farmers could be seen as a third-party 'detriment' that would be increased if there were to be a delay.

[3] It is obvious that the claim is out of time and unlikely to be granted an extension. It is necessary, though, to explain the legal reasons for reaching that conclusion with reference to the specific considerations the court would use.

[4] Mention of the issue of standing here shows the ability to see the links between different aspects of the case, but you should not discuss the sufficient interest test in detail here. It is important to deal with the procedural requirements in a logical order rather than skipping backwards and forwards.

Even if the court was prepared to extend the time limit, Marcia would struggle to show sufficient interest. The leave procedure is designed to filter out vexatious applications from 'busybodies, cranks and other mischief makers' (*IRC v Commissioners v National Federation of Self Employed and Small Businesses Ltd* [1982] AC 617) with strong views on a particular issue. Marcia's interest in the welfare of otters is unlikely to meet the test as she cannot show that the cull would impact on anything other than her feelings. After all, had she not happened to find the newspaper article, she may never have known about it.[5] Her best hope would be to see if the Otter Preservation Society would be willing to submit an application. Of course, they would face the same obstacles regarding the timing of the claim.[6] They may, though, be better placed to argue sufficient interest. In *R v Secretary of State for the Environment ex parte Rose Theatre Trust Co* [1990] 1 QB 504 it was held that a group could not obtain standing simply by banding together if no single member could have demonstrated it as an individual. In *R v Secretary of State for the Environment ex parte Greenpeace Ltd* [1994] 4 All ER 329, however, sufficient interest was granted to the organisation for a number of reasons. Firstly, Greenpeace had a large membership whom they could legitimately claim to represent. Secondly, some of those members could demonstrate individual standing, but Greenpeace had the resources to mount a more effective challenge. Finally, the decision concerned was one of general public interest, as it concerned the use of nuclear energy. Greenpeace had 400,000 members, so despite a membership of over 10,000, the court may not feel that the OPS are representing a sizeable section of the public in the same way.[7]

If the OPS were granted permission, the court would then consider whether or not any grounds for review were present. The grounds were categorised by Lord Diplock in *Council of Civil Service Unions v Minister for the Civil Service* [1985] AC 374 as illegality, irrationality and procedural impropriety. It is widely accepted that, as he predicted, the increasing influence of the European Convention of Human Rights has led to a fourth ground of proportionality.[8] In this case, Marcia should be advised that it is hard to identify any arguable grounds.[9] Her instructions suggest that she believes the decision to be illegal, on the basis that the Minister has failed to properly consider the evidence before reaching his decision and has therefore erroneously concluded that a cull would 'substantially reduce or eliminate' disease. The difficulty here, though, is that the power contained in the Act does not specify any particular factors which must be taken into account. It will, then, be for the court to determine what considerations are necessary to fulfil the purpose of the Act. It may be reasonable to argue that on any interpretation, scientific

---

[5] Here, the answer refers back to the point made about coming late and gives the explanation for it.

[6] There is no need to repeat the points made above about lateness here, but it is worth pointing out that they do still apply in order to make clear that it is also unlikely an extension would be given to OPS.

[7] The scenario included the information about member numbers. Whenever that kind of detail is provided, you should not ignore it. Ask yourself what aspect of the topic is being suggested to you and make sure you deal with it.

[8] There is no need to set out all the possible grounds for review. Focus on issues arising in the scenario.

[9] Students find it very hard to give negative advice. If you are certain that the case is weak, you should say so.

evidence must be required to determine necessity. The authorities are clear, however, that it will be for the decision-maker to decide what weight to give to each factor (***Tesco Stores Ltd v Secretary of State for the Environment*** [1995] 2 All ER 636).[10] Provided, then, that the minister could show that account had been taken of scientific evidence, it is highly unlikely that the court would interfere with the conclusions drawn unless it could be argued that they were irrational. This is a difficult argument to sustain as the test for irrationality requires the decision to be one that no reasonable decision-maker could have arrived at. Falling short of this, any criticism of the findings made by the minister would clearly go beyond the constitutional remit of the review process by commenting on the merits of the decision rather than the manner in which it was made.[11]

[10] This shows the examiner that the advice given is based upon a logical and careful application of law to facts. Showing this process is actually far more important than the conclusion reached.

Unfortunately, the advice given to Marcia will be a disappointment to her. It is highly unlikely that she would be able to bring a claim for judicial review in her own right, as she does not have sufficient interest in the matter. Even if the OPS were willing to mount a challenge and were able to show standing, they would struggle to persuade the court to permit a late claim in these circumstances. Assuming that permission were to be given, there do not appear to be any arguable grounds.[12] On this occasion, then, there are no legal avenues available to Marcia and she should be advised against attempting to apply for judicial review.

[11] This point makes it clear you understand how the topic of judicial review links with other areas of the syllabus.

[12] A brief summary of the identifiable difficulties is helpful as it leads into the inevitably negative concluding advice.

✓ Make your answer stand out

- By considering some additional cases regarding relevant and irrelevant considerations. You could discuss the case of *R* v *Somerset County Council ex parte Fewings* [1995] 3 All ER 20. The judgment addresses the difficulty in distinguishing between the grounds of relevant/irrelevant considerations and acting for an improper purpose, highlighting the 'grey' areas of the law.

- By recognising the similarities between the facts and those surrounding a court action attempting to challenge the decision to authorise a cull of badgers (*R (on the application of Badger Trust)* v *Secretary of State for the Environment* [2012] EWCA Civ 286). This would allow you to suggest that there is some precedent for permission being given to a wildlife campaigning group, reinforcing the advice that this case would be unlikely to be successful.

! Don't be tempted to . . .

■ Give detailed information about the facts of the cases mentioned. Marks are given for showing an understanding of the *ratio*, and an ability to apply this to the scenario given. For example, there is no need to tell your examiner anything about the facts of *Tesco Stores.* In order to explain the facts, you would need to be able to remember a lot of detail about planning law, and it would take up quite a lot of space in your answer.

■ Incorporate advice regarding the classification of a public body. There is no need to discuss the distinction between *R v Panel on Takeovers and Mergers ex parte Datafin plc* [1987] 2 WLR 69 and *R v Disciplinary Committee of the Jockey Club ex parte Aga Khan* [1993] 1 WLR 909 in this kind of question, where the decision-making authority is clearly a public body. A good answer will see what areas of discussion are highlighted by the question.

■ Assume that you must always find grounds for review. Sometimes, the advice that you need to give is negative.

Question 3

In the last 25 years, judicial review has developed as a formidable means of controlling the use of executive power and providing the citizen with redress.
Discuss.

Answer plan

➡ Explain the process of judicial review.

➡ Explain the relationship between judicial review and the separation of powers.

➡ Identify significant changes in the specified time period including the *GCHQ case*, and the introduction of the Human Rights Act 1998.

➡ Consider arguments for and against the suggestion that judicial review is an effective method of controlling the executive.

➡ Analyse any problems for the citizen in obtaining review.

Diagram plan

A printable version of this diagram plan is available from www.pearsoned.co.uk/lawexpressqa

Answer

Judicial review is the means by which the decision-making pro-cesses of the executive can be scrutinised and declared to be incorrect. Therefore, judicial review can be seen as a powerful tool allowing the judiciary to hold the executive to account. It could be argued that this is part of the system of checks and balances that exist between the organs of state to ensure a functional separation of powers, strengthening the constitutional arrangements of the United Kingdom and ensuring that the citizen is protected from the risk of the abuse of discretionary powers.[1] However, this must be balanced against the limitations that the judiciary accept upon their powers of review, and the difficulties which face the individual wishing to bring a claim.

[1] This question is not about the mechanics of judicial review, but rather, its constitutional role. Therefore, the introduction should make clear that the focus of the question has been understood.

The right of the court to review the actions of the executive is one that the judiciary robustly defend. The decision in *Anisminic Ltd* v *Foreign Compensation Commission* [1969] 2 AC 147 confirmed that any discretionary power which purports to deny the right of judicial review will be declared unlawful. More recently, in *obiter* comments, the Law Lords suggested that, if Parliament passed an act abolishing judicial review, the judiciary might countenance the constitutionally unprecedented step of refusing to apply an Act of Parliament (*R (Jackson)* v *Attorney General* [2005] UKHL 56).[2] The constitutional importance of the procedure, then, is clear.

[2] This is an important authority to cite, but you must make sure that you note the comments are *obiter*, to avoid giving the examiner the impression that you believe that this is a reality, rather than a hypothesis.

The mid-1980s can be selected as a starting point for an analysis of the function and scope of judicial review in modern times, as the seminal case *Council of Civil Service Unions* v *Minister for the*

[3] By asking for consideration of developments in the last 25 years, the question is inviting you to recognise the seminal *GCHQ case* as the starting point for discussion. It would be difficult to get good marks here without outlining the reasons why the case was so important.

Civil Service [1985] AC 374 (GCHQ case) signalled a shift in the attitude of the judiciary towards the Crown.[3] Previously, there had been an acceptance that the courts had no power to examine the exercise of a prerogative power, and the role of the judiciary would be limited to determining whether a claimed prerogative did indeed exist. This had the effect of ensuring that the exercise of all discretionary power by the executive can be examined and held to account, whether it derives from the prerogative or is delegated by statute. It is important to recognise, however, that the courts continued to accept that not every action of the government could be scrutinised, as 'excluded categories' remained. These included matters pertaining to the signing of treaties, foreign affairs, the prerogative of mercy, and issues affecting national security. The rationale for the existence of excluded categories is that certain matters of 'high policy' are for determination by the Crown and therefore judicial interference threatens the separation of powers.[4]

[4] Here, the answer refers back to the constitutional considerations outlined in the introduction, ensuring that the focus on the developing argument is maintained.

Since the decision in the *GCHQ case*, it is possible to argue that the courts have grown more willing to review the exercise of powers in a broader range of areas. For example, in *R v Secretary of State for Foreign Affairs ex parte Everett* [1989] QB 811, it was held that the issuing of passports (previously considered to fall within the area of foreign affairs) is reviewable. The exercise of the prerogative of mercy has been reviewed on more than one occasion, including the case of *R v Secretary of State for the Home Department ex parte Bentley* [1994] QB 349. In *R v Ministry of Defence ex parte Smith* [1996] QB 517, the courts rejected the government assertion that a decision to exclude homosexuals from the armed services was non-justiciable, despite the fact it concerned disposition of the armed forces.[5] It can be argued, therefore, that in recent decades judicial review has taken on increased importance in ensuring that the executive utilises its powers correctly.

[5] There are a variety of different cases that could be referenced, but one or two examples are required to support the suggestion that judicial review can be said to be used more effectively to control the executive.

[6] Marks will be given for recognising that the *GCHQ case* has not resulted in review of all areas of executive action.

Nonetheless, it should be noted that the judiciary are unwilling to review the exercise of any government power which concern matters that are clearly concerned with national security or diplomatic relations.[6] Therefore, in the cases of *R (Abbasi) v Secretary of State for Foreign and Commonwealth Affairs and Secretary of State for the Home Department* [2002] All ER (D) 70 and *R (Al Rawi) v Foreign Secretary* [2007] 2 WLR 1219 the court refused to interfere with the decision by government not to make representations on behalf of detainees at Guantanamo Bay, and in the case brought by **CND v Prime Minister of the United Kingdom** [2002] All ER 245 the courts refused to interfere with the government's determination of the legal effect of UN resolution 1441. Accordingly, the view that judicial review is able to control the use of executive power can only be given partial endorsement. The judiciary may not accept the existence of any non-justiciable categories, but deference to the executive remains to the extent that significant areas are still deemed to be the province of government.[7]

It is right to say that relatively few claims of judicial review will now be excluded on the basis that the subject matter cannot be reviewed. The vast majority of cases do not touch on matters of government policy or the use of prerogative powers. However, it is not the case that every citizen seeking review of the exercise of a statutory discretion will be able to avail themselves of the assistance of the courts.[8] Judicial review is not a right, and permission of the court is required. It is not possible to consider every aspect of the leave procedure here, but some of the potentially problematic areas can be considered.[9]

Only the actions of a public body are open to review, and further, only matters concerning public, rather than private, law. This is not always a straightforward determination as the boundaries between public and private bodies, and indeed, public and private law, can be indistinct. This can be seen by looking at the distinctions between **R v Disciplinary Committee of the Jockey Club ex parte Aga Khan** [1993] 1 WLR 909 and **R v Panel on Takeovers and Mergers ex parte Datafin plc** [1987] 2 WLR 699. The Jockey Club was declared to be a private body even though it had broad powers to regulate an important activity. The Panel was held to be a public body despite the fact the organisation was not acting on behalf of the state. The claimant will need to satisfy the court that the body is exercising powers analogous to those available to the state, which may mean redress is unavailable in some cases.[10]

A claim will be excluded if it is brought out of time. It is fair to say that the three-month limit imposed by CPR (r. 54) is not overly restrictive, and is indeed more generous than equivalent EU provisions, which allow for two months. However, partial ouster clauses are lawful (**R v Secretary of State for the Environment ex parte**

[7] At this stage of the argument, having looked at some evidence, it is possible to refer back to the question and draw some preliminary conclusions.

[8] The question raises two issues: the role of the courts in controlling the executive, and access to review for the citizen. The answer needs to ensure both matters are dealt with.

[9] As it is not possible to discuss every aspect of review in the time allowed, it is helpful to set out the parameters of the discussion.

[10] You must keep returning to the question at the end of every point you make.

Ostler [1977] QB 122), and these can make it difficult for an aggrieved citizen to lodge a claim. It will also be necessary to demonstrate 'sufficient interest' which can be viewed as a tool to exclude frivolous claims. However, the courts considered the meaning of sufficient interest in *Rossminster*, and concluded it was designed only to exclude 'mischief makers, busybodies and cranks', and, therefore, the majority of individuals who can claim to be affected by a decision will be granted standing.

[11] When answering an essay question, you must ensure that you conclude by addressing the issues that you were specifically asked to discuss. You must be prepared to offer an opinion on the material you have outlined.

Judicial review is not capable of challenging every executive action, nor can it protect every citizen. As has been shown, despite an increasing willingness by the judiciary to examine the actions of the state, limitations remain. Nonetheless, it is right to say that the scope of judicial review has increased significantly since the *GCHQ case*, and there is a greater willingness by the courts to scrutinise the use of government powers.[11]

✓ Make your answer stand out

- By expanding the discussion about the sufficient interest test and suggesting it is less onerous than it once was. You could cite the case of *R (Edwards)* v *Environment Agency* [2004] EWHC 736 (Admin), in which it was held the applicant had sufficient interest in a decision despite evidence that suggested he had displayed little interest in the issue during a long consultation process. This could be used to support the argument that the test does not prevent interested parties from lodging a claim.

- By considering the effect of the Human Rights Act on the constitutional role of judicial review. Jowell, J., (2000) Beyond the rule of law: towards constitutional judicial review *Public Law* 671–83 is a good starting point for additional reading. You could suggest that the HRA has resulted in a situation where judicial review is able to offer better protection for the citizen. This would show your examiner that you can see the connections between different areas of the syllabus.

- By outlining some of the contrasting academic argument about the role of judicial review in challenging legislation. Waldron has suggested that this poses a challenge to notions of democracy. Lever has rejected this argument. (Waldron, J. (2006), The core of the case against judicial review, *Yale Law Journal*, 115: 1346, and Lever, A. (2007), Is judicial review undemocratic *Public Law* 280–98). You must remember that it will not be enough to cite the views of academics, however, unless you use the arguments to answer the question your examiner has asked.

! Don't be tempted to . . .

- Provide statements about the role or effect of judicial review that you cannot support with authority, or examples. Marks cannot be given for unsupported opinion. A weaker answer might make the (valid) point that the judiciary will still defer to the executive when matters of foreign policy are in issue. More credit will be given to the student who can state that this can be ascertained from the decisions in *Abbasi*, or *Al Rawi*.

- Give a descriptive account of the process of judicial review. Students often expect this topic to appear as a problem scenario, and are therefore unprepared to engage in the kind of analysis needed here. Weak answers, then, tend to explain the various stages of the review process and outline the various grounds of a claim without using knowledge of the subject to offer an answer to the question. If you do not feel able to put together an argument about the role of judicial review, it would be better to avoid answering this question altogether.

? Question 4

Taylor wishes to open a bar in the Moorland area of Thurstown. He makes an application to the Council Licensing Committee for permission to sell alcohol for consumption on the premises. The Committee meets each month to consider applications, using the power delegated by the Licensing Act 2003, which provides, at section 4, that an application may be refused in order to comply with one of the following objectives:

(a) the prevention of crime and disorder;
(b) public safety;
(c) the prevention of public nuisance; and
(d) the protection of children from harm.

The Act further provides that any appeal against refusal of a licence must be made within four weeks.

Taylor is asked to address his application to Mr Greaves, the chair of the committee. Before posting the form, he decides to telephone Mr Greaves to make sure he has included everything relevant. During the course of the call, Mr Greaves tells Taylor not to worry, and that there are no reasons why the application should not be granted.

Two days after the committee meets Taylor receives a letter which simply states that the application has been refused. He telephones the council to ask why, but is told that the minutes will be made publicly available online in two weeks. Five weeks later, the minutes are finally posted online with a note explaining they are late due to staff shortages. The minutes regarding Taylor's application state:

The committee feels that there are too many bars in the area at present, and the commercial viability of existing licensed premises will be undermined if further applications are agreed.

Taylor seeks your advice about any action he can take.

Answer plan

→ Explain the process of judicial review.

→ Consider the problems raised by the timing of the application.

→ Identify and assess the merits of the potential grounds.

→ Draw some conclusions about the merits of Taylor's case.

Diagram plan

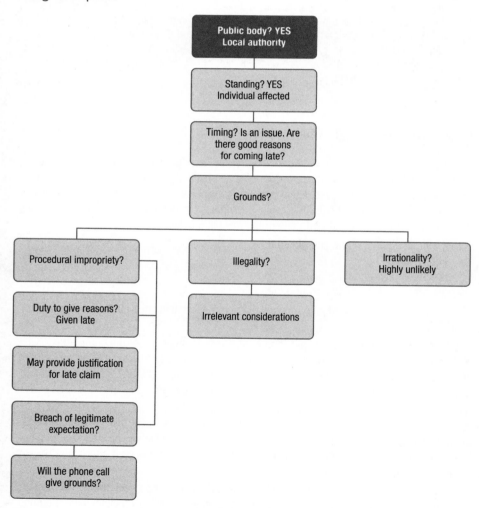

A printable version of this diagram plan is available from www.pearsoned.co.uk/lawexpressqa

Answer

Taylor should be advised to consider bringing a claim for judicial review of the decision not to grant a licence. Judicial review is the mechanism which allows the courts to scrutinise the decision-making process of executive bodies exercising discretionary powers. It should be noted that a judicial review is concerned with the manner in which a decision is reached, and is not an appeal on the merits.

The courts are only able to judicially review decisions reached by public bodies. Here, the local authority is clearly acting as a public body in the exercise of delegated power.

Judicial review is not a right, and Taylor will need to seek the leave of the court. The leave requirements are now set out at section 31 of the Senior Courts Act 1981. In order to obtain leave, he will need to demonstrate that he has sufficient interest in the matter complained of. Here, as he is directly affected by the decision then this will be unproblematic.[1]

[1] It is useful to show that all the requirements of the leave procedure are understood, but as standing is not problematic in this scenario, it should be dealt with swiftly.

The Senior Courts Act also requires claimants to lodge a claim 'promptly', and certainly no later than three months from the date of the decision complained of (Civil Procedure Rules, r. 54). Here, we are told that the statute imposes a time limit of less than three months. Rule 54.5 allows for the imposition of a shorter time limit; therefore Taylor is out of time. However, the court can exercise discretion and take the decision to allow the claim to proceed even though he is outside of the time limit. The court may exercise this discretion to allow late application if there are good, objective reasons for coming later (*R* v *Secretary of State for Trade and Industry ex parte Greenpeace* [1998] ELR 415). Here it seems that, as the minutes were not available at the correct time, Taylor was unaware of the grounds for the application until the deadline had passed, and it is arguable that this is a case in which the court should exercise its discretion.[2]

[2] The authority cited here allows the answer to draw conclusions about the likely outcome of this case.

Assuming that leave is granted, the court will then have to consider whether or not there are grounds for judicial review. There are three categories of grounds for judicial review, outlined in the *Council of Civil Service Unions* v *Minister for the Civil Service* [1985] AC 374 as illegality, procedural impropriety and irrationality. Taylor may have grounds falling under the headings of procedural impropriety and illegality.

Procedural impropriety can occur either through the failing to comply with statutory requirements, or through a general failure to comply with what are sometimes referred to as 'the rules of natural justice'. This somewhat ill-defined concept deals with the standards of fairness that the courts have seemed to consider demand protection in all proceedings.[3] There have been a number of cases in which a prior indication of the outcome of a decision has been held to create a 'legitimate expectation'. A legitimate expectation is not a 'legal right' but the courts can find circumstances where equity demands that it is given protection, as it would be unfair to thwart the expectation.[4] For example, in *R v Inland Revenue Commissioners ex parte Preston* [1985] AC 835 it was held it would amount to an abuse to allow the IRC to renege on an assurance given to taxpayers that their affairs would not be investigated provided certain conditions were complied with. Although it is clear then that a legitimate expectation can be created by an assurance, it is not certain that Taylor would be successful. A distinction can be drawn between the situation in the *Preston* case and the authority from *R v Liverpool Corporation ex parte Liverpool Taxi Fleet Operators* [1972] 2 QB 299 concerning an indication given regarding the probable grant of a licence, in which it was held that an undertaking given by a chair of the committee was *prima facie* unlawful as this would fetter the discretion of the decision-making body itself.[5] The expectation created in the minds of the taxpayers is, arguably, more worthy of protection as, if not honoured, the effect is punitive and potentially a threat to liberty. Here, the facts seem to be more analogous with the *Liverpool* case and it appears that the assurance given to Taylor will not give rise to an expectation that the courts will protect.[6]

There is no general duty to give reasons, so Taylor will be unable to argue that the failure to provide reasons automatically amounts to a procedural impropriety. However, as the council appears to accept that reasons should be given and provide a timescale, the issue requires some consideration and certainly, further investigation of the provisions of the enabling Act. If the legislation stipulates that reasons must be provided, and gives a timescale, then the failure to comply may be a procedural impropriety.[7] If that is the case, the court would need to determine whether or not the non-compliance

[3] You should attempt some explanation of 'natural justice', even though it is a vague concept. This reassures your examiner that you do understand this key concept.

[4] It is helpful to provide this brief definition. Not only have you shown the examiner that you know what it means, you have also shown you understand something about the legal status of an expectation.

[5] This is a really useful authority to cite, as the facts are similar to those in the problem. It can give a clear indication of the approach a court is likely to take when assessing the merits of Taylor's claim.

[6] You must remember to keep returning to the facts of the scenario, and using the law you have outlined to draw conclusions about the facts of the problem.

[7] It is a good idea to note the fact that the question has not specified that there is a requirement to give reasons. Some students will assume that there is because reasons have been provided. A better answer will make the point that there is a need to check the legislation carefully, as this is what a lawyer would do in practice.

[8] Marks will be given here for noting that the late reasons may provide procedural assistance, even if not part of the substantive claim.

[9] It is necessary to show that there are authorities to support this ground, but here, as there is little controversy about the applicability of the ground, it isn't necessary to explain the ratios or facts in any detail.

[10] Although it will be concluded that this ground is the most appropriate on which to base a claim, little space is given to it in the answer. This is because it is very straightforward, and more marks are available for exploring the more contentious issues in more detail.

should be considered to be 'substantial' following *R v Immigration Appeal Tribunal ex parte Jeyeanthan* [1999] 3 All ER 231. In this case, it is difficult to see how the late provision of reasons impacts on the decision-making process. This aspect of the case is more helpful in assisting Taylor to persuade the course to allow the late claim.[8]

Taylor may wish to argue that the decision should be considered to be illegal. Illegality can arise in a variety of ways. Where the statute provides that certain factors need to be considered in the decision-making process, it is not permissible to take account of other matters. The courts have been willing to hold a decision to be illegal where it has been taken on the basis of irrelevant matters in numerous cases including *Wheeler v Leicester City Council* [1985] AC 1054 and *R v Secretary of State for the Home Department ex parte Venables* [1997] 3 WLR 23.[9] Here, the statute sets out the matters that need to be considered, and the commercial effect on other businesses will therefore be deemed irrelevant. This would seem to be the ground that is most likely to succeed.[10]

If the application is successful, the court has the discretion to provide a remedy, and all remedies will have the effect of ensuring that the decision is taken again. Here, it is probable that a quashing order will be made to void the original decision.

✓ Make your answer stand out

- By spending more time discussing the issue of legitimate expectations which has attracted considerable academic comment. There is an excellent overview of the topic in Craig, P. (1992), 'Legitimate expectations: a conceptual analysis' *LQR*, 108: 79–98, which clearly explains the different circumstances in which an expectation could be said to arise.

- By incorporating some more recent case law that has addressed the issue of legitimate expectations. You may wish to start by considering the journal article Knight, C.J.S. (2009) Expectations in transition: recent developments in legitimate expectations *Public Law* 15–24, which discusses a number of important authorities. You will be rewarded if you can incorporate relevant academic comment.

- By giving more detail regarding the late provision of reasons. A clear explanation of this area can be found in Schaeffer, A. (2004) Reasons and rationalisations: late reasons in judicial review *JR* 151. This would show the examiner that you have a detailed understanding of the topic.

! **Don't be tempted to . . .**

- Speculate about the merits of the decision. It may seem self-evident that the licence should have been granted, given the wording of the statute. Students sometimes suggest that, as a result of a review, the decision will be reversed. You must remember, however, that the purpose of judicial review is to assess the manner in which the decision was made, and the effect of any remedy given is to ensure that the decision is made again, using the correct procedure.

- Use speculation to find potential grounds for review. Here, there is no suggestion of any improper purpose or bad faith, and yet a surprising number of students attempt to argue that, as the decision was plainly wrong, it must have been malicious. You must never make assumptions that are not based on facts that you have been given.

Question 5

An increasingly liberal approach to the grant of permission for judicial review means that the leave procedure can no longer effectively exclude 'busybodies, cranks and other mischief-makers' (Lord Scarman, *IRC* v *NFSESB* [1982] AC 617).
Discuss.

Answer plan

→ Explain the role of judicial review is supervisory.
→ Consider limitations preventing parties obtaining permission.
→ Outline the increasing willingness to review the prerogative.
→ Assess the relevance of the exclusivity principle.

Diagram plan

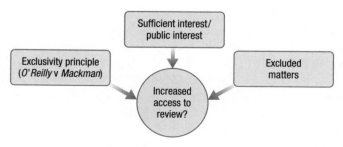

A printable version of this diagram plan is available from www.pearsoned.co.uk/lawexpressqa

Answer

Judicial review allows the courts to scrutinise the executive decision and provides a mechanism for individuals to challenge decisions which they feel have been improperly made. Judicial review is not, however, an examination of the merits of a particular decision, but a supervisory process to ensure that delegated powers are exercised correctly;[1] hence, it can be seen as part of a functional separation of powers. There has been a dramatic increase in the number of applications since the *IRC case*. In 1996, Lord Woolf suggested the expansion of judicial review was one of the most significant legal developments in 25 years (p. 250). In the same time period, there has been a decrease in the number of issues excluded from review, a more relaxed interpretation of the exclusivity principle and a more expansive interpretation of 'sufficient interest'.[2]

Scarman's description of 'busybodies and cranks' was intended to explain the need for the applicant to prove sufficient interest in the matter complained of[3] in order to obtain leave for judicial review (now mandated by the Senior Courts Act 1981, s. 31). Where an individual can show that the decision in question will have a direct impact upon them, this is straightforward.[4] Historically, the courts have not been prepared to accept that moral or political objections to a particular decision constitute 'sufficient' interest. This was the basis of the decision in *R v Secretary of State for the Environment ex parte Rose Theatre Trust Co* [1990] 1 QB 504 which held that the trust could not show sufficient interest simply because of the number of members if none could demonstrate standing as individuals.[5] More recently, however, a number of authorities appear to contradict that principle. *R v Secretary of State for Foreign Affairs ex parte World Development Movement* [1995] 1 All ER 655 allowed a pressure group to challenge a decision concerning overseas aid and justified this on the basis of the general public importance of the issue raised and respect for the rule of law. Similarly, strong feelings regarding the constitutional ramifications of the Maastricht treaty amounted to sufficient interest in *R v Secretary of State for Foreign Affairs ex parte Rees-Mogg* [1994] QB 552.[6] Arguably, then, the courts are now willing to equate 'public interest' with 'sufficient interest', which can be said to represent a significant extension of the function of judicial review.

[1] It is always crucial to be able to define judicial review, so exam preparation should include ensuring that you can accurately and succinctly explain the process.

[2] The majority of students will focus their answer solely upon the question of sufficient interest, but this is only one aspect of the leave procedure. More credit will be given to answers that demonstrate a broader understanding of this topic.

[3] Some students still refer to 'locus standi' but you should use the correct terminology introduced by the Senior Courts Act 1981.

[4] There is no need to discuss any cases in which individual standing has been granted as they are irrelevant to a consideration of changes to the sufficient interest test.

[5] This part of the judgment must be included; it is not the fact of the refusal that matters, only the reason for it.

[6] As you are suggesting that there has been a general trend towards liberalisation, it is helpful to cite more than one case to show that this conclusion is supported by a number of authorities.

Some argue that the shift in approach to the review process demonstrates an increase in judicial activism. Jonathan Sumption QC (2011), for example, observes a decline in judicial deference to both executive decisions and to the efficacy of Parliament's ability to hold the executive to account. Certainly, the courts have been willing to assert their ability to review a broader range of decisions, particularly those made using the exercise of a prerogative power. The presumption that prerogative powers were immune from scrutiny was overturned in *Council of Civil Service Unions v Minister for the Civil Service* [1985] AC 374 (the GCHQ case), but with the caveat that certain areas of executive decision making remained beyond the reach of judicial review.[7] The list of excluded matters included the making of treaties, defence of the realm, the grant of honours and the prerogative of mercy. The rationale was that certain matters were more properly a matter for the crown's discretion. Interference by the judiciary in these areas would contravene the functional separation of powers by straying into areas of policy.[8] Nonetheless, in the intervening years, the courts have reviewed decisions concerning matters excluded by the GCHQ case such as the prerogative of mercy (*R v Secretary of State for the Home Department ex parte Bentley* [1994] QB 349), and the issuing of passports (*R v Secretary of State for Foreign Affairs ex parte Everett* [1989] QB 811).[9] Issues of foreign policy, however, remain excluded (as evidenced by a number of authorities including *R (CND) v Prime Minister and others* [2002] EWHC 2777), although *R (on the application of Bancoult) v Secretary of State for Foreign and Commonwealth Affairs* [2008] UKHL 61, whilst unsuccessful on its merits, controversially held that orders in council may be subject to review.

As judicial review is concerned with scrutiny of executive decision making, it follows that only matters of public law can be reviewed. This was confirmed in the case of *O'Reilly v Mackman* [1982] 1 WLR 550 which upheld the 'exclusivity principle': a claim concerning public law matters must be brought by way of judicial review, not ordinary action.[10] Subsequent case law has diluted the 'rule' considerably. Where there is an overlap between public and private rights the claimant can effectively choose which action to take unless to do so can be seen as an abuse of process (*Mercury Communications Ltd v Director General of Telecommunications* [1996] 1 All ER 575). The distinction between 'public' and 'private' bodies remains

[7] You do need to mention this case, but do not give detail regarding the facts. The point you are making here is about the matters listed as 'non-justiciable'.

[8] It is important to highlight the constitutional basis for reluctance to review certain matters, as this links back to the argument made at the start of this paragraph about increased judicial activism.

[9] Again, it is a good idea to cite more than one case here, to make the point that there is a general move towards allowing more extensive review of the prerogative.

[10] You do need to take care here. Relaxation of the *O'Reilly v Mackman* rule could arguably lead to a reduction in review cases if private law is available, which runs counter to the argument. A detailed discussion of this may lead the examiner to think you have not understood this. Explain the rule as briefly as you can so that you can move on to the more relevant discussion about the 'flip-side'.

an important one, however, as decisions made by a private body cannot be reviewed. Loveland (2012) refers to the 'flip side of the O'Reilly coin' to denote cases where the applicant would prefer a public law remedy whilst the state wishes to assert that the matter is private (p. 523). The **Datafin case** is often cited as an example of the courts' willingness to consider the nature, rather than the source, of the power being exercised. That case was in some senses unique because, as Loveland points out, in the absence of the grant of judicial review, no alternative method of scrutinising the work of the panel could be found. Where an applicant can use private law, the courts remain generally unwilling to allow the applicant to choose judicial review instead (see, for example, **R v East Berkshire Health Authority ex parte Walsh** [1984] ICR 743).[11]

The authorities appear to show that the courts are increasingly willing to find that an applicant has sufficient interest in cases that they deem to be of public importance and the range of issues that can be considered has certainly grown. It is important not to overstate the practical effect of this, however. Bondy and Sunkin (2009) have found that between 1982 and 2006, there was an eleven-fold increase in applications for judicial review. The number of cases progressing past the permission stage merely doubled.[12] It cannot, then, be right to conclude that the floodgates have been opened to allow the 'busybodies and cranks' access to the courts.

[11] This is a useful case to include and an important part of this answer, as it helps reach the conclusion that the liberalisation of the leave procedure should not be exaggerated.

[12] Mention of the report is important here, as it provides an authoritative basis for the conclusion.

Make your answer stand out

■ By making connections between this topic and other constitutional considerations. The decline in judicial deference observed by Jonathan Sumption QC could be viewed as a threat to the functional separation of powers. Alternatively, you could argue that, if there is such a decline, it demonstrates that the judiciary enforce the rule of law.

■ By discussing the reasons for the rise in applications, and querying whether this is simply a reflection of an increase in the number of discretionary powers being devolved to executive bodies. This would allow you to discuss the possibility that this reflects the need to ensure that the judiciary are able to exercise the checks and balances required in the constitution.

■ By discussing additional relevant case law. You could, for example, look for additional authorities to illustrate the 'flip side' of the exclusivity principle. One interesting case is *R (Mullins)* v *Appeal Board of the Jockey Club and Another* [2005] EWHC 2197 (Admin), as it revisits issues raised in *R* v *Disciplinary Committee of the Jockey Club ex parte Aga Khan* [1993] 1 WLR 909. The judgment confirms that the definition of a 'public body' in that case is unchanged by the Human Rights Act 1998.

! Don't be tempted to . . .

■ Treat this question as an invitation to discuss other aspects of the permission stage. Demonstrating your knowledge about the time limits, for example, will not gather any marks. Your examiner wants you to be able to recognise which parts of the leave procedure are relevant.

■ Answer this question without reference to case law. It is really important not to make general assertions of opinion without providing authorities to support what you say. Your arguments are only persuasive if you set out the evidence that leads you to reach your conclusions.

www.pearsoned.co.uk/lawexpressqa

 Go online to access more revision support including additional essay and problem questions with diagram plans, You be the marker questions, and download all diagrams from the book.

The European Convention on Human Rights and the Human Rights Act 1998

5

How this topic may come up in exams

This topic lends itself to essay questions which ask you to consider the impact of the Human Rights Act 1998. This issue is pervasive and could overlap with any area of the syllabus. You could be asked to discuss the effect of Convention rights on the constitutional doctrines considered in Chapters 1 and 2, or to assess any number of the substantive rights in connection with laws concerning terrorism, police powers, or freedom of assembly. Problem questions could ask you to address the use of the Human Rights Act in challenging or creating domestic legislation.

Attack the question

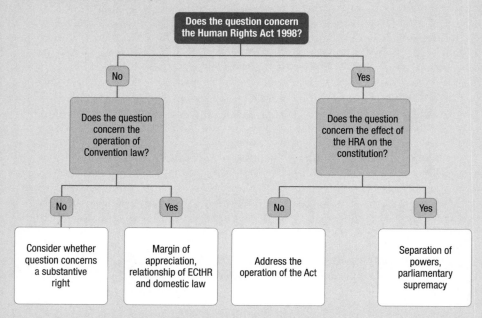

A printable version of this diagram is available from www.pearsoned.co.uk/lawexpressqa

🛈 Question 1

The (fictional) University Attendance Act 2010 aims to raise educational standards by ensuring that students take their studies seriously and get enough sleep. Section 10 makes it mandatory for all students to reside in university managed accommodation during their studies. All universities are required to fit computerised entry systems to residences. The system must record details of any student who returns to their room after midnight. If this occurs more than twice in a seven-day period, all bank accounts belonging to that student will be frozen for one week (s. 13). If the student continues to return late, the penalties increase, and can result in the loss of a university place (s. 15).

Jim is a mature student at university who, prior to starting his course, lived with his wife and family. No university residence could be found to accommodate his family. Therefore, he returns home every weekend from Friday to Monday to see them. He is very disturbed when his bank accounts are frozen, and he is told he may lose his place. He seeks advice about whether or not the Act of Parliament was made lawfully and whether or not Human Rights legislation can assist him.

Advise Jim.

Answer plan

➜ Identify the Convention rights infringed by the legislation.

➜ Discuss the legality of the Act of Parliament.

➜ Explain the possibility of a claim following the Human Rights Act 1998.

➜ Assess the likely approach of the court to the legislation using section 3 and section 4 of the Act.

➜ Draw conclusions about the likelihood of obtaining redress.

Diagram plan

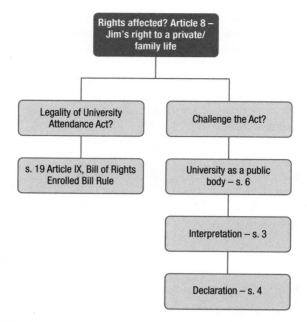

A printable version of this diagram plan is available from www.pearsoned.co.uk/lawexpressqa

[1] This succinct introduction shows an understanding of the issues that need to be discussed, and also suggests that a particular conclusion will be reached. This shows confidence with the material.

[2] Before launching into a discussion about how the Human Rights Act works, it is necessary to be able to demonstrate why the legislation should be challenged, by reference to Convention rights. This can be done swiftly, to ensure more weight is given to discussion of how the matters will be dealt with in the domestic courts.

Answer

It seems clear that the (fictitious) University Attendance Act (the Act) is in breach of Art. 8 of the European Convention on Human Rights. The Human Rights Act 1998 (HRA) provides a mechanism for the citizen to enforce Convention rights in the domestic courts; however, it is not clear that this will provide Jim with effective redress.[1]

Article 8 enshrines the right to a private and family life, and any interference must be justified for one of the reasons specified in Art. 8(2). It is not possible to construe the interference with Jim's family arrangements as 'necessary' for the purpose of protecting national security, public safety, health and morals, the rights of others, or to prevent disorder. Therefore, implementation of the Act leads to an unjustifiable interference with Jim's human rights.[2]

Jim queries whether the Act of Parliament is lawful. Regardless of whether or not legislative provisions conflict with Convention rights,

³ This gives a clear answer, but more explanation is needed because the question specifically asks for consideration of this issue.

⁴ When dealing with the HRA, the answer should refrain from making general statements about the effect of the legislation, and should ensure that specific sections are referenced.

⁵ Marks will be awarded for noticing that the type of organisation may pose a problem, as it shows familiarity with the procedural issues.

⁶ Evidence needs to be provided to support the conclusion that the university is a public body. There are a number of cases that could be cited here.

⁷ This is an important point to be aware of, and one that is often overlooked. Reference to horizontal effect shows an understanding of the operation of Convention law. There is no need to provide a detailed explanation as correct use of the term shows that the issue is understood.

any Act of Parliament is lawful and will be enforced in the courts.³ Section 19 of the Human Rights Act imposes a requirement that a minister introducing a Bill to Parliament must make a declaration of compatibility with the Convention or, if this is not possible, explain that the government wishes the legislation to be passed. Even if this requirement was not met during the passage of the legislation, then it appears that Art. 9 of the Bill of Rights will preclude the possibility of judicial interference with 'proceedings' in Parliament. The constitution rests upon the notion of the legislative supremacy of Parliament, which includes the notion (articulated by Dicey) that no person or body may question the validity of an Act of Parliament. The HRA does not alter this state of affairs, and explicitly protects the authority of Parliament by stating that its provisions do not affect the continued validity of any incompatible legislation (s. 3(2)(b), s. 4(6)).⁴

However, Jim may be able to seek a remedy in the domestic courts by bringing a claim against the university for breaching his Art. 8 rights. The HRA states that any person who is a victim of a breach of their rights may bring proceedings (s. 7). This will not be problematic for Jim as he is clearly directly affected. An action can only lie against a public authority (s. 6); this issue requires some consideration. Universities are independent organisations, although they may receive a degree of subsidy from the state.⁵ The courts have, in a number of cases, found that if the function of a body can be construed as governmental, then a claim can be actionable. In particular, any body permitted to exercise coercive powers against the individual will almost certainly be considered to be a public body (*R (Munjaz)* v *Mersey Care NHS Trust* [2005] UKHL 58). Considering the punitive powers given to the university, it seems highly probable that it will be dealt with as a public body.⁶ In any event, section 6 makes it clear that courts and tribunals are public bodies, creating an indirect horizontal effect.⁷ As a result, even if the university is a private body, when dealing with a dispute over the Act, the courts are required to uphold Jim's Convention rights.

The HRA imposes a duty on the courts to interpret existing legislation as compatible with convention rights 'in so far as it is possible to do so' (s. 3). The extent of the interpretative duty has been questioned in numerous cases since the Act came into effect. It is clear that the provision confers considerable powers on the court to interpret statutes as compliant even when the literal meaning of the words are unambiguous. On occasion, the judiciary have utilised the power to impose a meaning that 'linguistically may appear strained' (*R v A* [2001] UKHL 25, per Lord Steyn). This does not, however, extend so far as to allow the judiciary to engage in a process of interpretation tantamount to drafting legislation.[8] This point was stressed in *Re S* [2002] UKHL 10, in which the Lords confirmed that the HRA maintains the 'constitutional boundary', and preserves parliamentary sovereignty. The scenario above does not include the precise wording of the statute. However, the effect of these sections is to authorise substantial interference with the domestic and financial affairs of students and it is hard to see how the courts could read down or read into[9] such provisions to force compliance. Therefore, it would appear unlikely that the courts would be able to utilise section 3 to assist Jim.[10]

Where legislation conflicts with a Convention right, the superior courts have the discretion to make a declaration of incompatibility (s. 4, HRA). Referred to in *R v A* (above) as a 'last resort' a declaration will generally only be made where section 3 has been considered and it is deemed impossible to impose a Convention-compliant meaning on the wording. Once made, the government can determine whether any action is necessary. If it is felt appropriate to alter the legislation this can be done either by introducing a new statute or, under section 10, taking remedial action and amending the offending provisions by ministerial order. Any order should be limited to removing the incompatible portions of the legislation, and is subject to retrospective parliamentary approval.[11] Jim should be advised that a declaration of incompatibility is likely to be made in this case.

As highlighted above, section 4(6) makes it clear that a declaration does not affect the validity of the Act. Therefore, as expressly stated at section 4(6)(b), it is not binding on the parties to the case. The courts will enforce the law as it exists when dealing with the case. A declaration of incompatibility will not assist Jim in obtaining redress in the domestic courts.[12]

If a declaration of incompatibility is made by the superior court, then Jim could consider taking his case to the European Court of Human Rights to seek a remedy.[13] Where a declaration has been made, then the government is likely to wish to settle the matter as the outcome of the case would appear to be almost inevitable.

[8] The possibilities afforded by section 3 should not be overstated; marks will be given for recognising that it does not authorise rewriting legislation.

[9] This shows considerable confidence by referring to the judicial terminology.

[10] It is crucial to keep returning to the facts of the scenario and answering the question, which asks you to advise Jim.

[11] This section demonstrates awareness of the effect of a declaration.

[12] This is an important point, because the answer needs to focus not just on whether or not the courts will approve of the legislation, but on the impact of any decisions on Jim's situation.

[13] Because the question requires you to focus on advising Jim, you do need to acknowledge the fact that he has the option to take a claim to Strasbourg.

The Act includes provisions which infringe Jim's right to a private and family life. However, this does not render the statute unlawful, and it will be upheld by the court unless and until the government repeals or amends the law. Therefore, the HRA does not provide Jim with assistance in the short term, and he may still need to appeal to the European Court of Human Rights in order to obtain redress.[14]

[14] The conclusion needs to refer back to the issues that the question raised, and summarise the advice given.

✓ Make your answer stand out

- By providing more detail about the redress available in Strasbourg, and explaining the concept of a 'friendly settlement'. This will show the examiner you have a detailed understanding of the operation of Convention law. You must, of course, ensure that you relate this to Jim's situation.

- By explaining what is meant by indirect horizontal effect, and providing some authority to illustrate this point. A good example might be *Goodwin* v *UK* (1996) 22 EHRR 123, in which (as Loveland points out) the European Court concludes a state may be in breach if citizens can rely on legal provisions that restrict the access to Convention rights of others. (Loveland, I. (2012), *Constitutional Law, Administrative Law and Human Rights: A Critical Introduction* (6th edn). Oxford: Oxford University Press.)

! Don't be tempted to . . .

- Spend time discussing the limits of Art. 8. The focus of the question is not on the extent of Convention rights. It is not necessary, then, to enter into a detailed discussion about the margin of appreciation afforded to states in cases like *Handyside* v *UK*. You must make sure you focus on what action Jim may be able to take in this case.

- Refer to the HRA in general terms. It is very important that you do know which sections are relevant, and why. The more detail you can give, the better. For example, it is clearly right to say that the courts may make a declaration of incompatibility (s. 4). It is more impressive if you can also reference section 4(6) and explain that this has no effect on the case being determined. It is even better if you can highlight that this section serves to preserve the principle of parliamentary supremacy as this would show you are making links between the different areas of the syllabus.

Question 2

The Human Rights Act has strengthened the constitutional position of the judiciary, and weakened the position of the executive.

Discuss.

Answer plan

→ Outline briefly, the functions of the judiciary and the executive.

→ Explain the powers given to the judiciary by the HRA (s. 3, and s. 4).

→ Provide examples to demonstrate judicial 'strength'.

→ Consider the role of the European Court of Human Rights.

Diagram plan

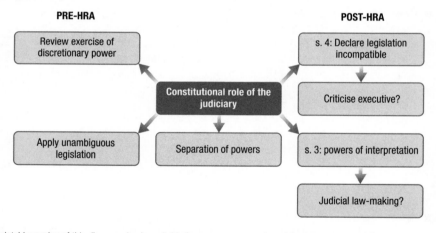

A printable version of this diagram plan is available from www.pearsoned.co.uk/lawexpressqa

Answer

The Labour government introduced the Human Rights Act (HRA) shortly after coming to power, proclaiming that it was 'bringing rights home'. A decade later, senior government figures are highly critical of the Act; Jack Straw as Justice Minister stated he was 'frustrated' by the Act in late 2008. The Conservative Party have stated that they will seek to abolish the Act and replace it with a British Bill of Rights.

It is clear, then, that the Act is a source of concern to the major political parties. Since 2000, there have been several cases in which the superior courts have utilised powers granted by the Human Rights Act to challenge legislation.[1] This may lead to the conclusion that the Human Rights Act has increased the ability of the judiciary to hold the other organs of state to account. It will be argued, however, that whilst there are instances in which the judiciary has appeared to challenge legislation supported by the executive, these can be best characterised as political, rather than constitutional issues.[2]

Although the United Kingdom does not have a written document which enshrines the authorities and functions of the organs of state, the doctrine of the separation of powers can be considered to be an integral part of the constitution.[3] According to the doctrine, the roles of the organs of state are distinct: Parliament is the supreme law-making body, the executive is responsible for introducing policy and administration, and the judiciary interprets and applies the law. The Human Rights Act granted new discretionary powers to the judiciary when considering statute. It would seem that, if there is a shift in the constitutional balance of power, the relationship between the legislature and the judiciary would be the one affected. The question presupposes an acceptance of the view famously promulgated by Lord Hailsham that there is the potential for an 'elected dictatorship' if a party of government enjoys a large majority in the Commons. Challenges made to legislation introduced by government could be viewed as, to some extent, undermining the ability of the executive to administer policy.[4]

It is perhaps appropriate to emphasise that the HRA did not increase or alter the rights of the citizen. The right of petition to the European Court of Human Rights has existed since 1966. The HRA aimed to ensure that Convention rights are incorporated into domestic law and accordingly are enforceable in domestic courts.

The HRA gives the judiciary powers to uphold Convention rights. Prior to the HRA, where an unambiguous legislative provision conflicted with a Convention right, the constitutional principle of parliamentary supremacy required the court to apply the statute in accordance with the clear meaning. Section 3 of the HRA grants the courts powers to interpret statutes as Convention compliant 'in so far as it is possible to do so'. It is clear that this allows the courts to read

[1] The question refers to the clash between the executive and the judiciary, but you will need to recognise that this arises through challenges made in the courts to legislative provisions.

[2] Many answers to this question will be too descriptive. Marks will be available for asserting a clear point of view.

[3] You will be rewarded for noting that this question is focused on the impact of the HRA on the separation of powers. You should not spend too long explaining the doctrine, but a brief explanation is needed,

[4] This question does pose some difficulty by requiring the focus to be on the relationship between the executive and the judiciary. The Human Rights Act is primarily concerned with approaches to legislation. This section explains why a discussion of the judicial approach to legislation is permissible, as most statute originates from government.

[5] The answer needs to ensure that it does have a clear focus on identifiable legal issues. The discussion must be centred on the provisions of the Human Rights Act rather than a broad, political, debate.

[6] There are numerous cases dealing with section 3. *R* v *A* is useful because it represents an example of a very broad use of the interpretative power. The phrase 'linguistically strained' is worth remembering, as it is a useful way of briefly explaining that the power can be used to alter the obvious meaning of a statutory provision.

[7] You should do more than explain the powers given to the courts by the HRA; this needs to be related to the issue of power within the constitution.

[8] Here, the developing argument refers back to the issue in the question, to maintain focus.

[9] A preliminary conclusion can be reached here, before moving on to the next part of the argument.

[10] The answer reminds the marker that the key issue is the relationship between the judiciary, and the executive.

down, or read into, provisions even where there is no ambiguity present.[5] The scope of this power is evident in cases such as **Ghaidan v Godin-Mendoza** [2004] UKHL 30, where the court was prepared to read additional words into the statute, or **R v A** [2001] UKHL 25, where the judiciary were prepared to infer a meaning that was 'linguistically strained'.[6]

Critics of the HRA could argue that section 3 has the potential to fundamentally alter the constitutional landscape, by granting a degree of legislative power to the judiciary, allowing them to subvert the intention of Parliament.[7] Consider the case of **R v A**, which concerned safeguards against the cross-examination of rape victims contained within section 41 of the Youth Justice and Criminal Evidence Act 1999. The clear aim of Parliament was to ensure that the trial process did not allow questions to be asked regarding sexual history, and yet the judiciary interpreted the provision as meaning that questions were permissible if necessary for a fair trial within the meaning of Art. 6. Decisions such as this lend weight to suggestions that the HRA gives power to unelected members of the judiciary in formulating policy.[8] However, this must be balanced against numerous instances where the courts have declared themselves unwilling to impose a meaning that goes 'against the grain' of the statute, as was said in **Ghaidan v Godin-Mendoza**. Therefore, it would seem that despite the additional powers contained at section 3, the judiciary remain largely respectful of constitutional boundaries and do not seek to stray beyond the 'outer limit' (**Re W (Care Plan)** [2001] EWCA Civ 757) by embarking on a process of drafting legislation.[9]

Where it is not possible for a statutory provision to be interpreted as compliant with conventions using section 3, then section 4 of the HRA gives the superior courts the discretion to issue a declaration of incompatibility. This has no effect on the parties in the case, but allows the judiciary to give a clear signal to the executive that the statute requires consideration.[10] The HRA contains a provision for the executive to take remedial action to amend the offending part of the legislation (s. 10). During the passage of the Human Rights Act through Parliament, the government envisaged that section 4 would rarely be invoked and this has proved to be the case. In the period 2000–2006 the government amended existing law or introduced new legislation in nine cases following a declaration of incompatibility. (Joint Committee on Human Rights (2006), 23rd Report).

The significance of section 4 should not be overstated, however, as the HRA is careful to preserve the supremacy of domestic law. A section 4 declaration cannot compel the executive to review the legislation, and unless government determines that change is necessary, the courts will continue to enforce the law. It can be argued then, that the constitutional balance is unchanged. Legislative change occurs not because of coercive pressure from the court, but as a result of political necessity.[11] A series of decisions concerning asylum and terrorism have indeed resulted in the judiciary making strong criticism of particular statutes and this has resulted in legislative change. In *A v Secretary of State for the Home Department* [2004] UKHL 56, the House of Lords declared that Part IV of the Anti-Terrorism, Crime and Security Act 2001 was unlawful, which resulted in repeal and a shift in policy as regards foreign terror suspects. It should be remembered that the courts are guided by Convention principles, and judgments of the Court in Strasbourg. If section 4 did not provide a means of resolving the issue domestically, then a negative judgment from Strasbourg would inevitably follow. Therefore, the pressure for change is extrinsic rather than domestic.[12]

[11] This is the crux of the argument suggested at the outset, and at this stage, evidence has been shown to support this assertion.

[12] This is a point worth making, as the courts are not creating new rights, but simply enforcing those protected by the Convention.

Political leaders may express concerns about the HRA, but on closer examination, it seems that the Act does not in fact make radical alteration to the constitutional position of the judiciary. Arguably, pressure on the executive regarding particular policy choices stems not from the judiciary in London, but from Strasbourg.

✓ Make your answer stand out

- By giving more consideration to the issue raised regarding extrinsic pressure on the executive. Some academics suggest that the domestic courts are beginning to adopt a more radical approach than that taken by Strasbourg (see, for example, Fenwick, H. (2007), *Civil Liberties and Human Rights* (4th edn) London: Routledge Cavendish, ch. 4).
- By keeping up to date with current developments. It will be interesting to see how the Coalition government balances the conflict between the pre-election commitment to the HRA expressed by the Liberal Democrats, and Conservative promises of radical reform. If you can comment on developments as they arise and set these in the context of the constitutional balance of power, this will impress upon your examiner that you are confident with the topic and able to form an opinion.

Don't be tempted to . . .

- Engage in a discussion of issues, without being able to pinpoint examples and cite authorities. A discursive essay of this kind has the potential to lose focus on legal issues and talk generally about the role of the courts. For example, make sure that you can give examples of when the courts have used section 3 to interpret statute in a manner that seems contrary to legislative intention.
- Ignore the fact that the question specifically refers to the clash between the executive and the judiciary. It is fine to use examples that, on the face of it, seem to be more concerned with conflict between the courts and the legislature provided that this is justified by explaining that the statutes in question represent executive policy.

Question 3

The wide margin afforded to signatory states undermines the concept of 'fundamental freedoms' in the United Kingdom.
Discuss.

Answer plan

→ Explain the terms 'qualified rights' and 'margin of appreciation'.
→ Outline the supervisory role of the European Court of Human Rights.
→ Consider the justification for differing margins for different rights.
→ Assess the role of the domestic courts in applying margins of appreciation.

Diagram plan

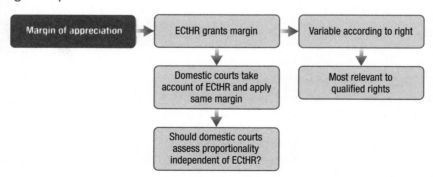

A printable version of this diagram plan is available from www.pearsoned.co.uk/lawexpressqa

Answer

The European Convention on Human Rights and Fundamental Freedoms was drafted in the aftermath of the Second World War, as the atrocities that occurred during the Nazi regime became apparent. Signatories to the Convention agree to secure the rights contained within the treaty, and the European Court of Human Rights (ECtHR) is empowered to determine whether an action by a state is compatible with that duty. In so doing, the ECtHR may afford the state a 'margin of appreciation'; it is the effect of this judicial concept that must be examined. It can be argued that the margin of appreciation has, on occasion, allowed the UK government to enact legislation that runs contrary to the spirit of the Convention.[1]

The Convention seeks to set a common standard of rights and freedoms for the signatory states. Art. 1 of the Convention places the primary responsibility for securing those rights upon the states. The role of the ECtHR can be seen as supervisory, to review the decisions made by states about how to achieve the objectives of the Treaty.[2] The notion of 'margin of appreciation' has emerged over time, as a result of the fact that the language of the Treaty permits restrictions on many of the Article rights. Few rights are 'absolute'; the majority are subject to qualification. For example, Art. 8 sets out the right to a private and family life, but Art. 8(2) recognises that a state may interfere with that right if it is 'necessary' for one of the following purposes: national security, public safety or economic well-being; to prevent crime and disorder; to protect health or morals, or to protect the freedoms of others. In determining whether the action of a state falls within one of the permitted qualifications, the ECtHR acknowledges that the domestic authorities may be better placed to judge what is necessary in the context of their own cultural values and norms; this degree of deference is the 'margin' of appreciation.[3]

Decisions of the ECtHR show that the 'margin' is not fixed, and the degree of flexibility granted to the state may vary according to the nature of the right itself, and also to the reason claimed for qualification.[4] In *Sunday Times v UK* (1979) 2 EHRR 245, the court drew a distinction between issues such as health and morals, and more 'objective' issues such as judicial autonomy (the qualification being

---

[1] The introduction signals that the key issue is going to be addressed, and that a view will be taken about the question.

[2] This is a key point to make here as it makes clear that you understand the respective roles of the signatory states and the ECtHR.

[3] It is essential to be able to give an explanation of the term 'margin of appreciation', and to do so, reference to the existence of qualifications on Convention rights is required.

[4] The imprecise boundaries of the margin of appreciation needs to be noted, as this forms part of the argument that will be developed about the need for domestic courts to be rigorous in assessing the validity of a particular qualification.

[5] *Handyside* is a useful authority, as it is a clear illustration of application of a margin of appreciation.

claimed in that case). When dealing with an objective issue, the court was not prepared to allow a wide margin, whereas in **Handyside v UK** (1976) 1 EHRR 737[5] the court refused to interfere with the domestic government's determination of the moral need for obscenity legislation. A broad margin is also evident when dealing with social policy issues, considered to be matters where there can be legitimate political difference and debate. Therefore, in **Hatton v UK** (2003) 37 EHRR 28 the court refused to hold that in allowing night flights from Heathrow the state interfered with the Art. 8 rights of the claimant. Here, the state was permitted to reach a determination that the interference was necessary for the economic well-being of the nation and the ECtHR deferred to that determination.

It is important to note that the existence of a margin of appreciation does not mean that the court will not review the exercise of discretion. However, as Fenwick (2007) notes, if the margin permitted is wide, then the ECtHR will engage in minimal supervision; limited largely to ensuring any discretion was exercised in good faith. If the margin is narrow, then there will be a more rigorous examination of the restriction to ensure it is proportionate to the aim. The notion of a margin of appreciation is controversial. As Loveland (2012) points out, viewed in a positive light, the concept shows an appropriate respect for the autonomy of democratically elected national governments. Alternatively, it could be argued that the ECtHR has on occasion abdicated responsibility for ensuring that the rights of minority groups are protected.[6]

[6] A willingness to acknowledge the academic debate ensures that the answer is not overly descriptive; analysis of the issue will be rewarded by the marker.

Matters of national security are conceded to be sensitive, and historically the ECtHR has been reluctant to interfere with a domestic determination of necessity. The case of **Brannigan and McBride v UK** (17 EHRR 539) caused considerable concern when the court upheld the legality of a derogation from Art. 5 applied by the government. The derogation arose following the judgment in **Brogan v UK** (1988) 11 EHRR 117, in which the ECtHR held that periods of detention authorised under terrorism legislation were an unjustified interference with the right to liberty. It is difficult to reconcile the decision in **Brannigan** with the ECtHR's role in ensuring robust protection for fundamental freedoms, as there appears to be a tacit endorsement of actions previously considered to be in breach of the Convention.[7]

[7] This is a useful case to cite, as it provides support for the suggestion in the question that fundamental freedoms are undermined by the application of a margin of appreciation.

It is possible to endorse the notion of the margin of appreciation, as it properly emphasises the role of the state in determining how best to balance the freedoms of the individual against the broader public interest. However, the approach of the domestic courts to the margin of appreciation could be viewed as leading to a 'watering down' of the convention, as Fenwick suggests.[8] Section 2 of the Human Rights Act requires the courts to give weight to the ECtHR judgments. There are a number of cases in which decisions appear to suggest that where Strasbourg has afforded a considerable margin to the state, the domestic courts should also give judicial deference to the decision-maker. For example, in the case of ***Gillan and Quinton v UK*** [2009] ECHR 28, the House of Lords had to determine whether the exercise of stop and search powers authorised by the Terrorism Act 2000 breached (*inter alia*) Art. 8. The state claimed that any interference was necessary in the interests of national security. The judgment suggests that, once deference is given on that issue, there can be no interference with the exercise of the power and no circumstance in which the use of the provision would be disproportionate. Fenwick (2007) refers to this as 'double deference'. As noted above, acknowledgement of a margin of appreciation does not mean the ECtHR will not address the restriction. In the case of **Gillan**, when the matter reached Strasbourg the court was unanimous in finding a breach of Art. 8.

There will always be a need to balance individual and majority freedoms, and there is unlikely to ever be a homogenous culture across Europe. The concept of a margin of appreciation, therefore, is helpful in acknowledging these facts whilst nevertheless seeking to maintain a common standard of rights and freedoms. It can be argued, however, that if deference to national autonomy is not followed by rigorous examination of executive power in the domestic courts, some of the protection for individual freedoms envisaged in the Convention will be lost.[9]

[8] The central argument, that the margin of appreciation has a detrimental effect on the protection of rights in the domestic courts, is being developed here. It would not be sufficient to refer to Fenwick's argument; the answer must also incorporate some illustrative authority to support this view.

[9] The conclusion is justified, as the argument has been developed throughout the answer.

Make your answer stand out

- By exploring some of the academic views referred to regarding deference in more detail. Fenwick (2007) is an excellent text (*Civil Liberties and Human Rights* (4th edn) London: Routledge).

- By acknowledging that the decisions of Strasbourg do not always lead to a clear conclusion about the existence of the margin of appreciation in respect of a particular Convention right. Although you have alluded to different justifications for restrictions on a right resulting in a differential approach (through *Sunday Times* and *Handyside*) you could make the point that this somewhat undermines the notion of a 'fundamental' right.

- By exploring the notion of 'double deference' in more detail. Good use has been made of the recent litigation concerning *Gillan*. You could question whether or not the Strasbourg decision marks a shift towards more stringent supervision from the ECtHR. This would show the ability to draw conclusions about the developing law.

! Don't be tempted to . . .

- Assume that the marker will know you understand the term 'margin of appreciation'. You do need to be able to give a definition.

- Use terminology incorrectly. A surprisingly large number of students refer to the permitted restrictions on Convention rights as 'derogations' and lose marks. Ensure you know the difference between qualifications upon a right for a permitted purpose, and the process of derogation which allows a state to withdraw from the obligation to protect a Convention right in certain limited circumstances.

- Fail to explain how the cases you cite support the argument. Too many students make statements along the lines of '*Handyside* v *UK* is an example of the margin of appreciation'. You need to explain that the judgment demonstrates that the ECtHR allowed the state the margin to determine the most appropriate standard of morality for its own population.

Question 4

The government publishes a consultation paper proposing a new bill provisionally entitled 'the Criminal Trial Bill'. The aim of the legislation is to ensure that more criminal convictions are obtained, by reversing the burden of proof so that defendants will need to prove their innocence in all cases.

Discuss the legality of these proposals, and the difficulties in passing and enforcing the legislation in light of the Human Rights Act 1998.

Answer plan

→ Explain the presumption of innocence in domestic law, and under Art. 6.

→ Explain the difference between a legal and evidential burden of proof, with examples.

→ Consider whether the proposals are in breach of Art. 6(2).

→ Outline the effect of section 19.

→ Analyse the likely approach of the courts in enforcing the legislation, in light of sections 3 and 4 of the HRA.

Diagram plan

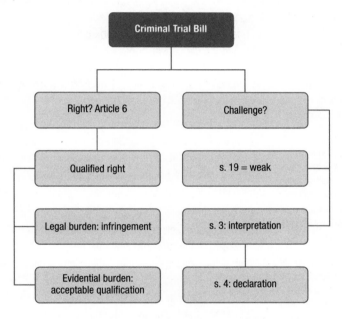

A printable version of this diagram plan is available from www.pearsoned.co.uk/lawexpressqa

Answer

[1] The question does not specify the reasons why the bill is problematic; credit will be given for being able to identify the issue.

The proposals contained in the bill would, if enacted, remove the presumption of innocence in criminal trials, described as the 'golden thread' running through the English legal system (**Woolmington v DPP** [1935] AC 462). The presumption of innocence in criminal trials is expressly protected by Art. 6(2) of the European Convention on Human Rights.[1] It is probable that these proposals could violate the

Convention. The Human Rights Act (HRA) would enable the domestic courts to seek to circumvent the effects of the proposals.

As a general principle, defendants in criminal trials are innocent until all elements of the crime are proved beyond reasonable doubt. However, the concept of a reversal of the burden of proof is not novel, particularly in relation to defences. A distinction should be drawn between an evidential and a legal burden. The imposition of an evidential burden upon the defendant can be understood as a partial reversal of the burden of proof: the defendant needs to raise some evidence of the existence of the defence, thereafter, the task reverts to the Crown to disprove the claim.[2] Often, all that is required is for the defendant to make the claim. For example, a person accused of an offence against the person can state they acted in self-defence. It is then for the Crown to provide evidence that their actions were not a legitimate use of reasonable force. An evidential burden does not equate to a presumption of guilt, and would not therefore, be considered a breach of Art. 6(2).[3]

The imposition of a legal burden is more onerous, and requires the defendant to prove a particular matter. A legal burden upon the defendant is rare at common law (the defence of insanity is a rare example), but may be imposed by statute (generally in relation to defences). A legal burden has the clear potential to violate Art. 6.

The European Court of Human Rights (ECtHR) makes it clear that Art. 6(2) is not absolute, confirming in **Salabiaku v France** (1988) 13 EHRR 379 that presumptions may be justified, provided that they remain within reasonable limits. When determining whether or not a particular presumption is justified, consideration will be given to what is at stake. The domestic courts have adopted a similar approach and stressed the importance of proportionality.[4] Therefore, whether or not the imposition of a legal burden is justifiable will depend on issues including the seriousness of the allegation, and whether or not the matter is one the defendant can reasonably be expected to prove. In the conjoined appeals **Sheldrake v DPP; Attorney General's Reference** (No. 4 of 2002) [2004] UKHL 43 [5] the House of Lords reached differing conclusions in each case. Sheldrake was charged with being in charge of a motor vehicle whilst under the influence. Statute provided a defence if he could prove that he was not intending to drive the vehicle. The legal burden in this instance was justified, as it was for a legitimate purpose (the protection of road

[2] Some knowledge of criminal law is needed, to be able to explain the different burdens of proof. This question cannot really be attempted without a specific appreciation of the rights conferred by Art. 6, and an understanding of the operation of the burden of proof.

[3] The focus is returned to human rights; it is important to return to the central issue even when referring to other areas of law to make sure that all material is utilised to answer the question.

[4] Discussion of the European approach was necessary, but the answer needs to move to consideration of the domestic application of Convention law.

[5] This is probably the most crucial case to include in the answer, as the judgment clearly sets out the matters that will be considered when assessing whether placing a burden on the defendant is justifiable.

users) and was a matter the defendant could reasonably be expected to adduce evidence about. This was distinct from the situation in the second case which concerned the offence of belonging to a proscribed organisation. Section 11(2) of the Terrorism Act 2000 provides for a defence where the defendant can show that they joined prior to the date of proscription and have had no involvement since that time. Here, the House held that this required the defendant to prove a negative which would be difficult to do, placing the provision in conflict with Art. 6. The suggested legislation, applicable to all offences, would certainly be in violation of Art. 6(2), as it is too broad and would encompass a requirement on the defendant to produce evidence about matters that it would be difficult, or impossible, to obtain.[6]

If the Bill were to be placed before Parliament, the HRA requires that the minister make a 'statement of compatibility' prior to the second reading (s. 19). This cannot be viewed as creating a particularly onerous obligation.[7] Since the HRA came into force, there has been a declaration of compatibility made in almost every case, barring the Communications Act 2003.[8] It should be noted that, where a declaration cannot be made, the minister is only required to state that the government wishes to proceed with the bill. In any event, no reasons are required to justify either the confirmation of compatibility, or why a non-compatible bill is still desirable. Section 19 has no relevance once a bill is enacted, as the principle of parliamentary sovereignty means that the court will not question the legality of proceedings in Parliament and cannot declare an enrolled Act to be unlawful.

The question of enforcement is more complex. Should the bill become law, it is likely that there would be numerous appeals against conviction on the basis that the provisions breach Art. 6(2). The HRA provides a mechanism for the citizen to enforce Convention rights in the domestic courts. Section 3 confers a power on the court to interpret legislation 'in so far as is possible' to make it compliant with Convention rights. In **Sheldrake**, the courts were prepared to read down into the Terrorism Act that the burden imposed was merely evidential. This was despite the unambiguous wording of the statute, and the fact that elsewhere in the Terrorism Act the legislation listed the provisions that conferred an evidential burden and did not include section 11(2) in that list.[9] Therefore, despite the apparently clear intention of the statute, the courts were prepared to declare that the legislation must have been intended to comply with

[6] Having outlined the authority, this must be used to answer the question posed about the suggested legislation.

[7] The question requires an explanation of the impact of the HRA on the passage of legislation, so section 19 must be explained. A confident answer can deal with this quickly as it is not controversial. This allows space to explore the effect of section 3 in more detail.

[8] This is a really useful detail to include, as it shows you are aware of the practical impact of particular statutory provisions.

[9] Even though you have already discussed Sheldrake, you need to give relevant detail from the judgment here, as you are making a different point, which is to do with the procedural approach of the court, rather than the decision that the statute breached Convention rights.

[10] The answer keeps focus by referring back to the question; you were asked to consider the difficulties that might arise in enforcing the legislation, and your conclusion is that the courts would not enforce the provisions.

[11] You should not spend too much time on considering possible government responses to a declaration of incompatibility because that would be beyond the scope of the question, which focuses on enforcement.

[12] All the evidence has been presented, and a clear conclusion can be succinctly set out.

Art. 6(2). It seems possible, then, that the aim of government in enacting the bill will be thwarted if the judiciary feel able to utilise their powers under section 3.[10]

Given the extremely broad scope of the proposals, it is possible that no interpretation by the courts will be able to make the legislation compliant. In that circumstance, the HRA enables the court to make a declaration of incompatibility (s. 4).[11] Whilst this does not impose any obligation on the executive to rectify the incompatibility, there could be political pressure to do so. It would seem certain that any claim to the ECtHR would have a good chance of success as such sweeping alterations to the trial process would be unlikely to satisfy the requirement of proportionality outlined in *Salabiaku*.

It can therefore be seen that although the bill would be 'lawful' if enacted, it would be difficult for it to be enforced as the HRA would allow the courts to seek to mitigate the effect of the proposals using section 3, or to declare it incompatible with the Convention using section 4.[12]

 Make your answer stand out

- By giving consideration to the suggestions raised in the case of *Jackson* v *Attorney General* [2005] All ER (D) 285 that there may be circumstances in which the courts would declare an Act to be unlawful. It could be argued that this bill, if enacted, would be unconscionable and could spark constitutional rebellion by the judiciary!
- By referring to some academic arguments on the role of the judiciary in upholding human rights. The journal *Public Law* is a good source of relevant material, including Hickman, T. (2008) The courts and politics after the Human Rights Act: a comment, *Public Law* 84. You should make a habit of checking the journal for up-to-date sources of opinion.

! Don't be tempted to . . .

- Be diverted into a general discussion about the morality, or otherwise, of the aims of the bill. Be sure to focus on the legal issues raised in relation to the Human Rights Act.
- Be diverted into a discussion about the criminal law. This is a fairly tricky question because you do need to be able to cross-reference your knowledge of the criminal law to explain the issue of burden of proof, but make sure you do bring the discussion back to the HRA.

Question 5

The Human Rights Act 1998 has had little impact in increasing the protection of rights and freedoms of citizens of the United Kingdom.

Discuss.

Answer plan

→ Briefly outline the position prior to the HRA.

→ Explain that the HRA has not introduced new rights.

→ Outline the ways in which the HRA allows the citizen to enforce human rights.

→ Analyse the effectiveness of the Act, with reference to authorities.

Diagram plan

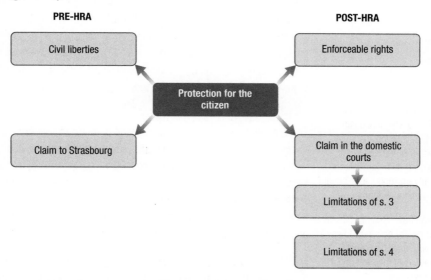

A printable version of this diagram plan is available from www.pearsoned.co.uk/lawexpressqa

[1] It is worth making sure that you have a concise summary of the purpose of the HRA at your fingertips, as many questions, like this one, ask you to assess how successful it has been in achieving its aims.

Answer

The Human Rights Act 1998 (HRA) incorporated the European Convention on Human Rights into domestic law and provides a mechanism for the individual to seek protection of their rights in the domestic courts.[1] The HRA has been the focus of considerable media and political attention as a result of a number of high profile cases involving contentious issues such as prisoner rights, but it is not clear that it has been consistently applied to increase the protection afforded to citizens.[2]

[2] A confident introduction sets out the approach that will be taken in the body of the answer.

Traditionally, the British subject enjoyed civil liberties rather than 'rights'.[3] Using this approach, an individual enjoys freedom to do any thing unless a law exists to prevent it. In Dicey's view of the constitution, the role of the judiciary is to ensure that civil liberties are maintained by preventing the arbitrary use of power. This traditional approach is perhaps best exemplified by the ruling in **Entick v Carrington** (1765) 19 State Tr 1029, in which the court held that, without legal authorisation, there was no power to enter an individual's home. Parliament is free to enact law on any subject, and accordingly, is able to remove or restrict the liberty of the citizen at will. Prior to the HRA, the courts would have no option but to enforce a statute, even when, as was the case in **IRC v Rossminster** [1980] AC 952, it was held that the interference with the privacy of the individual was 'breath-taking'. The Public Order Acts between the 1930s and the mid-1990s can be viewed as an incremental reduction in freedom to protest, and a corresponding increase in the powers of the police to regulate and control association.[4]

[3] In order to determine the impact of the HRA, the answer needs to briefly explain the 'traditional' approach to rights in the United Kingdom.

[4] Whilst there will be credit for being able to explain the Diceyean position, the strength of the answer is improved by being able to identify examples that explain the traditional approach.

The European Convention on Human Rights provided some measure of protection in the domestic courts as the provisions of the treaty were an aid to the interpretation of ambiguous legislation, and the judgments of the European Court of Human Rights (ECtHR) carried some persuasive force. In cases where there was no ambiguity, however, the citizen had no legal option but to seek redress by petition to the ECtHR, a costly and time-consuming process.

[5] If you have a clear opinion, then do not be afraid to say so; you must be prepared to provide evidence to support what you say.

[6] The cases referred to are used to make a specific point about the issue raised in the question. The facts are not important here; only the fact they show the broad scope of section 3, therefore you don't need to waste the word count explaining the background.

The HRA undoubtedly gives the judiciary greater scope to uphold the rights protected under the Convention.[5] The courts now have a duty to interpret legislation as compatible with the Convention 'so far as it is possible' (s. 3). The courts have been clear that the duty applies even where there is no ambiguity, and can allow an interpretation that is 'linguistically strained' (**R v A** [2001] UKHL 25), and even the reading in of additional phrases (**Ghaidan v Godin-Mendoza** [2004] UKHL 30). This can be viewed as a significant increase in protection for the rights of the citizen where the courts are willing to accept that the exercise of a statutory power infringes a Convention right.[6]

Where the court is unable to utilise interpretative powers to uphold a right, a declaration of incompatibility may be made (s. 4). This can result in remedial action by the executive to amend the offending legislation, or introduce new legislation (s. 10). However, it should be noted that the use of section 4 remains relatively rare, and a declaration of incompatibility cannot compel the executive to take action.[7] In addition, the HRA makes it clear that a declaration has no effect on the continued validity of the legislation and no impact on the parties to the case (s. 4(6)). Therefore, the citizen who has been affected by the provision in question will still have little option but to look to Strasbourg for redress.[8]

The HRA has created mechanisms to assist the courts in protecting the rights of the citizen where they find that there has, in fact, been a violation. The judiciary has often accepted that deference to the decisions made by the executive or legislature should be granted. This was the position set out in the leading case of **R v DPP ex parte Kebiline** [2000] 2 AC 326, in which the court explained the need for deference on democratic grounds. This does respect the principle of the separation of powers but, arguably, has greatly reduced the impact of the HRA in protecting the rights of the individual,[9] in particular, when dealing with matters of some political sensitivity such as issues pertaining to national security. In the case of **R (Gillan) v Commissioner of Police for the Metropolis** [2006] UKHL 12, having indicated that deference should be given to the executive regarding the need for legislation, the judgment went on to state that it was hard to conceive of a situation where the use of powers of stop and search authorised by the statute would be disproportionate. This case can be seen as an example of the courts failing to protect the Convention rights of the citizen, a point supported by the subsequent judgment of the ECtHR, which unanimously found the powers to be unlawful. This can be contrasted, however, with instances in which the courts have been proactive and vocal in their support for Convention rights, such as the case of **A v Secretary of State for the Home Department** [2004] UKHL 56, in which a declaration of incompatibility in respect of the Anti-Terrorism, Crime and Security Act 2001 was accompanied by stringent criticism.[10]

The HRA gives the citizen the right to bring a claim in respect of a violation of a Convention right by a 'public authority' (s. 6). Therefore,

[7] Most students will note the power to make a declaration of incompatibility; more marks will be given here for being able to comment on how little it has been used in practice. This shows you have done more than simply learn the sections of the HRA, and have understood how it operates.

[8] Again, the marker is reassured that each point made is relevant to the question.

[9] Reference to the separation of powers is useful here, as it shows that you understand the constitutional context.

[10] This paragraph, and the cases cited, are important as this material forms the basis of the conclusion that the judiciary are inconsistent in upholding individual rights.

all public authorities are required to seek to uphold individual rights. There has been some judicial difficulty in determining precisely how to determine whether or not a body is public. The case of **Anston Cantlow Parochial Church Council v Wallbank** [2003] UKHL 37 held that the authority should be 'governmental' and the test is primarily functional.[11] This may mean that there are instances where the individual has no claim against the body responsible for infringing their rights, but it should be remembered that section 6 specifies that courts and tribunals are public bodies which creates indirect horizontal effect.[12]

The HRA has significantly increased the protection that can be afforded to Convention rights in the domestic courts, by providing a route for redress against public bodies. However, the efficacy of the Act depends in large part on the attitude of the judiciary to assessing the proportionality of executive action and this, as has been suggested, has not been consistent.[13]

[11] In this instance, there is no need to give the facts of Anston; only the fact that it is authority for the fact that the function of the body in question must be considered.

[12] The final point made, again, refers back to the question by focusing on the effect of the HRA for individuals.

[13] The conclusion is quite brief, but the argument has been developed throughout the answer so can be summarised succinctly here.

✓ Make your answer stand out

- By considering the effect of section 6(2), which affords a defence to a public authority that it is acting in accordance with primary legislation. This leaves the citizen in the unsatisfactory position of seeking a declaration under section 4 which, as the answer shows, has no bearing on the parties to a case. By making this point, you reinforce the argument that the HRA does not provide the individual with adequate redress.

- By expanding the argument that the ECtHR still has an important role in providing protection for UK citizens. You could do so by referencing cases in which the ECtHR has overturned domestic decisions and ruled that UK legislation is unlawful. *Gillan* v *UK* is a good, recent, example to cite here.

! Don't be tempted to . . .

- Simply describe the provisions of the HRA. It is important to show an understanding of how the Act works, but the answer must use the material to offer analysis of how effective it is in protecting individual rights.

- Spend too long outlining the position prior to the HRA. The focus of your answer must be on how effective the changes have been.

 Question 6

The Human Rights Act is a significant factor in the loss of parliamentary sovereignty. Discuss.

Answer plan

→ Briefly outline the key components of the doctrine of parliamentary sovereignty.

→ Describe the major effects of the HRA.

→ Assess the impact of the HRA on the passage of legislation.

→ Analyse the impact of the HRA on existing legislation and consider whether or not this undermines the supremacy of Parliament.

Diagram plan

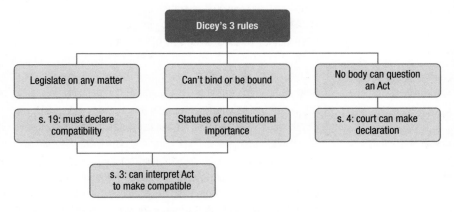

A printable version of this diagram plan is available from www.pearsoned.co.uk/lawexpressqa

Answer

Dicey, writing in the nineteenth century, argued that parliamentary supremacy was the cornerstone of the British constitution. His exposition of the doctrine acts as a starting point to assess whether or not the Human Rights Act (HRA) has had any significant effect on the position of the legislature.[1] It will be argued that there has been little real alteration to the constitutional arrangement of the United Kingdom.

[1] Any question that requires an explanation of parliamentary sovereignty requires the answer to show familiarity with the views of Dicey.

According to Dicey, the doctrine of parliamentary supremacy encompasses three aspects. Firstly, Parliament is free to legislate on any subject matter. Secondly, Parliament cannot be bound by a predecessor or bind a successor. Lastly, no person or body can question the validity of an Act of Parliament. The effect of the HRA can be evaluated against these precepts in turn.[2]

[2] This is helpful, as it shows the marker that there will be a clear, logical structure.

In the case of **Madzimbamuto v Lardner-Burke** [1969] AC 645, Lord Reid observed that there were no constitutional or legal mechanisms to prevent Parliament acting, even if morally or politically 'highly improper'.[3] The HRA requires Parliament to be mindful of the European Convention of Human Rights in respect of all legislation. Section 19 stipulates that a minister introducing legislation must make a statement of compatibility prior to the second reading of the bill. If it is not possible, then the minister must confirm that government still wishes to proceed. It is not necessary to give reasons to support either position. It is submitted that the effect of section 19 is limited.[4] Since the HRA came into force in 2000, there has only been one instance of a bill being laid before Parliament without a statement of compatibility (enacted as the Communications Act 2003). A statement can be made even where there has been a derogation from an articled right in order to achieve compatibility (in respect of Art. 5 and the Anti-Terrorism Crime and Security Act 2001). Even if a statement is not made, or if an unsupportable statement is made, it is difficult to see how any challenge could be made, as deference to the legislative autonomy of Parliament would prevent this.[5] Article 9 of the Bill of Rights protects proceedings in Parliament from judicial scrutiny, even where there have been allegations that Parliament has been defrauded (**British Railways Board v Pickin** [1974] AC 765). Although section 19 may require Parliament to follow a particular process, the lack of sanction for non-compliance undermines the claim that this can be viewed as constitutionally significant.[6]

[3] Whilst the answer could simply state that Parliament was entitled to legislate as it chose, the case is a useful illustration. The facts aren't required; the key point is the comment in the judgment that the moral content of a statute was constitutionally irrelevant.

[4] Credit will be given for setting out an opinion, but this must be followed with some illustrative examples to support the assertion.

[5] This is a useful point to make, as it shows that the HRA does not infringe the principle of legislative supremacy.

[6] This kind of 'mini conclusion' is a useful habit to get into, when you reach the end of each point,. You can then be certain that you make sure you are focused on the question posed throughout your answer.

According to the Diceyan view, each successive Parliament is supreme, and cannot be bound by legislation enacted by a predecessor. Therefore, no statute can become entrenched. This aspect of the doctrine is illustrated by **Vauxhall Estates Ltd v Liverpool Corporation** [1932] 1 KB 733.[7] The case concerned a dispute regarding the compensation scheme applicable in a compulsory purchase of land. The Acquisition of Land (Assessment of Compensation) Act 1919 laid down a scheme, and further stated

[7] It is not necessary to provide the facts of cases but here a brief explanation of this key authority will demonstrate that the doctrine of implied repeal has been understood.

[8] It is not enough to state that the HRA may be a statute of constitutional significance; you must state this suggests the doctrine of implied repeal does not apply because it is this fact that impacts upon the principle of parliamentary supremacy.

[9] The operation of section 3 is almost always crucial to a discussion about the HRA, so it is worth making sure you know the critical wording from the section.

[10] It is important to use the authorities properly to help you build your answer to the question. Here, *Ghaidan* v *Godin-Mendoza* is used to show that there you can provide an example of words being read into a statute; but there is no need to give the facts.

[11] These are important cases that generally serve interchangeable purposes as they both give examples of the use of section 3. Here, the use of these two short phrases from the judgment allows you to make a point about the limits of the interpretative power.

[12] Simply explaining the effect of section 4 will not be sufficient, if this isn't related back to consideration of the sovereignty of Parliament.

that any inconsistent provision would be ineffective. The Housing Act of 1925 created a different payment scheme, without expressly repealing the earlier Act. It was held that the later Act impliedly repealed the earlier provisions. More recently, it has been suggested that some statutes are entrenched. Case law has tended to centre on the European Communities Act 1972 (in particular, the series of cases concerning *Factortame*) but the arguments are equally applicable to the HRA. Indeed, Laws LJ included the Act in a list of statutes he suggested were 'of constitutional significance' and, therefore, not subject to the doctrine of implied repeal.[8]

The HRA imposes a duty on the judiciary to interpret legislation as compatible with convention rights 'so far as is possible to do so' (s. 3).[9] The courts have, in a number of cases, indicated that this obligation extends to cover unambiguous statutory provisions, and even authorises the judiciary to read words into statute (see, for example, ***Ghaidan* v *Godin-Mendoza*** [2004] UKHL 30). It could be argued that this veers close to judicial legislation and therefore, an erosion of the legislative supremacy of Parliament.[10] Although there have been cases where it could be argued that the intention of Parliament has been subverted by the imposition of an interpretation that is 'linguistically strained' (***R* v *A*** [2001] UKHL 25), the courts have been clear that a meaning cannot be imposed that goes 'against the grain' of the legislation (***Ghaidan* v *Godin-Mendoza***).[11]

If the courts are faced with a piece of legislation that cannot be read as compliant using section 3, then section 4 allows a declaration of incompatibility to be made. Hence, the judiciary make a clear statement to the executive that legislation is unsatisfactory. This could be viewed as permitting the judiciary to question the validity of an Act of Parliament, thereby undermining the last of the Diceyean precepts.[12] It should be noted that the judiciary view section 4 as a last resort, and declarations of incompatibility are relatively rare. Even when a declaration is made, the supremacy of Parliament is preserved, as the section provides that the making of a declaration has no effect on the validity of the legislation, or on the parties to the case in which it is made. It may be the case that, where a declaration is made, the executive feels pressed to react, but this could be seen as a political choice rather than a constitutional requirement.

It may appear that, in passing the Human Rights Act, Parliament has voluntarily ceded some constitutional authority to the judiciary. The

[13] The conclusion can draw together the material and focus directly on the constitutional impact of the Act.

impact should not be overstated, however, as the language of the Act is careful to maintain the supremacy of Parliament.[13] The effect of section 19 is, in reality, minimal, and has little effect on the ability of the House to legislate as it sees fit. The power to make a declaration of incompatibility is rarely used, and certainly does not empower the judiciary to ignore or overturn a legislative provision. The greatest threat to the autonomy of Parliament, then, is the interpretative duty imposed by section 3, but it is possible to argue that in utilising their powers, the judiciary are mindful of the intention of Parliament and respectful of the constitutional boundary between interpretation and legislation. Although it may be the case that the doctrine of implied repeal does not apply, the Act is not entrenched, as express repeal is a possibility; indeed, the Conservative Party have pledged to make this a reality.[14] The Human Rights Act has undoubtedly had significant impact as it allows the courts to evaluate the compatibility of legislation with the Convention, but the constitutional supremacy of Parliament is preserved.

[14] Reference to the Conservative Party plans demonstrates an ability to place the subject in context.

✓ Make your answer stand out

- By expanding the discussion regarding 'statutes of constitutional significance', as the issue has been the subject of considerable academic debate. A good article commenting on the implications of *Thoburn* is Campbell, D. and Young, J. (2002), The metric martyrs and the entrenchment jurisprudence of Lord Justice Laws *Public Law* 399. It is possible to argue that this is not a new argument; Bradley, A. and Ewing, K. (2010) *Constitutional and Administrative Law* (15th edn) London: Pearson, pp. 62–70, outline statutes that could be said to be, practically, at least, entrenched.

- By discussing the voluntary nature of any cessation of supremacy in more detail. Although linked to the issue of entrenchment, you could consider the political criticism of the HRA (including Conservative Party calls during the 2010 election campaign for it to be repealed and replaced) and ask whether this is feasible. This would show an ability to comment on new developments.

! Don't be tempted to . . .

■ Provide an answer that concentrates on a general discussion regarding the doctrine of parliamentary supremacy. Although it is crucial to set out the Diceyean criteria, these must be used as a springboard to consider the constitutional effect of the HRA.

■ Simply describe the different provisions of section 3 and section 4. You must be prepared, when dealing with a question like this, to reach some conclusions and state an opinion about the impact of the Act on parliamentary supremacy. Remember, marks are given for analysis of the law, not for simply restating it.

❓ Question 7

Yvonne and Zahir are both studying law at college and often discuss legal issues during breaks from class. One day, Yvonne appears quite upset, and Zahir asks why. Yvonne tells Zahir that she attended her local authority leisure centre to take part in an exercise class, and was surprised to be greeted by a security guard demanding to search her bag before allowing her into the centre. When she asked why, she was told that it was because the (fictional) Healthy Choice Act of 2012 had come into force, which states that persons wishing to use local authority facilities are required to submit to 'spot checks' to ensure they are not in possession of cigarettes or tobacco. Persons with those items would be required to pay an additional entry fee of twenty pounds or denied access to the facilities.

Yvonne is a smoker, but she did not have the twenty pound fee. Therefore she did not go to the class. Zahir is outraged by the story and suggests to Yvonne that she should go to court about the incident to protest about the infringement of her human rights.

Yvonne is not keen on the idea. Zahir, however, would like to pursue the matter if possible.

Advise Yvonne and Zahir whether or not the Human Rights Act can assist them.

Answer plan

→ Identify the convention right that could be engaged.

→ Explain the operation of qualified rights.

→ Consider how section 3 and section 4 could be applied in this case.

→ Explain the effect of section 7.

Diagram plan

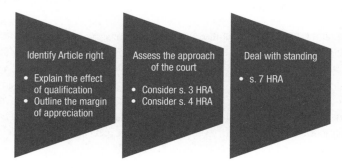

A printable version of this diagram plan is available from www.pearsoned.co.uk/lawexpressqa

Answer

The Human Rights Act 1998 (HRA) incorporated the European Convention on Human Rights and Fundamental Freedoms (ECHR) into domestic law. As a result, individual citizens who believe that one or more of the rights protected by the Convention have been infringed can seek a remedy in the domestic courts.[1] To advise Yvonne and Zahir, it will be necessary to consider whether there are any relevant Convention rights engaged in this scenario, before discussing how the HRA could be applied.

[1] It is not necessary to explain the relationship between the Convention and domestic law in detail here, but a brief summary shows understanding of the effect of the HRA.

The (fictional) Healthy Choice Act of 2012 (HCA) authorises local authorities to carry out searches of individuals, and impose penalties on smokers by requiring them to provide additional payment. On these facts, the most relevant part of the ECHR is Art. 8 (right to respect for private and family life). Although Yvonne may feel that being prevented from entering the building during the search is a restriction of liberty (contravening Art. 5), it is unlikely that this would be a successful argument as the time period would be too short. In **Stork v Germany** (2006) 43 EHRR 6, the European Court of Human Rights (ECtHR) held that a deprivation of liberty under Art. 5 requires (firstly) a restriction to a particular place for a 'not negligible' length of time.[2]

[2] Here, even though Art. 5 is dismissed, the answer makes it clear how the decision has been reached. You should always try to ensure your examiner can see your reasoning.

Article 8 is a qualified right, meaning that it is permissible to place restrictions upon the right in accordance with the provisions of

Art. 8(2). Restrictions must be prescribed by law, and necessary to achieve a specified aim. In this scenario, the HCA could be intended either to protect 'health and morals' or to protect the rights of others.[3] These are both a legitimate basis for interference with the right, provided that they are a proportionate method of achieving the aim. When considering whether or not the provisions could be considered a legitimate restriction, it should be noted that the ECtHR would apply a 'margin of appreciation'; a degree of deference to the ability of the signatory state to judge the requirements of (in this case) health and morals in their own territory more effectively than the court itself. In this way, the Convention recognises that the signatory states of Europe do not share a homogeneous social or political culture.

The width of the margin may vary depending on the importance of the right claimed, and the reason for the restriction. In **Handyside v UK** (1976) 1 EHRR 737 the claimant was unsuccessful in arguing that a prosecution under the Obscene Publications Act 1959 for distributing pornographic materials breached his Art. 10 right to freedom of expression, as a broad margin was applied. In this case, the courts would have to balance the objective of reducing the incidence and financial burden of smoking to the state, against the interference with Yvonne's right to make autonomous decisions about her health.[4] The issue of smokers' rights was considered by the Joint Committee of Human Rights during the passage of the Health Act 2006 which introduced a ban on smoking in public places. They argued that, although the ban clearly did engage the Art. 8 rights of smokers, the restrictions were a proportionate means of protecting the rights of non-smokers to be free from the effects of second-hand smoke. It is worth noting, however, that they reached that conclusion on the basis that the ban did not extend to private homes. (Joint Committee on Human Rights (2005)). It may be possible to argue that the provisions in question here are more severe and cannot be similarly justified as there is no need to balance the rights of smokers and non-smokers.[5]

If Yvonne did decide to bring a claim against the local authority, the court would deal with the case in accordance with the provisions set out in the HRA. Section 6 makes it clear that a claim can be made against any public body which in this case is not problematic.[6] Section 6 makes it clear that where a local authority is merely complying with obligations imposed by statute they will have a defence.

[3] It is really important that you explain what is meant by qualified rights, but it is a bad idea to set out all of permissible reasons for restriction. It is far better to identify those that could be claimed in this scenario.

[4] You must remember to keep bringing the focus of your answer back to the facts in the question.

[5] This is a good point as it shows an ability to use existing material to develop an argument in a different situation.

[6] There is no need to consider the case law around the definition of a public body where the question does not give any indication that this is an issue.

[7] This part of the answer makes it clear that you understand the procedural application of the HRA.

[8] In any problem concerning the HRA you will almost certainly have to explain the operation of section 3, so as part of your revision you should ensure that you can do so succinctly and clearly.

[9] Do not forget to use the law that you have explained to reach conclusions about Yvonne's case.

[10] This is such an important point to note about section 4 when advising an individual about the HRA, but one that is often missed. Make sure you do remember to explain the practical impact of a declaration of incompatibility.

[11] There is no need to spend any further time considering a potential claim to Strasbourg as the question pointed you to consider domestic Human Rights legislation.

[12] Although you should not overlook this issue, as you were specifically asked to deal with Zahir's position, the position is very straightforward and needs no elaboration.

The court, however, is also a public body and therefore obliged to comply with the ECHR, creating indirect horizontal effect. In determining whether or not the actions of the local authority were lawful, the court would need to consider the provisions of the HCA for compatibility with Art. 8.[7] If on a literal interpretation the provisions are found to exceed permissible qualifications, section 3 imposes a duty on the court to apply a compatible interpretation 'in so far as is possible'. The courts have been prepared to use section 3 to read down additional words into a statutory provision, provided that the interpretation can be said to 'go with the grain' of the legislation (***Ghaidan v Godin-Mendoza*** [2004] UKHL 30).[8] However, where the language of the statute is clear and unambiguous the courts will be unable to force compatibility through a process of interpretation. In this case, if the courts consider that the imposition of a financial penalty on persons found in possession of cigarettes does infringe Art. 8, it is difficult to see how any interpretation of the language could change this and allow the court to find in Yvonne's favour.[9] She should be advised, therefore, that this may be a case in which a declaration of incompatibility is made.

A declaration of incompatibility (s. 4) can be made by a superior court. If a declaration is made, the government may choose to use the procedure set out in section 10 to expedite amending legislation. This would not assist Yvonne in the short term, however, as a declaration of incompatibility has no effect upon the parties to a case (s. 4(6)).[10] To protect the principle of parliamentary sovereignty, the courts must apply the law until such time as it is amended or repealed. If that were to be the case, Yvonne may wish to consider pursuing an appeal to the ECtHR, as the domestic declaration could be said to be a clear indication that an infringement would be found in Strasbourg.[11]

Zahir will not be able to pursue the matter on Yvonne's behalf. Section 7 provides that a claim may only be made by a person who is the victim of an act infringing their rights.[12]

Although the government's aim of reducing smoking may be laudable, it would seem arguable that the imposition of fines authorised by the HCA are an unjustifiable infringement on the Art. 8 rights of smokers. Yvonne should be advised that she could bring a claim but that, even were she to be successful, it is unlikely that the HRA could be used to find a remedy in the domestic courts.

Make your answer stand out

- By considering the case of *N,R (on the application of)* v *Secretary of State for Health* [2009] EWCA Civ 79 in which the Court of Appeal considered whether or not a smoking ban at Rampton Hospital infringed the Art. 8 rights of patients. It is a useful case to consider as the judges reach differing conclusions about whether or not smoking is within the ambit of Art. 8.
- By explaining the effect of the margin of appreciation in more detail here, and making clear the relationship between the jurisprudence of Strasbourg and the domestic courts. Arguably, when considering an area where Strasbourg has awarded a wide margin, the domestic courts will defer more readily to the executive.
- By discussing the issue of horizontal effect in more detail. Bamforth (2001) maintains that the courts' position is determined not by section 6, but by the operation of section 3 (The True 'Horizontal Effect' of the Human Rights Act 1998) *LQR*, 117: 34.

! **Don't be tempted to . . .**

- Spend too much time considering what the result of any action would be, or the potential remedies that may be available. This is not a question about Yvonne's Art. 8 rights, it is a question designed to test your understanding of the Human Rights Act.
- Set out the provisions of section 3 or section 4 without making an attempt to analyse how they may be applied in this case. Your examiner wants to see your ability to apply the law, not just your ability to describe it.

Question 8

'The judiciary bears not the slightest responsibility for protecting the public and sometimes seems utterly unaware of the implications of their decisions for our society' (Charles Clarke, former Home Secretary cited by the Rt Hon Lord Phillips in the Gresham Special Lecture 2010).

Discuss the extent to which the judiciary have utilised the Human Rights Act to undermine legislative efforts to combat terrorism.

Answer plan

→ Outline the provisions that will be the focus of discussion: indefinite detention; closed evidence; control orders.

→ Set out a number of cases in which the judiciary have refused to approve legislative provisions dealing with terrorism.

→ Analyse the extent to which these 'undermine' government policy.

→ Consider parliamentary supremacy and the role of the judiciary.

Diagram plan

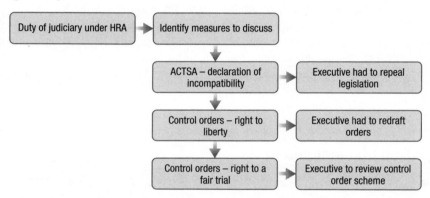

A printable version of this diagram plan is available from www.pearsoned.co.uk/lawexpressqa

Answer

[1] The question requires a discussion of the tension between the judiciary and the executive so it is important to show that this has been understood. In addition, the introduction recognises that the HRA imposes an obligation on the judiciary.

[2] It is perfectly acceptable to limit the discussion in this way, and indeed, you should, as it is not possible to consider more than one or two areas in sufficient depth.

The Human Rights Act came into force in 2000, one year before the terrorist attacks on New York demonstrated the scale of the threat posed by global extremism. The Terrorism Act 2000 had already been enacted, but further legislation followed to control and contain the threat. The United Kingdom currently has five statutes directly concerned with the prevention, investigation and prosecution of terrorism. The Human Rights Act obliges the judiciary to give effect to Convention rights when interpreting statutes. Legislative provisions concerning terrorism have given rise to a large number of human rights cases, and significant judicial decisions which run counter to the intention of the executive.[1] This discussion will focus on key decisions concerning the indefinite detention without trial of foreign nationals and the implementation of control orders.[2]

A v Secretary of State for the Home Department [2004] UKHL 56 considered the legality of provisions made in the Anti-Terrorism Crime and Security Act 2001, which allowed foreign nationals suspected of terrorist activity to be detained indefinitely without trial.[3] The legislation was designed to contain the threat posed by a number of individuals resident in the United Kingdom who, if returned to their country of origin, may have faced torture, or inhuman and degrading treatment. *Chahal v UK* (1996) 23 EHRR 413 established that, if the government returns an individual to a nation knowing that there is such a risk, this will be a breach of its obligations under Art. 3. Criminal prosecution could not take place owing to the need to keep sensitive security information secret, but the individuals were felt to be a grave risk. The government felt that the risk to society posed by terrorism constituted a 'national emergency' justifying a derogation from Art. 5 in respect of the detainees. Lord Hoffmann felt that the derogation was unjustified, and memorably commented: 'The real threat to the life of the nation . . . comes not from terrorism but from laws such as these. That is the true measure of what terrorism may achieve.'[4]

The remaining judges felt that the circumstances did permit derogation, but all agreed that the measures in the Act went beyond those strictly required by the situation and were, therefore, disproportionate.[5] A declaration of incompatibility was made in accordance with section 4 of the Human Rights Act. In reaching the decision, the Lords rejected government submissions that it was for the executive to assess the proportionality of legislative responses to terrorism.[6] Lord Bingham stated that the role of the independent judiciary in interpretation and application of statute is 'a cornerstone of the rule of law itself'. The legislation was repealed, and replaced with the system of control orders. The case is perhaps the clearest illustration of the conflict between the judiciary and the executive in respect of measures enacted to prevent terrorist activity, but it is not an isolated example.

The control order regime, established by the Prevention of Terrorism Act 2005 to replace indefinite detention, was itself the subject of numerous human rights claims. A control order was a civil order which imposed obligations and restrictions on the suspect to limit the risk of terrorist activity. A series of linked judgments considered the range of conditions applied to various individuals to assess whether

[3] Although there are a number of areas that can be discussed, this is a useful case to include because it is a clear illustration of the conflict between the executive and the judiciary.

[4] This is an excellent quote to include as it is a very strong and clear criticism of the legislation. If you cannot remember the wording, you should ensure that you can paraphrase the comments.

[5] The concept of proportionality is crucial to Convention jurisprudence. Use of the correct terminology demonstrates that this has been understood.

[6] It is useful to include this point from the judgment, as it shows that the government and the judiciary were not in agreement about their respective roles.

or not the orders were in breach of Art. 5. Some of the orders were assessed as acceptable; however, in **Secretary of State for the Home Department v JJ** [2007] UKHL 45, the majority found the orders imposed on the applicants to be incompatible with Art. 5. The Lords referred to **Guzzardi v Italy** (1980) 3 EHRR 333, in which it was held that the combined and cumulative effect of restrictions could amount to a deprivation in circumstances falling short of imprisonment.[7] In reaching the decision, the Lords expressly rejected the government argument that the acceptability of the orders must be assessed in light of the serious risk posed by the individuals concerned. Lord Brown stated that such claims must be 'firmly resisted'. As a result, the government redrafted some of the orders, with less stringent conditions.[8]

The judiciary also assessed the use of 'closed evidence' and the Special Advocate procedure in hearings concerning control orders to consider whether this can be compatible with Art. 6 rights to a fair hearing. In **Secretary of State for the Home Department v MB** [2007] UKHL 46, it was held that the Special Advocate procedure provided adequate safeguards for Art. 6 rights in all but the most exceptional cases. Two years later, following the Strasbourg ruling in **A v UK** [2009] ECHR 3455/05, the Lords reconsidered the issue and held that an individual must always be told sufficient information about the evidence to enable them to provide instructions to a Special Advocate (**Secretary of State for the Home Department v AF** (No. 3) [2009] UKHL 28).[9] Lord Hoffmann, dissenting, felt that the Strasbourg decision was wrong, and could result in the destruction of the control order system which he described as an important part of the defence against terrorism. He was proved right, as the Coalition government abolished control orders, replacing them with Terrorism Prevention and Investigation Measures (TPIMs). The new legislative scheme, then, can be seen as a direct response to judicial criticism.

It is clear that the judiciary have reached decisions which have forced the executive to revisit measures enacted to combat terrorist activity. In assessing how far this should be viewed as 'undermining' the aims of government, it must be noted that the Human Rights Act charged the courts with the obligation to uphold Convention rights.[10] As Lord Philips noted in the Gresham lecture, Parliament asked the courts to protect the rights, and therefore the judiciary have a specific, democratic, obligation to do so.

[7] The ECtHR decision should be cited, as the domestic courts have followed this authority.

[8] The answer should explain the impact of the court rulings to illustrate how judicial decisions have affected government efforts to control terrorism.

[9] Here, the answer demonstrates knowledge of how domestic law develops in conjunction with decisions reached in the ECtHR.

[10] This is a point worth making, as arguably the courts are doing no more than is required by statute.

Make your answer stand out

- There is scope to broaden the discussion to consider the operation of the separation of powers within the constitution. In particular, the case law could be used to show how judicial deference to executive decisions concerning 'national security' has evolved since the *GCHQ case (Council of Civil Service Ministers* v *Minister for the Civil Service* [1985] AC 374). You could refer to more recent decisions in *R (Al Rawi)* v *Foreign Secretary* [2007] 2 WLR 1219 to make the point that foreign policy is still held to be non-justiciable; but you can certainly argue that the control order cases suggest that the HRA has resulted in a clearer system of 'checks and balances' between the institutions of state.

- You could spend more time considering the ECtHR jurisprudence regarding *Chahal* and the later case of *Saadi* v *Italy* (2008) (Application 37201/06), which appears to confirm that the position regarding deportation and Art. 3 has not altered following 9/11.

- By incorporating a broader range of academic opinion. The following article argues that the judiciary are still extremely deferential to parliamentary supremacy: Ewing, K.D. and Tham, J. (2008) The continuing futility of the Human Rights Act *Public Law* 668–93.

- By spending more time discussing how far TPIMs will resolve the problems identified with control orders.

‼ Don't be tempted to . . .

- Engage in detailed discussion of which conditions the judiciary considered incompatible with Art. 5 in the control order cases. The detail is not important, only the fact that the judiciary and the government reached different decisions.

- Ignore the effect of decisions made in Strasbourg. The judiciary are, after all, guided by precedent from the ECtHR. Failure to address this fact would result in an overly simplistic approach. It should be recognised that, since becoming a signatory to the Convention, decisions have been persuasive precedent and therefore the impact of the HRA is perhaps less dramatic than the quotation in the question suggests.

www.pearsoned.co.uk/lawexpressqa

 Go online to access more revision support including additional essay and problem questions with diagram plans, You be the marker questions, and download all diagrams from the book.

Freedom of association and assembly

6

How this topic may come up in exams

This topic is commonly examined by problem scenarios, which often require an evaluation of the provisions of the Public Order Act 1986. These questions are generally fairly straightforward provided you have a good understanding of the statutory provisions. Essay questions often concern the compatibility of statutory and common law powers with rights under Articles 10 and 11 of the Convention. Students should be aware of provisions contained in other legislation that impact on freedom of assembly. An understanding of the common law powers available to the police to prevent a breach of the peace is crucial.

■ Attack the question

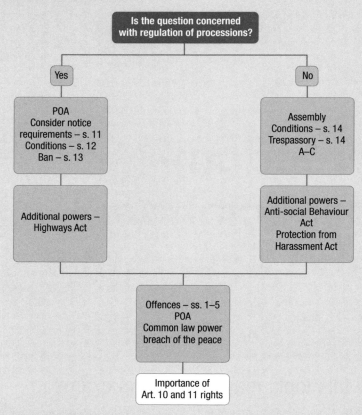

Is the question concerned
with regulation of processions?

Yes

No

POA
Consider notice
requirements – s. 11
Conditions – s. 12
Ban – s. 13

Assembly
Conditions – s. 14
Trespassory – s. 14
A–C

Additional powers –
Highways Act

Additional powers –
Anti-social Behaviour
Act
Protection from
Harassment Act

Offences – ss. 1–5
POA
Common law power
breach of the peace

Importance of
Art. 10 and 11 rights

A printable version of this diagram is available from www.pearsoned.co.uk/lawexpressqa

❓ Question 1

Brendan and Simon are the organisers of a group called 'Citizen Beats', who believe that the public should have greater access to more free music events. At the annual general meeting, a campaign strategy for the months ahead is agreed.

Brendan agrees to take responsibility for organising a march to protest about recent changes to licensing laws for music venues. The march is to take place in ten days' time, and he hopes that about 200 people will attend. A route is planned that starts from the Town Hall in Carthorpe, and will follow a circular, mile long, route around the City Centre. Brendan intends that the marchers will walk in the centre of the road, to cause maximum disruption to the city and create attention for the cause. The day that Brendan intends to hold the event also coincides with a procession that an organisation called 'Silent Nights' has planned for the same day, on the same route. 'Silent Nights' believe that loud music should be banned. The two groups are known to be very hostile to each other.

Simon decides to hold a free music event in a field on the outskirts of Headingley. He arranges the hire of a large sound system, to ensure that the music will be able to be heard in the surrounding area. The event is intended to last from 11pm to 6am and is arranged to take place in one month's time.

Brendan and Simon begin to distribute leaflets advertising their planned events. One of the leaflets is found by Chief Superintendent Didson, who seeks your advice about whether he is able to stop the events going ahead.

Please advise Chief Superintendent Didson of his powers, and consider whether or not it matters that the owner of the field is aware of the planned event.

Answer plan

- → Provide definitions of 'procession' and 'assembly'.
- → Explain the requirements of section 11 that Brendan should comply with.
- → Outline the powers available under section 12 and section 13.
- → Outline the powers available under section 14, and section 14A in the event the landowner has not given permission.
- → Consider powers of arrest at common law and under the Public Order Act.

Diagram plan

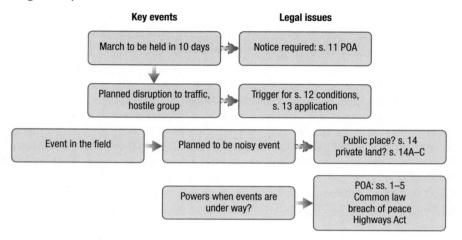

Key events   **Legal issues**

March to be held in 10 days → Notice required: s. 11 POA

Planned disruption to traffic, hostile group → Trigger for s. 12 conditions, s. 13 application

Event in the field → Planned to be noisy event → Public place? s. 14 private land? s. 14A–C

Powers when events are under way? → POA: ss. 1–5 Common law breach of peace Highways Act

A printable version of this diagram plan is available from www.pearsoned.co.uk/lawexpressqa

Answer

Brendan and Simon are planning two events to raise public aware-ness of their campaign. The freedom to protest is seen as central to political democracy and therefore the freedom of assembly is pro-tected by Art. 10 of the European Convention of Human Rights. The Convention recognises legitimate reasons to interfere with the right, such as the prevention of disorder or crime; permitted qualifications are listed at Art. 10(2).[1] The main restrictions on the freedom of assembly are contained within the Public Order Act 1986, which imposes obligations on the organisers of protests, and gives the police powers to control public gatherings. Chief Superintendent Didson will need to be advised about these provisions, and some additional statutory and common law powers.

A procession is defined at common law as 'a body of persons moving along a route' (***Flockhart v Robinson*** [1950] 2 KB 498).[2] Sec-tion 11 of the Public Order Act 1986 (POA) requires the organisers of processions to give written notice of their intentions, provided the procession is for one of the specified purposes. These include events designed to show support for, or to publicise, a campaign. Brendan

[1] It is useful to demonstrate an awareness of the Convention rights engaged by the issues raised in the question.

[2] This area of the syllabus can feel a little short on case law authority, so where there is a relevant case it will always be helpful to cite it.

should have provided written notice six days in advance of the planned event, including details of the route, expected numbers, the duration, and his details, unless it is not reasonably practicable to provide notice (s. 11(1)). Chief Superintendent Didson should be aware that, if the notice does not arrive in the next four days, Brendan will be liable for a summary offence unless he can claim he was not aware of the notice requirements (s. 11(8)).[3]

[3] The question states that advice should be given to Superintendent Didson. A good answer needs to remember this and use the information to set out the powers available to the police.

Section 12 gives the police powers to impose conditions on a procession if there is a risk of serious damage to property, serious disruption to the life of the community, or serious public disorder (s. 12(1)(a)), or if it is felt the purpose of the march is to intimidate others (s. 12(1)(b)).[4] If these conditions are met, any necessary conditions can be imposed to address the risk, including the route. The route is intended to cause disruption, and to ensure confrontation with the rival group. It would seem there are reasonable grounds to impose conditions on the route, time or duration.[5] Chief Superintendent Didson should notify Brendan of these in writing (s. 12(3)). Failure to comply will be an arrestable offence.

[4] The majority of students know that section 12 allows conditions to be imposed, but many fail to note that this is not an absolute power and is dependent on identifying one of the specified risk factors.

[5] It is not sufficient to set out the powers given by section 12; these must be used to analyse the information provided.

In addition, the most senior officer present at the procession is authorised to impose new or additional conditions that appear necessary, thereby allowing the police to react to any unforeseen risks that may arise on the day.

[6] Students often make the mistake of stating that the option to apply for a ban is available, without qualifying this by pointing out that it is a draconian power that is rarely justified.

If there are no conditions that could be imposed that would be sufficient to mitigate the risks outlined above, an application can be made to the local authority to ban the procession (s. 13). The Chief Superintendent should note that a ban cannot be imposed on a particular organisation or event, but will apply to all (or a class of) processions within a specified area for a period of time not exceeding three months. Therefore, a ban will only be granted if the risks posed by the event are extremely serious.[6] The limitations on this section perhaps highlight the general importance of the Art. 10 right and the unwillingness of the legislature to contemplate a situation where legitimate public protest is curtailed without good reason.[7] In this scenario it should be noted that both planned processions would be unable to go ahead if a ban is granted.

[7] The fact that notice is not needed for an assembly is a very simple point that is often overlooked, but marks will be given for noting the differences between the two kinds of public order events.

[8] Awareness of this distinction from processing will be rewarded by the examiner.

The planned assembly is not subject to notice requirements.[8] The POA gives powers to impose conditions on an assembly in a public place (defined at s. 16), mirroring the provisions at section 12. Although the noisy event is likely to cause 'serious disruption', it is not clear whether the POA will assist, as it appears it will be on private land. It will, therefore, be critical to ascertain whether or not the landowner has given permission, and whether there are any limits on that permission. If the landowner has not given permission, or if the event is likely to go beyond the limits, it will be considered a trespassory assembly as defined at section 14(a) of the POA. Sections 14(a)–(c) of the POA were inserted by the Criminal Justice and Public Order Act 1994, specifically to allow for the control of 'raves', which were prevalent at the time.[9] Chief Superintendent Didson can make an application to ban trespassory assemblies in a designated area for a period of time no longer than four days. Unlike the powers contained at section 13, there is no need to demonstrate that conditions have been considered and exhausted prior to making an application. Once a ban is in place, Simon should be informed of the order. Once aware, continuing with the event is an offence (s. 14(b)). In addition, the police are empowered to stop vehicles or persons en route to the event and direct them to turn away (s. 14(c)).

[9] The question requires the answer to consider the provisions pertaining to trespassory assemblies. It is important to make the point that unless this applies, the Public Order Act does not confer any power on the Chief Superintendent; that is why this point is crucial.

If the procession is allowed to go ahead, with or without conditions, criminal offences are created by sections 1–5 of the POA in the event of disorder. These range from riot (s. 1) to disorderly conduct (s. 5).[10] Section 137 of the Highways Act makes obstruction of the highway an arrestable offence. Obstruction can be construed as any behaviour other than passing along the highway, or activities reasonably incidental to the activity. Chief Superintendent Didson should note that the courts have, on occasion, taken a liberal view of permissible 'incidental' activities in order to protect the right to protest (*Hirst and Agu v Chief Constable of West Yorkshire* (1987) 85 Cr App R 143).[11] The police have the common law power of arrest for breach of the peace, or to prevent an imminent breach of the peace. This power is potentially extremely broad, as the officers present have considerable discretion to determine what constitutes a threat to the peace. The House of Lords, in *R (Laporte) v Chief Constable of Yorkshire* [2006] UKHL 55 have, however, confirmed that an arrest will not be justified unless it can be demonstrated that there is an immediate threat. The decision pointed out that the Public Order Act created carefully defined powers and offences to deal with protest, whilst allowing for democratic demonstrations, and

[10] You do not need to give a lot of detail about the offences in the Public Order Act here, there is certainly no need to describe the constituent elements of the crimes.

[11] Questions concerning public order tend to invite statute-based answers; where possible and appropriate, case law should be used to demonstrate how the courts interpret statutory provisions.

[12] This case allows the answer to be a little more discursive and demonstrate a broader knowledge of the relationship between the Public Order Act and human rights law.

[13] As with all problem scenarios, a summary of the advice given is a useful way to conclude the answer.

that therefore, co-existing common law powers could not be used disproportionately and indiscriminately. The Chief Superintendent should note this decision, and be aware that, since the Human Rights Act, the courts have been less willing to automatically endorse the discretionary decisions of the police.[12]

Chief Superintendent Didson can try to impose prior controls on the procession, and his officers are empowered to deal with any disorder that occurs. His powers in relation to the assembly will depend on whether or not it is a trespassory event.[13]

✓ Make your answer stand out

- By expanding the discussion regarding the imposition of conditions. The officer could be advised about the types of conditions that have been endorsed by the courts in cases such as *Police* v *Reid* [1987] Crim LR 702, or more recently, *Austin and Saxby* v *Commissioner of Police of the Metropolis* [2005] HRLR 20. This would allow you to demonstrate your ability to consider the effect of a variety of judgments on the facts you are dealing with.

- By discussing the implications of the broad sweep of discretionary powers available to the police, and considering whether or not judicial review can be an adequate protection for Convention rights in this context. You could suggest that any review of decisions taken during a demonstration will occur after the opportunity to rectify the decision has passed.

! Don't be tempted to . . .

- Simply outline the relevant sections of the Public Order Act. Answers on this topic have a tendency to be rather descriptive. There is a danger that students will just set out the statutory provisions, and fail to apply these to provide advice as required.

- Make the mistake of outlining the law without being specific about tailoring the advice for the police officer. This is a popular topic in exams, and most students will be able to state the powers given in the Public Order Act. In order to get higher marks, you will need to make sure that your answer concentrates on assessing the powers given to the police (rather than the responsibilities of organisers).

❓ Question 2

You are approached by the leader of the Student Union on Monday morning, seeking your advice. Westchester City Council has recently begun to publicise their intention to ban 'student nights' in all city centre pubs, bars and clubs. The Student Union intends to invite students to gather in Central Square outside the City Council offices at 2pm on Friday afternoon to protest. This has been chosen as a suitable time because the licensing committee meets at 2.15pm and the protesters will be able to protest at members of the committee as they enter for the meeting.

It is then intended that the students march to Westchester Park, past the University campus, before holding a rally in the Park.

The Student Union anticipates that a large number of students will attend.

Please advise the Student Union of the following matters:

As organisers, are there any steps that should be taken before the protest?

What powers, if any will the police have prior to, and during the protest?

Answer plan

→ Define 'procession' and 'assembly'.

→ Outline the powers available to the police during the first assembly.

→ Explain the obligations on the organisers of the procession.

→ Discuss the powers of arrest available to the police.

Diagram plan

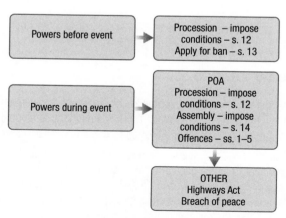

Answer

The right to protest is considered to be central to fair and open democracy, and as such is protected by Art. 10 of the European Convention of Human Rights. The Convention acknowledges that protest could lead to disorder, and disruption to society, hence, qualifications are permitted at Art. 10(2). The Public Order Act 1986 contains the main statutory controls that are likely to affect the planned activities of the student union, although they will also need to be advised of additional powers in the Highways Act, and at common law.[1]

The gathering outside the Council offices will be an assembly in a public place (defined at s. 16),[2] within the scope of the POA. Since the Anti-Social Behaviour Act 2003 amended section 16, only two persons need attend for the powers of restraint to arise. It is not necessary for the organisers to take any particular steps prior to the assembly, but they should be advised of the powers that can be utilised to control the protest once it is in progress.[3] Section 14 of the Public Order Act enables the most senior officer on the scene[4] to impose such conditions as he or she believes are necessary to prevent serious damage, disorder or disruption to the life of the community; or if it is felt that the purpose of the protest is to intimidate others. The case of **Police v Reid** [1987] Crim LR 702 concerned a protest outside an embassy in which participants shouted at persons entering the building. It was held that conditions imposed to prevent this were unlawful, as intimidation is more than mere discomfort. This is one of the few cases concerning the use of section 14 in which the domestic courts have been prepared to interfere with the discretion of the police.[5] In **R (Brehony) v Chief Constable of Greater Manchester** [2005] EWHC 640, it was held that section 6 of the HRA imposes a requirement for any condition to be proportionate to the risk involved, but the court decided that inconvenience to Christmas shoppers could be construed as 'serious disruption' to the life of the community. The House of Lords have agreed that the controversial technique of detaining protesters in a location for a period of time (kettling) can be a lawful condition and compliant with Arts. 5, 10 and 11, provided it is used sparingly and when necessary (**Austin and Saxby v Commissioner of Police of the Metropolis** [2005] HRLR 20, a decision upheld in the European Court of Human

[1] The introduction identifies the key legal provisions that need to be addressed. This is a good way to begin an answer to a problem question, and certainly better than simply rewriting the facts.

[2] It is not necessary to reproduce the sections of the statute that apply in their entirety. It is clear from the reference to section 16 here that there is an understanding of its effect.

[3] It is a good idea to keep reminding the examiner that you are using the law to advise the parties as required, by applying the points made about the law to the facts.

[4] Most students will state that 'the police' can impose conditions; so inclusion of this additional detail will show that you have read the statute thoroughly.

[5] By making this point, you show the examiner firstly that you are familiar with a broader range of cases, and secondly, that you can evaluate the effect of the judgment.

[6] Knowledge of the case law allows for a more analytical approach to the problem. Rather than simply listing the powers available to the police, a view can be given about the legality of any conditions imposed.

[7] There will be no additional marks given for repeating the same information that you have already provided.

[8] You must distinguish between the two types of protest which occur in this scenario.

[9] It is important to offer some solutions to the Union, rather than just setting out the law which applies.

[10] There is no need to reiterate the grounds here as they have been explained above, it would be a waste of your word count, but you should make it clear you know that the grounds are set out at section 12 in respect of the procession.

[11] Students very often state that section 13 gives the police the power to ban processions. You will be rewarded for noting that the power is only to make the application.

Rights ***Austin and Others* v *United Kingdom*** (2012) 55 EHRR 14).[6] Once a condition has been made, failure to comply will be an offence. The planned rally in the park will also be an assembly, and all the same considerations apply.[7] The organisers need to note that there is no means available to appeal the conditions at the time, and any subsequent review is unlikely to be successful, given the existing authorities.

Once the students begin the march to the park, the protest becomes a procession,[8] defined at common law as 'a body of persons moving along a route' (***Flockhart* v *Robinson*** [1950] 2 KB 498). As the intention is to express support for, and publicise, a campaign, it is governed by section 11 of the POA, which imposes an obligation on the organisers to give advance notice of the event. The notice must be in writing, and must contain details of the date, time, route and duration of the march, together with details of those organising the event. Failure to provide the notice (unless it is not reasonably practicable to do so) is an offence (s. 11(7)). The notice must be given six clear days before the planned event. Therefore, the Student Union will be unable to comply with this requirement and may wish to consider putting the event back.[9] Section 11 requires notice to be given, but there is no need to seek authorisation for the event.

Once notice has been received by the police, conditions can be imposed on the conduct of the march on the same grounds which justify the imposition of conditions on an assembly (s. 12).[10] If imposed in advance, the conditions must be authorised by the Chief of Police and notified to the organisers in writing. Failure to comply with a condition will be a criminal offence. In addition, the most senior police officer on the scene will be able to react to changing circumstances on the date of the event and can impose additional conditions as necessary. The organisers will be liable for a failure to comply with a condition, unless they can argue in defence that the failure arose from circumstances beyond their control (s. 12(4)).

If the Chief of Police does not feel that any conditions are sufficient to prevent disorder, then section 13 allows for an application to be made to ban the procession.[11] The local authority can issue a banning order if it is felt that the march will lead to serious public disorder, but the ban will be applicable to any procession in a specified area for a period of up to three months. This power has rarely been used since the POA came into force, perhaps because the powers contained in section 12 are broad enough to allow the police to contain and control disorder. There is no power to ban an assembly in a public place (although a ban could be sought if either assembly was due to take place on private land (s. 14(a)).

Once the protest is under way, the police have considerable powers to control any disorder which may arise. The POA creates arrestable offences ranging in seriousness from riot (s. 1) to the minor offence of disorderly conduct (s. 5).[12] Arguably these offences give the police sufficient powers to contain any disorder, but there are additional powers available. The march along the public highway could lead to obstruction of the highway which is an offence contrary to section 137 of the Highways Act. It should be noted that the courts have been willing to protect the right to protest by holding that an otherwise lawful protest march can be considered a legitimate use of the highway (**Hirst and Agu v Chief Constable of West Yorkshire** (1987) 85 Cr App R 143). Perhaps the broadest ranging power available is the common law power of arrest for breach of the peace, or to prevent an imminent breach of the peace. Fenwick (2009) suggests that this power is so broad, and so 'bewilderingly imprecise' that it makes the protection afforded to the right to protest in statute almost irrelevant. It is right to say that the power gives an individual officer considerable discretion to decide that a breach may occur and therefore make a pre-emptive arrest. However, the courts do make it clear that only a person creating a threat should be arrested (**Beatty v Gilbanks** (1882) LR 9 QBD 308), and that it is necessary to show the threat is immediate (**R (Laporte) v Chief Constable of Yorkshire** [2006] UKHL 55). The power should not be used indiscriminately and disproportionately (**Laporte**).

The Student Union have no obligations prior to the planned assemblies, but have failed to provide adequate notice of the procession and should reconsider the date in order to comply with their legal obligations. As organisers, they should be aware that they will be liable for the failure of protesters to comply with any conditions imposed. The police have considerable powers to control any disorder which arises during the event.[13]

[12] It isn't necessary to outline the differing requirements for each offence.

[13] The conclusion should briefly summarise the advice given, and demonstrate how each aspect of the question has been addressed.

Make your answer stand out

- By considering in more detail the broad scope of powers of arrest available to the police, particularly in respect of breach of the peace. It could be argued that this places a potentially significant limitation on the freedom of the Student Union to conduct an effective protest.

- By expanding your argument to consider the impact of the discretion afforded to the police on Convention rights. There is a great deal of academic comment about this issue. Useful articles include Fenwick, H. (2009) Marginalising human rights: breach of the peace, 'kettling', the Human Rights Act and public protest *Public Law* 737 and Stone, R. (2001) 'Breach of the peace: the case for abolition' 2 *WebJCLI*.

- When discussing the case of *Austin*, you could contrast the decision with that in *Gillan and Quinton* v *UK* [2009] ECHR 28 which criticised stop and search powers under the Terrorism Act 2000 as disproportionate due to their indiscriminate nature.

! Don't be tempted to . . .

- Reproduce large sections of statute in your answer. Try to summarise the key points that apply to the problem. Some universities allow you to take a statute book into your exam and some unconfident students do copy whole chunks of legislation into the answer. This is never a good strategy. You need to show your examiner that you understand the provisions, and to do this you need to be able to explain the law in your own words.

- Ignore powers that the police have in addition to those set out in the Public Order Act 1986. This question is not limited in this way; you are asked to address all the powers available to deal with disorder. You must, therefore, note the common law powers in respect of breach of the peace, and you should also mention the Highways Act.

Question 3

The creation of offences of aggravated trespass, and the use of civil injunctions have led to a situation where greater weight is given to the rights of businesses than to the right to protest.

Discuss.

Answer plan

→ Explain the rights at Arts. 10 and 11.

→ Distinguish between protest and disruptive action.

→ Explain the need to balance the rights of competing interest groups.

→ Assess the effect of section 68 CJPOA.

→ Consider the use of injunctions under the Protection from Harassment Act 1997.

Diagram plan

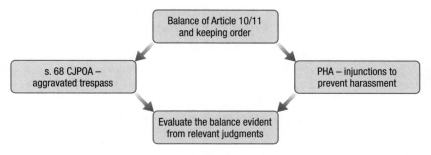

A printable version of this diagram plan is available from www.pearsoned.co.uk/lawexpressqa

Answer

Freedom of expression, association and assembly are expressly protected by the European Convention on Human Rights at Arts. 10 and 11. These rights are considered central to the democratic process, which should tolerate and encourage the expression of minority views. There are limits upon such freedoms, however, as any government may legitimately seek to keep order and ensure that individuals can go about their business without fear of criminal interference.[1] Article 11 protects only peaceful assembly; therefore, there is no protection for violent protest.

In the United Kingdom, despite numerous statutory and common law provisions which entitle the state to control public processions, and assemblies, the basic right to engage in political protests of this type is supported. The Public Order Act 1986 provides the key legislative framework, and although the police have powers to impose conditions on processions or static assemblies in public places, the assumption

[1] By referring to the two separate interests (business and protest), the examiner is asking you to consider the balancing act that the judiciary have to perform when considering Convention rights and by raising this in the introduction you demonstrate that you have understood the question.

[2] This question asks for a discussion of provisions in the Criminal Justice and Public Order Act, and civil injunctions. An explanation of the main statutory controls on protest demonstrates knowledge and gives the discussion some helpful context, but must be brief.

[3] It is always a good idea to give an illustrative example of the law in operation as this will provide support for the point raised, and show that you really understand the issue.

[4] You need to keep returning to the balancing exercise conducted by the courts, as you have identified this as the central issue. All the points you discuss should be related to the central argument.

[5] It will be difficult to obtain good marks for this question without a reasonably detailed knowledge of some key cases, as you must show how the courts have addressed the balance to be struck between competing interests.

[6] Having considered the case law under section 68, the discussion needs to return to the central theme, whether the balance between competing interests has been struck appropriately.

appears to be that they should be permitted to proceed save in the most extreme circumstances.[2] For example, section 11 states organisers of a procession must give notification, but they are not required to seek permission. Only where there is a grave risk to public order that cannot be addressed by the imposition of conditions can the police make an application for a ban (s. 13).[3]

The position is, arguably, more complex when the aim of a protest is not simply the expression of a view, but rather, to disrupt or prevent others from engaging in lawful activity. Here, there has been a tension between civil and criminal sanctions which can be invoked to curb direct action and protest, and the duty imposed on the court to uphold Convention rights by the Human Rights Act 1998. The courts are asked to strike a balance between the rights of competing interest groups.[4]

The Criminal Justice and Public Order Act 1994 introduced measures to address problems caused by protesters who sought to enter land or premises and disrupt activity by criminalising 'aggravated trespass', and has been utilised to prosecute individuals and groups engaged in protests regarding, *inter alia*, foreign policy in Iraq, experimentation on animals, and genetically modified crops. The case of *R v Jones* [2006] UKHL 16 involved defendants who trespassed on to military bases with the intention of disrupting activity, to protest against involvement in the war with Iraq.[5] The defendants sought to argue that the conflict was an 'aggressive war', and therefore illegal under international law. If there was no 'lawful' activity taking place, it followed that there could be no intention to commit the offences outlined in section 68. The House of Lords were not prepared to entertain the argument. Lord Hoffmann plainly considered that the argument was simply an attempt to gain further publicity during the court case, a form of protest through litigation. The majority of case law decided regarding section 68 has rejected a claim that interference with the activities of others is justifiable. It is submitted that this is not contentious, as the offence seeks to protect the rights of individuals going about their lawful business, and therefore the legislation falls squarely within the qualifications permitted by Arts. 10 and 11. Civil disobedience may, or may not, have a moral or philosophical justification in any given instance, but there appears to have been no compelling legal excuse promulgated by the protesters in these cases.[6]

[7] The question does not
explicitly specify the
Protection from Harassment
Act but reference to
injunctions implies you
should discuss it.

[8] Here, a detailed knowledge
of case law is key, as this will
help you to identify a relevant
aspect of civil law and this
will be rewarded.

[9] The use of the contrasting
cases is helpful here as it
allows the answer to examine
the key argument, which
is how the courts have
attempted to balance
business interests and article
rights. You must ensure,
though, that you use the
case law to help you draw
some conclusions about
the development of the
judicial approach.

[10] If you can, it is worth
revising a few short quotes
such as this one, which
neatly encapsulate an idea.

More controversial is the use of civil injunctions to restrain or prevent
protest under the Protection from Harassment Act 1997.[7] The Act
was designed to address the problem of 'stalking', and permits a
civil injunction to be granted where a course of conduct creates
harassment, alarm or distress. Breach of the injunction is a criminal
offence. There have been a series of cases involving protests about
animal experimentation, in which civil injunctions have been obtained
to restrain the activities of both individuals and groups.[8] In an early
case, **Huntingdon Life Sciences Ltd v Curtin** (1997) *The Times*,
11 December, the judge refused to allow the Act to be used to injunct
a group, stating that it could not have been Parliament's intention
that the statute would be used to suppress public protest. However,
later cases have sanctioned the use of the Act to restrain the
activities of protesters, including placing limitations on protesting
at a laboratory save at specified times in the case of **University of
Oxford v Broughton** [2004] EWHC 2543 (QB). In the latter case,
the judiciary were clearly mindful of the need to balance the competing rights of protesters with the Art. 8 rights of employees and con-
tractors of the university. A recent decision was more supportive of
the rights of protesters, and refused to allow an injunction to prevent
protesters outside a facility using megaphones, wearing blood spat-
tered clothing and masks (**Novartis Pharmaceuticals UK Ltd v
Stop Huntingdon Animal Cruelty** [2010] HRLR 8).[9] It was held
that, whilst there could be occasions when protest crossed a line and
became harassment, opinions that some find offensive should nevertheless be able to be expressed. As was said in **Redmond-Bate
v DPP** [1999] Crim LR 998: 'Freedom only to speak inoffensively is
not worth having.'[10] The courts continue to take a dim view of civil
disobedience when this infringes upon the rights of others.

It is hard to see why the right to protest should extend into the cur-
tailment of the liberties of others, by allowing protest to prevent
individuals or companies carrying out their business. It is important,
however, that the right to protest, and to protest robustly, is supported and upheld. If this does not occur, then there is a danger that
the interest and opinions of businesses and corporations will be
afforded undue weight in any debate, and those of minority groups
may not be heard. This was a point stressed in the judgment of the
European Court of Human Rights in **Steel and Morris v United
Kingdom** (2005) 41 EHRR 22, in which it was held that refusing to

[11] It is important to conclude by offering a view regarding the central argument. There is no 'correct' answer, as such, but you should ensure that the conclusions you reach are supported by the evidence provided in your argument.

grant the applicants legal aid to defend a libel action instigated by McDonalds infringed Art. 10. The public interest demands that those 'outside the mainstream' can disseminate information and ideas. It is submitted that the judicial approach in response to section 68, and the Protection from Harassment Act, has sought to strike an appropriate balance by supporting the right to air controversial opinions, but preventing behaviour that unduly interferes with the lawful activity of others.[11]

Make your answer stand out

- By considering the implications of the use of the Protection from Harassment Act in more detail. Is it appropriate that it has been utilised to deal with public protest, when this was not the problem Parliament had in mind? You should refer to the discussion of the use of the Act in Fenwick, H. (2007) *Civil Liberties and Human Rights* (4th edn) London: Routledge-Cavendish, pp. 787–98 for a detailed analysis of the issue.
- By incorporating academic comment in your answer, as well as assessment of relevant case law. This will add weight to your arguments. Fenwick is an excellent starting point, as is Stone, R. (2012) *Textbook on Civil Liberties and Human Rights* (9th edn) Oxford: Oxford University Press.

! Don't be tempted to . . .

- Talk generally about powers to restrain protest; this question is focused on two particular provisions. You should not attempt this question if you have focused your revision on the application of the Public Order Act 1986. 'Question spotting' is a dangerous revision strategy. Students who expect this topic to be dealt with by a problem scenario focusing on the POA will be in trouble if forced to attempt this question!
- Attempt this question without knowledge of a range of cases that illustrate how the courts approach protests that impinge on business interests. Without this, you will not be able to obtain good marks as your answer will lack analysis.

❓ Question 4

'Trainers not traffic' is the name given to an event that takes place once a month in Fetcham City Centre, to protest against pollution caused by too much traffic. The participants, all joggers, congregate outside the Town Hall on the last Friday of the month, and at 5pm set off jogging for one hour. They take up as much room on the road as possible, to disrupt the traffic. Sunil organised the first event, and pays for a notice in the local paper inviting people to attend. The route is never decided in advance, as whoever jogs the fastest decides where to go.

One Friday, as the joggers congregate, the police hand out flyers which state: 'This is an illegal procession, because no notice has been given. Therefore, taking part is a crime.'

One of the joggers, a law student, says this is rubbish, and the event goes ahead. After 20 minutes, the police arrest Sunil.

The following day, several joggers climb over a wall into the local authority bus garage, and chain themselves to a bus. They are carrying placards that state 'Pollution is a crime. Prevent crime'. It is several hours before the chains are cut and the buses can set off. All the protesters are arrested.

The next day, 20 joggers congregate on a patch of land outside a privately owned coach garage and shout at coach drivers as they arrive for work. The police are called but decide not to attend. Several coach drivers are too frightened to go into work, and a considerable amount of money is lost. The coach company is considering whether or not to take legal action against the police for failing to act, and to prevent the protesters from attending again.

Consider the legality of the activities described, and whether the police have acted properly.

Answer plan

→ Outline the notice requirements in section 11 of the Public Order Act.

→ Analyse the legality of the police actions, and consider the case of *Kay*.

→ Assess the legality of the protest at the bus garage, in the light of section 68 CJPOA.

→ Discuss the conduct of the assembly at the coach depot.

Diagram plan

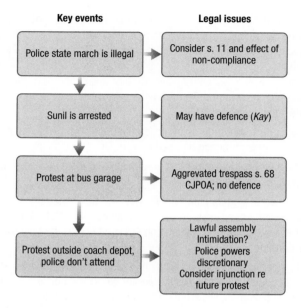

Key events	Legal issues
Police state march is illegal	Consider s. 11 and effect of non-compliance
Sunil is arrested	May have defence (*Kay*)
Protest at bus garage	Aggrevated trespass s. 68 CJPOA; no defence
Protest outside coach depot, police don't attend	Lawful assembly Intimidation? Police powers discretionary Consider injunction re future protest

A printable version of this diagram plan is available from www.pearsoned.co.uk/lawexpressqa

Answer

This scenario deals with the freedom of individuals and organisations to engage in forms of protest. Articles 10 and 11 of the European Convention of Human Rights protect the rights of expression, and assembly, in recognition of the fact that tolerating protest and dissent is seen as one of the hallmarks of a democracy. It is accepted, however, that a state may have legitimate reason to limit these rights, and the permitted qualifications are listed within the Convention. In order to advise the joggers, it will be necessary to consider the restrictions on protest contained in the Public Order Act 1986 (POA), the Criminal Justice and Public Order Act 1994 (CJPOA), as well as civil sanctions created by the Protection from Harassment Act 1997 (PHA).[1]

The monthly event in Fetcham City Centre is a procession, as defined in ***Flockhart v Robinson*** [1950] 2 KB 498 as 'a body of persons moving along a route'. The Public Order Act 1986 imposes obligations

[1] The facts of this problem raise issues about several different legal provisions. Setting them out in the introduction shows the marker that the key issues have been identified.

on the organisers of most processions including those which are designed to publicise or show support for a campaign, as is the case here.[2] Section 11 requires the organisers of such processions to give written notice to the police, six days in advance, including details of the route. Failure to do so renders the organisers liable for a criminal offence. The flyer distributed by the police, however, does not accurately reflect the legal position. Section 11 requires the organisers of particular processions to give notice, but failure to do so does not render the procession itself unlawful. Those in the procession are not committing an offence simply by taking part.[3]

Following the decision in **Kay v Commissioner of Police of the Metropolis** [2008] UKHL 69, Sunil may be able to deny liability for an offence.[4] That case concerned an analogous event, the monthly 'critical mass' cycle ride in London which took place on the last Friday of every month at a specific time, with no particular route. The House of Lords were only asked to consider whether or not the event was 'customary' and therefore exempt from notice provisions at section 11. Lord Philips also made a number of *obiter* statements regarding the applicability of notice requirements to such events. The case turned on whether or not a procession with a route that varied each week could be considered to be customary. It was held that, despite a variable route, each monthly event shared sufficient common features to be able to state that it was a common event. Therefore, Sunil may be able to argue that the 'Trainers not traffic' events are exempt from the notice requirements at section 11.[5]

Further, Lord Philips rejected the submission that, unless customary, it would be impossible to arrange a procession of this type that did not have a planned route. The submission was based on the proposition that section 11 imposes a requirement to give notice of the route, and criminal liability if a different route is taken. This was, in the view of Lord Philips, 'draconian'. It would seem, then, that the event was lawful, and Sunil will have an arguable defence.

The position of the joggers who enter the bus garage is less certain. It is likely that the bus garage is private land, and therefore, entry will constitute civil trespass. Section 68 of the CJPOA creates an offence of 'aggravated trespass', committed by entry onto private land with the intention of disrupting or obstructing lawful activity. Here, the offence appears to be made out. It would appear that, based on the

[2] You don't need to list all the processions listed at section 11 here; far better to mention those which are relevant to help you advise the joggers, as this shows you can pick the parts of the statute which are applicable.

[3] It is important to note this, as the question asks for comment on the police conduct. To do well in this question, you do need to have read the scenario closely, as there are a lot of details which are all included for a reason. The distribution of the flyer is one of these and there are marks available for dealing with the issue.

[4] The facts of the first part of the scenario are based on those in the case of *Kay*. The answer is greatly assisted by having a good knowledge of this case, and because the facts are analogous, it is worth giving more detail than is normally required.

[5] It is critical to make sure that, having set out the facts of *Kay*, you make sure you do relate this to the facts of the scenario.

[6] Marks will be given for noting the significance of the wording on the posters. This is a further example of the value of making sure you consider every detail of the scenario to ensure you maximise your marks.

[7] *Jones* is probably the key case regarding the application of section 68, and certainly is the leading authority regarding the attempted defence argument that the activities disrupted are unlawful.

[8] You do need to note that there are distinct types of protest, and explain how each event will be classified.

[9] The question states that the company are considering legal proceedings against the police; there will be credit for a brief discussion of the form this might take. This is linked to the analysis required of whether the police have acted correctly.

[10] *Police* v *Reid* is a really useful case, as it provides assistance with the interpretation that should be applied to the statutory provisions that allow conditions to be imposed on assemblies that intimidate.

posters, the joggers may seek to argue they were acting in order to prevent a crime, but there is no precedent which would support this.[6] Although section 3 of the Criminal Law Act 1967 authorises 'public defence' to prevent criminal activity, **Blake v DPP** [1993] Crim LR 586 rejected a similar claim on the basis that the section was designed to excuse conduct involving a degree of force. It will also be difficult to point to a particular criminal offence alleged against the owners of the bus garage. Similar arguments were explored in detail, and comprehensively rejected, by the House of Lords in **R v Jones** [2006] UKHL 16, who declined to support direct action as a form of legitimate protest where this involved interference with the lawful activities of others. Therefore, the joggers will be liable for the offence of aggravated trespass and do not appear to have a defence.[7]

The protest outside the garage appears to take place on public land, and will therefore constitute an assembly as defined at section 16 of the Public Order Act.[8] There is no requirement to give notice of an assembly. Once called, the police could impose conditions on the conduct of the assembly if satisfied that these are necessary to combat a serious risk of public disorder, damage to property, disruption to the life of the community, or if the purpose of the gathering is to intimidate others. The police choose not to take action despite the fact that the protesters are shouting at drivers. The coach company may seek judicial review of this decision, on the basis that the police did not exercise their discretion correctly.[9] This is unlikely to succeed because, first, there may not be grounds to impose conditions on the assembly due to the abuse; as the case of **Police v Reid** [1987] Crim LR 702 is authority for the fact that 'intimidation' is more than 'mere discomfort'.[10] Secondly, the courts are unwilling to interfere with police discretion, as evidenced in **R v Chief Constable of Devon and Cornwall ex parte Central Electricity Generating Board** [1982] QB 458, where the courts refused to criticise an operational decision not to police a demonstration.

It would be open to the company to seek an injunction under the Protection from Harassment Act 1997 to restrain future protest, but the authorities do not provide support in these circumstances, as this protest is unlikely to be considered to be harassment. The decision in **Novartis Pharmaceuticals UK Ltd v Stop Huntingdon Animal Cruelty** [2010] HRLR 8 upheld the right to protest outside a facility in bloodstained clothes, with megaphones, despite the fact this would cause some offence. Despite the inconvenience caused to the company, this would appear to be a legitimate protest.

To summarise, it appears that the actions of the joggers in the original event, and outside the coach garage, are lawful. However, those who enter the bus garage and physically prevent the company from conducting business will be liable for aggravated trespass.

✓ Make your answer stand out

- By discussing whether or not the police could arrest the joggers for obstruction of the highway, including a discussion of *Hirst and Agu* v *Chief Constable of West Yorkshire* (1987) 85 Cr App R 143. That case suggested that the courts have been willing to accept that protest may be a legitimate use of the highway. Although this is not the key issue raised by the question, a thorough answer should note all matters of relevance.
- When discussing the protest outside the coach company, outline the powers of arrest under sections 4 and 5 of the Public Order Act, and the common law power to prevent a breach of the peace. This would show a comprehensive knowledge of the available powers.
- By including academic comment to expand the discussion. You could consider the assessment of the use of section 5, POA as a restraint on free speech in Geddis, A. (2004) Free speech martyrs or unreasonable threats to social peace – 'insulting' expression and section 5 of the Public Order Act 1986 *Public Law* 853.

! Don't be tempted to . . .

- Ignore the detail you are given in this question. All the information you are given will be included for a reason. Therefore, consider the significance of every piece of information. For example, the examiner has told you the precise wording on the placards used. This is because you are being invited to consider cases in which protesters sought to argue they acted in the legitimate prevention of crime.
- Fail to explain your reasoning fully. Students often make the mistake of thinking that because a particular argument cannot succeed, there is no need to address the issue. Here, you are told that the coach company are considering legal action. It is clear that there is no basis for judicial review here, but you need to show the examiner how you have reached that conclusion in order to get full credit for this point.

❓ Question 5

Frangton is a small town renowned for its peaceful atmosphere and scenic town square. Residents are, therefore, horrified to hear of plans to construct a large superstore in the centre of the town and to turn the school playing fields into a car park. Qaleem decides to organise a protest against the development. He types up some notices and sticks them up around the town centre on lamp-posts and outside the church. The notices state that a march will be held at 2pm on a Saturday in two weeks' time, from the school playing field to the local authority offices, where a public meeting will take place. It provides Qaleem's email address and phone number as a point of contact.

PC Cutter happens to see one of the notices. She reports the matter to her Chief Constable. Two days later, Qaleem receives an email from the police advising him that the proposed march is illegal and any person attending the protest will face arrest and any marches or processions in Frangton are banned for the foreseeable future.

Qaleem quickly removes as many notices as he can and contacts everyone he can think of to stop them attending. Despite Qaleem's efforts, five people do meet and go to the local authority offices carrying banners saying 'Death to Supermarket-Supporting Scum' and yelling abuse at local authority employees entering the building.

PC Cutter approaches the protesters and informs them that the protest is unlawful as no notice has been given. She tells them to put down the banners and stop shouting, or they will be arrested. Qaleem, who is out shopping, sees what is happening and comes across to reason with the protesters and ask them to stop. The protesters yell at him, calling him a traitor, and waving their banners in a menacing manner. PC Cutter arrests Qaleem to prevent a breach of the peace.

Advise Qaleem on the legalities of the police response.

Answer plan

→ Explain the difference between assemblies and processions.

→ Consider the effect of sections 11–13 of the Public Order Act 1986.

→ Assess PC Cutter's attempt to control the assembly.

→ Analyse the legality of the arrest to prevent a breach of the peace.

Diagram plan

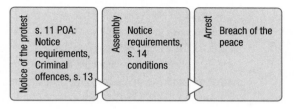

A printable version of this diagram plan is available from www.pearsoned.co.uk/lawexpressqa

Answer

Public protest plays an important part in the democratic process, as it can be an effective means of influencing the executive and focusing attention on a particular issue. In 2010 and 2011, the Arab Spring saw a wave of protests across the region which effected massive change. In the UK, protests against the planned community charge in 1990 led to a change in government policy. The importance of protest is recognised by the European Convention of Human Rights which protects freedom of assembly at Art. 11, and freedom of expression at Art. 10. These are both qualified rights and can therefore be subject to limitations in order to achieve a purpose recognised in the convention such as the prevention of crime, or preservation of order. There are a number of statutory powers that can be used to regulate protest for these purposes but this scenario raises issues concerning the operation of the Public Order Act 1986 (POA) and the common law powers in respect of breach of the peace.[1]

The POA gave the police powers to control public protest in order to prevent disorder occurring, and established a range of criminal offences to deal with disorder if it were to arise. The Act treats processions and static assemblies differently, imposing more limitations on the former. This recognises the fact that a procession poses more challenges for the police and has a greater potential to disrupt traffic or otherwise impede non-participants.[2] Although 'procession' is not further defined in the POA, **_Flockhart v Robinson_** [1950] 2KB 498 described it as 'body of persons moving along a route'. Section 11 states a procession will be subject to control under the Act if it is to

[1] Here, the answer demonstrates awareness of the range of potential public order controls, but there is no need to list them. A clear statement of the relevant areas shows more confidence with the material.

[2] This comment about the reasons for the difference demonstrates an ability to understand and assess the law, rather than simply remember the statutory provisions.

[3] It is much better to apply each statement of law to the facts as you work through the requirements, rather than setting out all the legal issues in section 11 and then discussing how they affect Qaleem. It will make it much easier for the reader to follow the advice.

[4] The question implies that Qaleem has little experience in organising protest events, which should alert you to the need to consider the statutory defence.

[5] Take care how this point is phrased, as you must not imply that the police had any legal duty to advise Qaleem that he could still give notice.

[6] This is a crucial point to include and requires you to be familiar with the judgment of Kay.

[7] It is important to note that the case was primarily concerned with a different issue, as it shows the examiner that you have read and understood the authority carefully and considered how it may apply here.

[8] Do not be afraid to make a definite statement about this as it shows you are confident with the material.

commemorate an event, show support or opposition for a policy or viewpoint, or to publicise a campaign. It is clear that the march that Qaleem plans falls within the ambit of section 11.[3] As the organiser, Qaleem has a duty to provide written notice of the procession to the police. This must be delivered six clear days before the planned procession and must include details of the route, start time and name and address of the organiser. Failure to comply with these requirements is a criminal offence (s. 11(7)). It is clear that in this case Qaleem has not given adequate notice; posters on lampposts will not suffice. Section 11(8) provides a defence if the organiser can prove he did not know of the requirements.[4] It seems Qaleem was unaware of his obligations and therefore he may well be able to rely upon that defence.

The email which Qaleem receives from the police raises concerns. Firstly, it should be noted that there would appear to be ample time for Qaleem to comply with the notice provisions and he could have been advised of this.[5] Section 11 imposes a requirement to inform the police of a planned protest, but it does not impose a requirement to obtain permission for the event. Failure to obtain permission could result in criminal charges against Qaleem but it would not render the march unlawful, or criminalise other participants.[6] *Kay v Commissioner of the Police of the Metropolis* [2008] UKHL 69 concerned a protest in central London attended by officers who handed out fliers to participants prior to the event warning them that they would be participating in an illegal event. The main issue in the case was the precise nature of notice requirements, but the judgment made it clear that the fliers were a misstatement of law.[7]

The email also states that the police have banned all marches for the foreseeable future. This is not lawful.[8] Section 13 of the POA states that the police may make an application to the local authority (or, in the City of London, to the Home Secretary) for a ban on processions in a geographical area for no more than three months. This is clearly intended to be a last resort. Section 12 allows the police to impose conditions on a procession (such as changes to the route, duration or time) if necessary to prevent serious disorder, serious damage to property, serious risk of disruption to the life of the community, or if the purpose is to intimidate others. An application under section 13 for a ban of no more than three months can only be made where there are no conditions that could be imposed which would adequately deal

⁹ It is surprising how frequently this important point is omitted. You will be rewarded for recognising that the power can only rarely be used.

with the risks.⁹ It follows that banning orders are relatively rare and it does not seem that any such order would have been made in this case, even if the police had made application to the local authority.

There are no notice requirements in relation to a static assembly. Therefore, PC Cutter's statement to the protesters is incorrect and the assembly would have been lawful.¹⁰ Section 16 of the POA (as amended by the Anti-Social Behaviour Act 2003) defines an assembly as a gathering of two or more persons in a public place wholly or partly open to the air. The protest falls within this definition. Section 14 mirrors section 12, and allows the police to impose conditions on an assembly for the reasons outlined above.¹¹ Failure to comply with a condition will be an arrestable offence. Conditions can be imposed by the most senior officer at the scene, so PC Cutter may be entitled to tell the protesters to put down the placards and stop shouting. She may argue that the protesters' purpose is intimidation. **Police v Reid** [1987] Crim LR 702 held that 'intimidation' is more than mere discomfort and it could therefore be argued that the imposition of conditions in this case is disproportionate. However, the courts are generally reluctant to interfere with operational decisions made by the police (see, for example, **R (on the application of Brehony) v Chief Constable of Greater Manchester** [2005] EWHC 640).¹²

¹⁰ Again, this is a point that can be confidently and plainly stated.

¹¹ As you have already set out the conditions in section 12, there is no need to write out the provisions of section 14 in full here.

¹² Where there are seemingly contradictory authorities, it is better to include both and acknowledge that you cannot be certain of which will be followed, rather than choosing the one that suits the advice you would like to give.

¹³ There are a number of authorities that could be used here. Do make sure that at least one is provided.

Qaleem should not have been arrested to prevent a breach of the peace. Although police have extremely broad common law powers to take steps to prevent a breach of the peace, the authorities are clear that an arrest can only be made when there is an imminent threat to the peace by the person who is arrested (**Bibby v Chief Constable of Essex**, *The Times*, 24 April 2000).¹³ In this scenario, the threat comes from the protesters rather than Qaleem so his arrest is unlawful.

The police have not acted lawfully in this situation. The email Qaleem received stated that a ban had been imposed, despite there being no legal power for the police to put one in place, and incorrectly advised him of the consequence of going ahead with the event. PC Cutter may have been entitled to impose conditions, but not to arrest Qaleem.

Make your answer stand out

- By discussing whether or not the display of slogans could constitute 'harassment, alarm or distress' sufficient for an offence under section 5 of the Public Order Act 1986. The broad scope of this power could be considered. The matter has been considered in a number of cases that you could consider, including *Percy* v *DPP* [2001] EHWC Admin 1125. In that case, the conviction for section 5 was overturned, but on the grounds that the reasoning at first instance was flawed; leaving open the possibility that conduct considered to be deliberately insulting could constitute an offence. Comment on this, or similar cases, shows that you have a detailed knowledge of authorities relevant to the problem.

- You could draw links between the matters raised in relation to section 5 and recent judicial decisions on the use of injunctions to restrain protest (consider the *Novartis Pharmaceuticals* case), in which a more robust defence of the right to cause offence can be seen. This would demonstrate confidence in drawing parallels between cases dealing with different legal provisions.

Don't be tempted to . . .

- Engage in a general discussion about the powers available to the police. The answer needs to keep a focus on whether or not the exercise of the powers has been lawful in this case, and on any remedies that may be available to Qaleem.

- Assume that the police are exercising the discretionary powers regarding breach of the peace lawfully. Students are occasionally misled in this scenario, by the fact that there is a potential for public order disturbance. You do need to say that the arrest of Qaleem is unlawful.

🖎 Question 6

A number of recent decisions demonstrate an increasing acceptance of broad discretionary powers of the state to restrict the freedom to protest.
Discuss.

Answer plan

→ Identify breach of the peace as the main focus of discussion.
→ Consider the effect of *Laporte*.
→ Contrast *Laporte* with recent 'kettling' cases.
→ Conclude that the courts are unwilling to interfere with police discretion.

Diagram plan

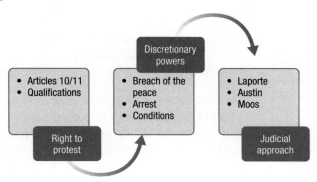

A printable version of this diagram plan is available from www.pearsoned.co.uk/lawexpressqa

Answer

The right to protest is seen as a necessary part of the democratic process. Protest movements can ensure that an issue receives media and public attention and can also exert a powerful influence on government policy. In the United Kingdom, for example, protest against the community charge led to its abolition.[1] The European Convention on Human Rights obliges signatory states to protect that right by Arts. 10 and 11. Article 10 protects the right to freedom of expression, which includes the right to express ideas and support or opposition for a cause.[2] Article 11 protects the right of peaceful assembly and association. Both rights are qualified and can therefore be restricted to the extent required to achieve a specific objective such as the maintenance of public order, or the protection of the rights of others (Art. 10(2) and Art. 11(2)).

There is a balance to be struck between allowing peaceful protest and the need to prevent public disorder and minimise disruption. The police use discretionary powers granted by statute and at common law to control protest. Statutory powers are largely contained in the Public Order Act 1986, but these are supplemented by (*inter alia*) the Criminal Justice and Public Order Act 1994, the Anti-Social Behaviour Act 2003, the Serious Organised Crime and Policing Act 2005 and the Police Reform and Social Responsibility Act 2011. Despite the numerous legislative provisions, the police often rely upon the common

[1] It is important to use an example here, as otherwise the statement about the effect of protest movements is simply an assertion of opinion. You should always try to provide evidence in support of a proposition.

[2] The relevance of Art. 10 to questions about the freedom to protest is often overlooked, so it should be specifically mentioned.

law powers to prevent a breach of the peace. It is these powers that confer the broadest discretion and which have attracted the most academic criticism. There have been a number of significant cases considering the use of these powers, which can be examined in order to assess how the judiciary attempt to assess the balancing exercise between protecting protest and supporting public order controls.[3]

[3] You cannot possibly hope to deal with all the available public order controls in the time allowed. It is far better to decide the aspect you are going to concentrate on, and explain why. Here, because the question refers to broad discretionary powers, it is pointing towards a discussion of the breach of the peace which is often criticised for being too broad.

At common law, the police have the power to take steps to prevent a breach of the peace. This includes arrest, but also allows an officer to take other steps to keep the peace such as the imposition of conditions upon a protest, dispersal or containment through the use of police cordons (commonly referred to as 'kettling'). It is not possible to provide a comprehensive list of actions that can be taken to prevent a breach of the peace because there is no statutory framework governing the common law powers; instead, the judiciary have had to determine what sort of conduct constitutes a breach of the peace and assess the legality of the police response on a case by case basis. This lack of definition has attracted criticism. For example, Fenwick (2009) described the powers as 'bewilderingly imprecise'.[4]

[4] It would not be enough to simply state that there is criticism; you must provide some evidence of this by citing one or more sources.

In *R v Howell* [1982] QB 416, it was said that a breach of the peace occurs whenever a person (or in their presence, their property) is harmed, or caused to fear such harm by 'an assault, an affray, a riot, unlawful assembly, or other disturbance.[5] It would not be sufficient, therefore, for the police to take steps to prevent unruly conduct falling short of this: there must be a threat of violence or damage to property. Where a disturbance is already in progress, there is little difficulty in endorsing arrests made in order to bring it to an end (although, arguably, there are other statutory offences that could be used instead). The more contentious use of the power, however, arises when the police take steps to prevent an anticipated breach of the peace.[6]

[5] You must include this definition, but do not be diverted into a lengthy discussion about the judicial debate surrounding the meaning of the term. Your answer needs to focus largely on the legality of responses to a breach.

[6] Here, the answer explains why the focus of the answer will be on one particular aspect of the topic, which then enables the discussion to ignore authorities that deal with matters outside of those parameters.

Where a breach of the peace has not yet occurred and the detainee has not yet engaged in any unlawful conduct, the courts have stressed that the discretionary power of arrest must be used sparingly and only if certain conditions are met (outlined in *Bibby v Chief Constable of Essex*, The Times, 24 April 2000).[7] However, steps falling short of arrest may be taken which effectively curtail protest. These were considered by the House of Lords in *R (Laporte) v Chief Constable*

[7] As the answer is not going to focus on the power of arrest, there is no need to list the conditions contained in *Bibby*.

of Gloucestershire [2006] UKHL 55. In that case, the police stopped three coaches carrying individuals to a planned protest and after searching the vehicles ordered them to return to London. The coaches were escorted by police and were not permitted to stop en route. The House of Lords, on this occasion, declared the police actions unlawful. Not only was the de facto detention on the coaches during the return journey held to be disproportionate, but preventing them travelling to the demonstration was also unjustified. Powers can only legitimately be used to prevent an imminent breach of the peace and imminent means in the immediate future. This authority, then, is an example of the judiciary placing clear limits on the use of police discretion in order to uphold the right to protest.[8]

Since that case there have been highly publicised uses by the police of the use of police cordons to contain protesters in a geographical area (sometimes for long periods) to prevent a breach of the peace. These have been challenged by claimants, arguing the detention was unlawful and a disproportionate use of the power which failed to discriminate between protesters whose conduct threatened the peace and those who were acting lawfully.[9] Despite the decision in *Laporte*, such challenges have failed. In *Austin v Commissioner of Police of the Metropolis* [2009] UKHL 5 the House of Lords declared that 'kettling' had not constituted a breach of Art. 5 in the 'unusually difficult' circumstances the police had faced. The Court of Appeal in *R (on the application of Mclure and Moos)* v *Commissioner of the Police for the Metropolis* [2012] EWCA Civ 12[10] also endorsed the use of kettling and made it clear the consideration will be whether or not the police decision was reasonable in the circumstances, rather than the court reaching its own conclusion. These two cases can be seen as something of a retreat from *Laporte* and a restatement of judicial deference to the operational discretion of the police.[11]

Given the plethora of statutory controls, it is perhaps surprising that the police still rely on the common law in public order situations. It seems that one explanation may well be the extent to which the judiciary have been prepared to approve of the use of such a vague, and broad, power. Although *Laporte* is an example of judicial attempts to impose limitations, more recent authorities do suggest that the courts are prepared to countenance significant restrictions on the freedom to protest in order to prevent a breach of the peace.[12]

[8] Having set out the relevant law, it is crucial to explicitly relate the authority back to the question so the examiner can see that law is being applied to develop the argument.

[9] You do not need to set out the facts surrounding *Austin* or *Moos* in any detail. It is far more important to set out the legal issue common to both cases.

[10] The question specifically mentions 'recent' decisions, so the answer should discuss the most up-to-date authorities.

[11] Here, the answer again refers back to the central question.

[12] This conclusion can be clearly and briefly stated because the arguments have been set out in the body of the answer.

✓ **Make your answer stand out**

- By providing a more detailed discussion of the case law. More detail could be given about the kinds of conditions endorsed in *Austin and Saxby* v *Commissioner of Police of the Metropolis* [1987] Crim LR 702. This could allow for a broader debate about the role of the judiciary in supervising the executive under the Human Rights Act. If you are able to use this material to comment upon the separation of powers, then you will be showing the examiner that you can consider the topic of freedom of assembly in the context of your study of the constitution.

- By incorporating additional academic comment into your answer. Comment on the *Austin* case can be found in Mead, D. (2009) 'Of kettles, cordon and crowd control – Austin, Commissioner of Police for the Metropolis and the meaning of "deprivation of liberty"' EHRLR 376.

- By discussing the approach of the European Court of Human Rights, and contrasting the decisions in *Gillan and Quinton* v *UK* [2009] ECHR 28 and *Austin and others* v *UK* (2012) 55 EHRR 14. The latter case endorses the deference to police discretion, whereas the former criticised powers seen as disproportionate and indiscriminate.

! **Don't be tempted to . . .**

- Include too much detail about 'old' authorities dealing with breach of the peace. As the question specifies 'recent' decisions, you should avoid explaining cases such as *Beatty* v *Gilbanks* (1882) LR 9 QBD.

- Try to deal with too many areas of discretionary power. It is far better to identify one or two topics that you wish to discuss and deal with them in detail than to skim the surface of a large number of issues.

- Ignore the issue of Convention rights. Although the question does not expressly reference the Convention, you cannot do well in this question without considering the application of Art. 5.

www.pearsoned.co.uk/lawexpressqa

 Go online to access more revision support including additional essay and problem questions with diagram plans, You be the marker questions, and download all diagrams from the book.

Freedom of expression, freedom of information

7

How this topic may come up in exams

This topic lends itself to either essay questions, or problem scenarios. Questions will tend to focus either on the ability of the individual to protect personal information from scrutiny; or upon the access to information held by the state, so you will need to be able to identify the subject matter of the particular question. In either case, you will need to be familiar with the relevant statutory provisions and a considerable amount of case law. The topic overlaps with the study of the European Convention of Human Rights, as questions typically demand analysis of how the Human Rights Act has affected domestic law.

■ Attack the question

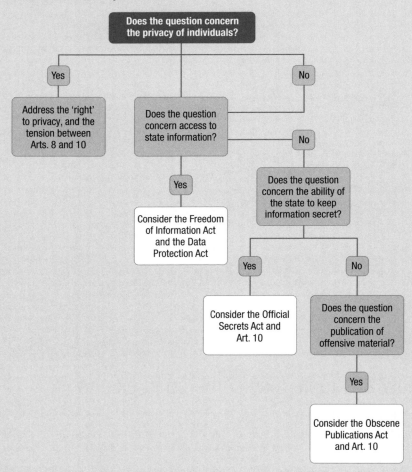

A printable version of this diagram is available from www.pearsoned.co.uk/lawexpressqa

❓ Question 1

Simone Jenkins is a celebrity who presents a children's television programme. She has a lucrative career which includes advertising campaigns aimed at children. She has been interviewed for magazines and other media outlets, and has made statements condemning infidelity and drug use. For a number of months, rumours have been circulating that Simone has been unfaithful to her partner. Simone has been advised by a relative employed by a newspaper that, next Sunday, there will be a tabloid story including an interview with an individual claiming to have had a long-running affair with her, and photographs of her seemingly taking drugs at a party.

Simone fears that, if any details about these allegations are made public, her reputation and consequently her career will be damaged. She would like to know what she can do to prevent the story being published, and whether or not she should have been contacted by the paper to advise her of their plans.

Her relative does not know which newspaper intends to publish the story, or who the individual is that has supplied the photographs.

Advise Simone of any action she can take.

Answer plan

→ Briefly explain the nature of the competing rights under Arts. 8 and 10.

→ Discuss the requirements of a breach of confidence claim.

→ Explore the issues concerning prior restraint with reference to recent cases.

→ Discuss the effect of a failure to give prior notification.

Diagram plan

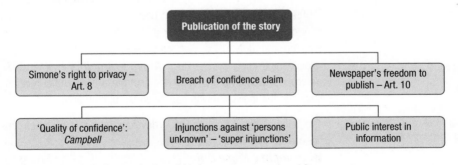

A printable version of this diagram plan is available from www.pearsoned.co.uk/lawexpressqa

Answer

Article 8 of the European Convention of Human Rights provides that an individual is entitled to respect for their private and family life. Article 10 protects freedom of expression. When a newspaper seeks to expose facts about an individual that the individual would rather keep private, a conflict between these Convention rights arises.[1] Simone's potential claim for injunctive relief will be considered in the light of recent decisions concerning the appropriate way to resolve the conflict of competing rights.

[1] You will be rewarded for recognising that the discussion must take place in the context of conflicting rights, so it is worth highlighting this in the introduction.

When untrue information is published about an individual, then that individual can seek redress through an action in defamation.[2] This may not provide a satisfactory remedy for Simone. Firstly, it will not assist if either allegation can be shown to be true, and secondly, it could be argued that any remedy given after publication is ineffective as the information is, by then, in the public domain. Therefore, Simone may wish to consider a claim for breach of confidence, and seek an injunction to prevent publication of the information.[3]

[2] This is not a question about defamation, so there is no need to demonstrate any knowledge of this topic.

[3] This is the key issue, as it addresses the specific concern of the person seeking advice; how to stop publication.

Prior to the Human Rights Act, it was clear that there was no substantive right to privacy in English law. An individual could, however, protect information through the doctrine of confidence. In order to be successful, it would need to be shown that the confidential information had been disclosed in circumstances giving rise to a duty of confidence; and that further disclosure would be detrimental to the applicant.[4] An action could restrain disclosure by third parties under the 'Spycatcher' principle (*A-G v Guardian Newspapers* (No. 2) [1990] 1 AC 109[5] Simone would have no difficulty in arguing that information from a partner, or ex-partner, fell within circumstances creating the duty. It is well established that intimate personal relationships imply such a duty (*Argyll v Argyll* [1967] Ch 302). However, it would be harder to demonstrate a confidential relationship with the individual who had taken the photographs.

[4] Make sure you do not spend long on outlining the previous law. Summarise the test as succinctly as possible.

[5] There is no need to give the facts of the 'Spycatcher' case; all that is required is a demonstration that you understand that it establishes a test for restraint of third parties.

The Human Rights Act has led to developments of the law of confidence which would assist. The House of Lords confirmed in *Wainwright v Home Office* [2004] 2 AC 406 that the HRA did not introduce a right to privacy.[6] However, *Campbell v MGN Ltd* [2004] 2 AC 457 significantly reformed the law on breach of confidence, to the extent that it now incorporates the tort of misuse of private

[6] It is worth making this point as some students confuse the incorporation of the right to respect for private life with a right to privacy. Mention of this authority will show confidence in the subject matter.

information. This may assist in restraining publication of all the material here. Following **Campbell**, it is clear that the courts will first ask whether or not the information concerned has a 'reasonable expectation of privacy'. This test is less restrictive, as there is no need to establish the pre-existing relationship. The law is less concerned with the context in which the information was obtained than with the nature of the content. There is some authority to support the suggestion that covert photographs may attract special protection, as arguably a picture has the potential to be more intrusive and damaging than the written word[7] (**Douglas v Hello!** (No. 3) [2006] QB 125). If the information can be said to be private, then the court must ask whether this is outweighed by arguments in favour of publication, either because the material is in the public domain; or that publication is in the public interest. Here, the courts must balance the Art. 8 rights of the applicant against the Art. 10 rights which protect free expression in the press.[8] It appears that this will be done on a case-by-case basis and therefore the court will seek to balance the threat posed to Simone's interests against the right of the public to be informed about activities of individuals who are in the public eye.

Simone will seek an injunction to restrain publication pending resolution of a claim for misuse of private information and/or breach of confidence. There is a need for the careful scrutiny of such applications, as it is accepted that the value of news may diminish if delayed (**The Observer and the Guardian v United Kingdom** (1992) 14 EHRR 153). Here, however, the particular issues for consideration are whom the application should be made against, and how far any prohibition on publication should extend.

It is possible to seek an injunction against 'persons unknown'.[9] It is not uncommon for a celebrity to become aware that an unidentified individual possesses private information that they intend to disclose. By obtaining an injunction against an unspecified respondent, newspaper groups can be restrained from publication as third party recipients of the information under the 'Spycatcher' principle. (See, for example, **TUV v Person or Persons Unknown** [2010] EWHC 853.) Thus, Simone can seek to restrain publication of the photographs from an unknown source.

A similar situation arose in the case concerning the footballer, John Terry, who sought to prevent publication of a story concerning his

[7] The explanation of what is meant by 'expectation of privacy' allows the examiner to see that you can relate the law to the specific issues raised in the problem scenario.

[8] Although this is not a case about 'human rights law' per se, the balance of rights should be mentioned, as all authorities since the HRA are concerned with how this balance should be struck.

[9] This may seem like a fairly minor point, but marks will be awarded for dealing with this issue. The scenario clearly states that Simone cannot locate the source of the information, and therefore a comprehensive response should cover the issue.

affair with a team mate's partner (*John Terry (previously referred to as LNS)* v *Persons Unknown* [2010] EWHC 119 (QB)). Simone appears to want to suppress any mention of the story. If she were to apply for an injunction, a report of her success could arouse public speculation. Terry sought (and was initially granted) what has been referred to as a 'super-injunction', restraining publication not only of the information but of mention even of the proceedings themselves. The use of such broad injunctions has been the subject of considerable academic, media and political criticism but, in any event, following *Terry*, it appears that Simone will be unsuccessful. The judge refused to renew the injunction on the basis that on the facts, he did not feel there would be an actionable claim and further, that even if there was, damage to Terry's commercial interests could be addressed by compensation. In this situation, it seems possible that the courts would determine that the freedom of the press did indeed outweigh Simone's right to privacy, as an adequate remedy exists for any harm resulting from publication.[10] Simone is not entitled to prior notification from the press. This matter was considered by the European Court in *Mosley* v *United Kingdom* [2012] EMLR 1.[11] The applicant claimed that the failure of the state to impose an obligation for prior notification on the press breached his Art. 8 and 13 rights, as if notification is not given, then an effective remedy is denied as restraint cannot be obtained. The European Court rejected the argument as to impose an obligation for prior notification in all cases would be a disproportionate restriction upon press freedom.

It seems that Simone would be best advised to bring an action for breach of confidence and misuse of private information, and to seek an interim injunction to restrain publication. She is unlikely to be able to obtain a so-called 'super-injunction', and is not able to obtain redress for the absence of prior notification.[12]

[10] Where there is a direct parallel between a reported case and the situation in a scenario, then it is worth explaining this. The aim is not to demonstrate that you know the facts, but rather, to draw some conclusions about how the precedent will be applied in the instant case.

[11] Credit will be given for reference to this matter, as it demonstrates that you have an awareness of the law as it is evolving, beyond the issues covered by the text books.

[12] As the issues have been discussed in the body of the answer, the conclusion can be a brief summation of the key points covered.

Make your answer stand out

- The *Mosley* case has been the subject of academic debate. You would be rewarded for examining the arguments regarding notification in more detail. Helpful comment and analysis can be found in Phillipson, G. (2009) Max Mosley goes to Strasbourg; Article 8, claimant notification and interim injunctions *Journal of Media Law*, 1: 73, and a response by Andrew Scott (2010) Prior notification in privacy case: a reply to Professor Phillipson, *Journal of Media Law*, 2(1): 49–65.

- The issue of 'super-injunctions' has been the focus of political attention, and a committee headed by Lord Neuberger (2011b) was established to consider the issue. The report was published in 2011 and is a useful resource. 'Report of the Committee on Superinjunctions: Superinjunctions, Anonymised Injunctions and Open Justice', 2011, available at http://www.judiciary.gov.uk/Resources/JCO/Documents/Reports/super-injunction-report-20052011.pdf.

- You should make sure you keep up to date with emerging case law. You may find links to recent cases, and some commentary, via the International Forum for Responsible Media (http://inform.wordpress.com/).

! Don't be tempted to . . .

- Discuss the facts of the cases. It can be particularly tempting here, as you will probably remember the details easily due to the publicity they received. Do remember that only the *ratio* is important!

- Lose sight of the facts of the scenario. Students sometimes set out the law clearly, but do not use the points made to draw conclusions about the particular facts provided.

 Question 2

'It is well known that in English law there is no right to privacy' (Glidewell J) in *Kaye* v *Robertson* [1991] FSR 62.

Assess this statement in the light of developments following the Human Rights Act 1998.

Answer plan

→ Briefly explain the traditional approach to privacy in English law.

→ Outline the effect of the HRA.

→ Assess the development of the law by focusing on major cases.

→ Consider the extension to the law of confidence.

→ Analyse how far this provides effective protection of personal privacy.

Diagram plan

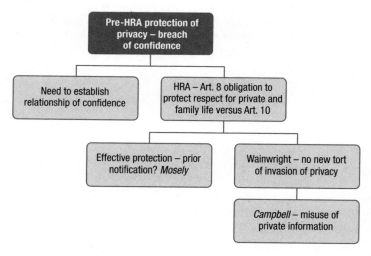

A printable version of this diagram plan is available from www.pearsoned.co.uk/lawexpressqa

Answer

The case of **Kaye v Robertson** [1991] FSR 62 was decided prior to the HRA, which incorporated the European Convention of Human Rights into domestic law. Article 8 protects the right to respect for private and family life. Nonetheless, in 2004, the House of Lords emphatically denied that the HRA had created a new action for invasion of privacy (**Wainwright v Home Office** [2004] 2 AC 406). It will be argued that the HRA has allowed the judiciary to provide more robust protection for individual privacy.[1]

[1] Setting out the conclusion at the start of the essay shows confidence and the ability to reach an informed view.

[2] This question asks you to evaluate how the law has changed since 2000, when the HRA came into effect. Therefore, it is essential to set out the position prior to that point.

[3] The parameters of the discussion need to be established. Here, you have stated clearly what the focus of the answer will be but, importantly, explained to your examiner why you have made that choice.

[4] These two cases are critical as they each mark a significant development in the law. In any question dealing with actions for breach of confidence, you will need to show that you recognise why they were important.

[5] You need to be able to highlight the limitations of an action for breach of confidence in order to evaluate whether the HRA has been effective in remedying any of these issues.

[6] This is a key point to make, as it will be suggested that the post-HRA balance between Arts. 8 and 10 is, to an extent, dealing with the same issue.

Prior to 1998, private information could be protected in a number of circumstances.[2] First, information regarding court proceedings could be protected by way of a court order, and in respect of juvenile proceedings, the order would be made unless a successful application was made to lift reporting restrictions in the public interest. Further, an individual was able to protect personal information from dissemination if it could be established that publication would amount to a breach of confidence. It is this issue that requires discussion, as this is the area where it can be said that the HRA has had the most impact.[3] Confidence arises from a particular relationship. Often, this arises from contractual obligations. **Argyll v Argyll** [1967] Ch 302 established that marriage was an intimate relationship giving rise to a duty of confidence. The principle developed further in **A-G v Guardian Newspapers** (No. 2) [1990] 1 AC 109 (the '**Spycatcher**' **case**),[4] in which it was held that third parties who received information obtained in a confidential relationship were also subject to restraint. Hence, a measure of protection existed for celebrities, politicians, and others who wished to prevent details of their private lives being exposed in the press.

To establish an action for breach of confidence prior to the HRA, the applicant would need to demonstrate that the information had 'the quality of confidence', and was obtained in circumstances creating a duty of confidence. Further, it would need to be shown that the unauthorised use of the information would be detrimental. Thus, information already in the public domain could not be restrained.[5] It could be argued that it is in the public interest to reveal certain kinds of private information, if this exposes corruption, or hypocrisy.[6] In **Woodward v Hutchins** [1971] 1 WLR 760, the court declared there is 'no confidence in iniquity'. In that case, a celebrity who had sought publicity could not complain about coverage of his private life.

Even in cases where it was clear that a gross intrusion of privacy had occurred, in the absence of a confidential relationship, there was little effective protection. This was the situation in **Kaye v Robertson** which prompted Glidewell LJ to suggest that Parliament should review the issue. Following the inception of the HRA, the courts, as a public body (s. 6), have a responsibility to provide a remedy for an individual who can demonstrate that their Art. 8 rights have been infringed. It should be noted, however, that there is a concurrent duty to uphold the protection of freedom of expression guaranteed by Art. 10. In dealing with cases where restraint of publication of private information is sought, the judiciary are required to conduct a balancing exercise between the competing rights. Therefore, it cannot be said that an individual is always entitled to privacy, and indeed it could be argued that the matters that will fall to be considered are scarcely different from those which were relevant before 1998.[7] Sebastian Coe was unable to prevent publication of details of an extra-marital affair on the grounds that, on balance, the freedom of the press and public interest outweighed his desire to keep the matter private (**Lord Coe v Mirror Group Newspapers** (2004, QBD, unreported)).

[7] The answer highlighted the potential for 'public interest' that existed in pre-HRA actions for breach of confidence earlier, so there is no need to repeat the points here.

There is, as emphasised in **Wainwright**, no new tort of invasion of privacy. What is clear, however, is that the judiciary have felt enabled to develop the doctrine of confidence, so that it can now be said to incorporate an action for the misuse of private information.[8] The critical case is that of **Campbell v MGN** [2004] 2 AC 457,[9] concerning an action in respect of publication of photographs of the model Naomi Campbell entering a drug rehabilitation unit, having previously denied taking drugs. The key distinction is that there is no longer a requirement to demonstrate a pre-existing relationship of confidence provided that it can be shown that the information carries with it a reasonable expectation of privacy.[10] This allowed Campbell to seek redress for the publication of photographs taken by a stranger. Once the threshold of reasonable expectation is passed, the courts will then consider whether or not the information is already in the public domain and, finally, whether there is a public interest in publication. It can be seen, then, that the case represents a significant extension to the legal protection for individual privacy, as it enables an action to be brought in a broader range of circumstances. The judiciary, however, have emphasised that Art. 8 rights do not have primacy over those contained in Art. 10 and, therefore, there will always be a careful balance to be struck.

[8] It is absolutely critical to include this point as the extension to the law of confidence is, without doubt, the most significant development in this area resulting from the HRA.

[9] *Campbell* is the most important case in this area and must be included.

[10] Marks will be awarded here, as the answer doesn't just give the *ratio* of the case, it also explains clearly how this represents a change in the law. This shows real understanding.

Even where an action can be brought in confidence, on the basis that private information has been misused, this will not always provide the protection that an individual may hope for.[11] Many cases contain an application for injunctive relief to prevent publication pending the resolution of the matter. However, where the individual does not have notice of the impending publication, any action after the event will be unable to prevent the material entering the public domain. Redress

[11] The question asked for consideration of the individual's right to privacy, so having shown how the law has developed, there should be an evaluation of the limitations of the protection now provided.

is only available through complaint to the Press Complaints Commission, or by obtaining damages for breach of confidence. The matter was considered by the European Court of Human Rights in **Mosley v United Kingdom** [2012] EMLR 1 where the applicant argued that, without an enforceable right to prior notice of publication, he was denied an effective remedy. His application failed as it was held that a blanket requirement for prior notification would be a disproportionate limitation on press freedom.

It is fair to say that, even before the advent of the HRA, the courts were mindful of the need to balance the rights of the individual against the importance of the freedom of the press. The incorporation of the right to respect for privacy has undoubtedly obliged the court to provide a measure of protection in a broader range of circumstances. It seems that, had **Kaye v Robertson** been decided today, the action for breach of confidence would have been successful, as the information carried the reasonable expectation of confidence outlined in **Campbell**. It cannot be said that this creates an automatic right to privacy in every case, as the courts must still balance the individual's wishes against the freedom of the press.

 Make your answer stand out

- You could expand the discussion about limits on the protection of privacy that still exist by exploring the developing stance of the judiciary in relation to 'super injunctions', and what this suggests about the appropriate balance between Arts. 8 and 10. Ensure that you keep up to date with new authorities as they emerge. The UK Human Rights Blog is run by Crown Office Chambers, and provides a free updating service that should alert you to new cases: http://ukhumanrightsblog.com.

- By considering the potential impact of the Leveson Inquiry. At the time of writing, the report is still anticipated but it is almost certain to contain sections concerning press intrusions upon privacy.

- By incorporating additional academic opinion on the law of privacy. A good starting point would be the *Journal of Media Law*, which often contains relevant material for this topic. Although the law has developed since publication, the textbook by Feldman, D. (2002) *Civil Liberties and Human Rights in England and Wales*. Oxford: Oxford University Press, remains an authoritative resource.

! Don't be tempted to . . .

- Engage in a lengthy explanation of Convention law. You do need to explain the need to balance Arts. 8 and 10 but your focus should be on application of the law in the domestic courts.

- Spend too much time outlining the law prior to the Human Rights Act. When you are asked to evaluate an area of law in light of the HRA, your examiner does require you to consider how far the Act has signalled a change; therefore you have got to outline the 'old' law but try to ensure the bulk of the answer considers the current position.

- Ignore the issue of effective remedies. Even if it is accepted that the law now does seem to protect more kinds of private information, we can see that there is debate about whether prior restraint is effective.

? Question 3

Jenna obtains a part-time job as an administrative assistant with the Home Office. On commencing her employment, she was asked to sign the Official Secrets Act. She did this, but paid it little attention.

Whilst filing some documents, Jenna comes across a memorandum marked 'classified', which warns that a large number of persons who entered the United Kingdom are no longer traceable. The memorandum further states that many of these individuals originate from countries characterised by high levels of terrorist activity. Later that day, Jenna hears on the news that the minister responsible for immigration answered a question in Parliament about security, and claimed that the tracking procedures for asylum seekers are excellent.

Jenna feels that this is highly misleading. She discusses this matter with her brother, Karl. Karl is a freelance journalist and he writes an article for the *Sunday Record*. In the week prior to publication, the paper begins to show television adverts claiming that 'insider information' from the Home Office will expose ministerial lies.

All employees in Jenna's department are told there will be an investigation into the leak. Advise Jenna of any possible consequences for her, and her brother.

Answer plan

→ Outline the main provisions of the Official Secrets Act.

→ Specify the nature of the information protected.

→ Distinguish between the obligations of (and consequences for) Jenna and Karl.

→ Consider any possible defences.

→ Briefly consider additional measures that could be taken for breach of contract, or breach of confidence.

Diagram plan

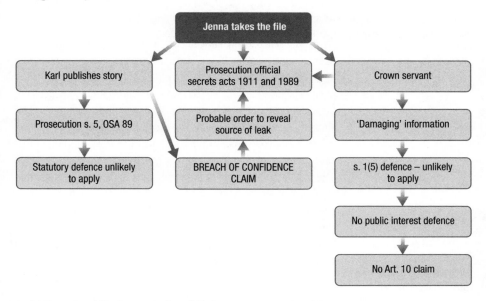

A printable version of this diagram plan is available from www.pearsoned.co.uk/lawexpressqa

Answer

[1] A brief introduction can show that you have been able to see all the key issues highlighted by the scenario.

[2] You should aim to summarise the purpose of the law as succinctly as you can, so that you can begin to focus on the issues relevant to the parties as soon as possible.

[3] As you have decided this is unlikely to be relevant, you should avoid spending time discussing the Official Secrets Act 1911.

Jenna and Karl may be subject to prosecution for offences contrary to the Official Secrets Acts 1911 and 1989. In addition, Jenna could face an action for breach of confidence and breach of contract. The Official Secrets Act 1989 does provide some defences, and the efficacy of these will be considered.[1] The liability of the parties will be considered separately, as there is variance between their positions.

The Official Secrets Acts aim to protect the interests of the state by preventing the unauthorised disclosure of information held by various government departments.[2] Section 1 of the 1911 Act remains in force, and prohibits the disclosure of information that could assist an enemy for a purpose prejudicial to the state. This is a serious offence, and is generally concerned with activities that could be classified as espionage. It is unlikely that Jenna will be prosecuted under the 1911 Act.[3] The 1989 Act categorises types of information that are protected, from security and intelligence (s. 1), defence (s. 2), interests abroad (s. 3) or criminal investigations (s. 4). It seems likely that the information regarding asylum seekers could be categorised as information concerning security and intelligence.[4]

[4] There is no need to give any detail about those categories that are not going to be relevant to Jenna.

As Jenna is a Crown servant, she may face prosecution for an offence under section 1(3). In order to be liable, it will be necessary for the Crown to prove that the information meets the 'harm' test; it must be shown that it is, or is likely to be, 'damaging'. Damage is not further defined in the Act; however, it appears likely that this will be straightforward for the Crown. The case of **Chandler v DPP** [1964] AC 763 was concerned with section 1 of the 1911 Act but, in that case, it was held that it was for the government to determine what constitutes the 'interests of the state'. This appears to suggest that the judiciary are likely to defer to executive determinations of harm. The statute does afford Jenna with a defence under section 1(5) if she is able to prove that she did not know or have reason to believe that the disclosure was damaging.[5] On a literal interpretation, this imposes a reverse burden of proof upon the defendant. This has been held to be contrary to the provisions of Art. 6(2) of the European Convention of Human Rights, as it infringes the right to a fair trial (**R v Keogh** [2007] 1 WLR 1500). Section 3 of the Human Rights Act will be utilised to read the provision as conferring only an evidential burden. If Jenna is able to raise some evidence that she did not know the information was damaging, then it will be for the Crown to disprove that assertion. Given that the memorandum was marked as 'classified', and she has confirmed awareness of her obligations by signing the Act, it is probable that the defence will fail.[6]

[5] As you are asked to advise Jenna and explore possible defences, you do need to spend time setting out the relevant legal principles and applying them to the facts, even if it might seem obvious that they will not apply. A diligent lawyer will carefully examine all the options to ensure that the client is properly advised.

[6] You will be rewarded for being able to reach a clear conclusion about the likely application of the law to these facts.

Jenna may wish to argue that she disclosed the information because it was in the public interest.[7] It may seem desirable that a public servant who uncovers evidence that Parliament has been misled should be entitled to act as a 'whistleblower'. Under the 1911 Act, Sarah Tisdall was prosecuted and imprisoned for disclosing information to journalists. She had done so as she believed that a minister had made false statements to the Commons. The case, and that of **R v Ponting** [1985] Crim LR 318, caused considerable disquiet and, arguably, led to the 1989 Act. The statute does not, however, provide any defence of public interest. This was confirmed in **R v Shayler** [2003] 1 AC 247, in which the House of Lords confirmed that the 1989 Act provides a mechanism for reporting concerns to a superior who may authorise disclosure (s. 7), and this would have been the

[7] The question explicitly states that Jenna feels the information is misleading, which is an invitation to discuss whether or not there is a 'public interest' defence.

correct procedure. Nor can Jenna argue that a prosecution would infringe her Art. 10 right to freedom of expression, a point also dismissed in the **Shayler** litigation. Article 10 is a qualified right, and infringement is permitted if necessary for national security.

Jenna does not appear to have any defence available to her. Her best hope is that the Crown may feel that the adverse publicity that could accompany any trial outweighs the need for a prosecution.[8] Katharine Gun was prosecuted under the Official Secrets Act in 2003 after disclosing information obtained in the course of her employment to the *Observer* concerning an American request to the United Kingdom to assist in surveillance of foreign diplomats. She intended to argue that she had the defence of necessity, on the basis she acted to prevent an illegal war. It is clear, following **Shayler** (above), that there was no prospect of success. Nevertheless, the Crown offered no evidence, as it appeared that the airing of the matter in court would have been damaging.

The Crown will wish to prevent publication of the material. The most straightforward means will be to seek an injunction for breach of confidence as the material was obtained in circumstances imposing a duty of confidence. An action can be brought against the paper, and it is by this means that the Crown will be able to determine that Jenna is the source of the information. Although section 10 of the Contempt of Court Act allows journalists to protect their sources, this can be overridden in the interests of national security. It was through such an action that Tisdall was identified; **A-G v Guardian Newspapers** (No. 2) [1990] 1 AC 109.[9]

Both Karl and the proprietors of the newspaper will be liable for an offence contrary to section 5 of the 1989 Act, which makes it an offence for a person who receives classified or confidential information to further disclose it.[10] There is a requirement to prove that the disclosure was made with relevant mens rea, that the defendant knew, or had reason to believe, the information would be damaging. Fenwick (2007) suggests that this may afford some degree of protection for journalistic freedom, as it could feasibly be argued that the journalist took the view that disclosure was in fact beneficial to the public interest (p. 603). There are as yet no authorities to confirm this view and nor does it seem that there is special protection afforded to the Art. 10 rights of the press when issues of security are

[8] Here, the answer demonstrates an awareness that proceedings in this area are concerned with matters that are not strictly legal, as there is a broader, political, implication.

[9] A good answer will be able to show the connection between actions against the newspaper and investigation of the source of the leak.

[10] Although you are advising Jenna, you were asked to address the implications for her brother so you must address the possible offences under section 5.

engaged. In ***Attorney General* v *The Times*** [2001] 1 WLR 885 an injunction was refused, with regard paid in the judgment to Art. 10, but in that case, the primary reason to allow publication was that the information was already in the public domain. That is not the case here, and therefore the authority does not assist Karl.

[11] The conclusion briefly summarises the advice given, demonstrating that you have applied your knowledge to answer the specific questions asked.

Jenna and Karl both face prosecution under the Official Secrets Act 1989 in respect of the disclosure of the information. Karl will be unable to protect Jenna's identification as the source of the information. The Human Rights Act does not offer any solace for either party and there do not appear to be any arguable defences.[11]

✓ Make your answer stand out

- By expanding the discussion of the relationship between the Contempt of Court Act and Convention rights. A good discussion of this topic can be found in Stone, R. (2012) *Civil Liberties and Human Rights* (9th edn). Oxford: Oxford University Press.

- By engaging in a more critical analysis of the 'harm' test which is applicable to the section 1 offence. It has been argued that the test is potentially broad in scope and lacks definition. See the criticisms of the Act contained in Fenwick, H. and Phillipson, G. (2006) *Media Law*. Oxford: Oxford University Press, pp. 923–48. This would demonstrate an awareness of the academic arguments raised by the facts in this scenario. You must make sure that you do not stray too far from the objective of advising the parties. So, for example, in this instance you may incorporate reference to the criticisms raised by Fenwick and Phillipson that 'damage' is so poorly defined that any disclosure Jenna makes could be interpreted as 'damaging'.

- By exploring the issues raised in the *Shayler* litigation regarding Art. 10 in more detail. Similar issues were addressed in the case of *Attorney General* v *Blake* [2001] 1 AC 268, in which the House of Lords declined to determine whether section 1 was too widely drawn. Reference to additional cases, where relevant, shows familiarity with the subject material.

! Don't be tempted to . . .

- Discuss the historical development of the law. This question does not require you to consider the reasons why the 1989 Act came into existence. You need to be applying the law which is relevant, and drawing conclusions what is likely to happen to Jenna and Karl.

- Engage in a lengthy discussion of section 1 of the 1911 Act. It can be tempting to show the examiner that you have remembered everything about the topic, but you will get better marks for focusing on the law relevant to the parties here.

- Making statements about what is likely to happen to the parties without providing support from the authorities. Whilst you would be given a mark for noting that there is no 'public interest defence', more credit will be awarded for stating that this proposition of law is confirmed in the *Shayler* case.

Question 4

'Unnecessary secrecy in government leads to arrogance in governance and defective decision-making . . . People expect much greater openness and accountability from government than they used to.' White Paper, *Your Right to Know*, Cm. 3818.

To what extent has the Freedom of Information Act 2000 succeeded in creating open government?

Answer plan

→ Outline the aims of the Act.

→ Identify the categories of information available and discuss the process of making a request.

→ Assess the impact of the Act with reference to particular examples.

→ Draw conclusions about the effectiveness of the legislation in meeting its aims.

Diagram plan

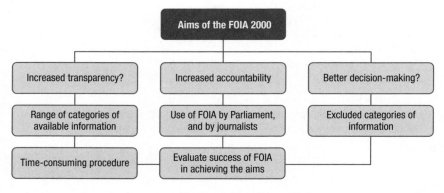

A printable version of this diagram plan is available from www.pearsoned.co.uk/lawexpressqa

Answer

The Labour Party made a manifesto commitment to increase open government prior to election in 1997. In December of that year, the White Paper *Your Right to Know: White Paper on Freedom of Information* (Cm. 3818, London: HMSO) was published, and this led to the Freedom of Information Act 2000, fully implemented in 2005. The Act allows the public rights of access to information held by public bodies, subject to certain exceptions and limitations. Perhaps the most notorious use of the Act thus far has been in respect of requests made concerning expenses claims made by MPs, leading to the scandal in 2009. It will be argued that, whilst the Act may have led to greater transparency, the effect upon the process of government decision-making has been minimal.[1]

The Data Protection Act 1998 granted individuals access to information held about them to ensure accuracy. The Freedom of Information Act, however, conferred a broader right of access to information held by a range of public bodies including local and central government, Parliament, the police, schools and colleges, and the NHS. The Act aimed to increase transparency and accountability, improve the decision-making process of government, and also to increase public trust and participation in government.[2] Worthy and Hazell (2010) have argued that the Act has succeeded in achieving the first of these aims, but has

[1] Here, the answer suggests that a fairly complex argument is going to be developed, drawing a distinction between openness and better government.

[2] In order to evaluate the impact of the Act, it is necessary to show that you understand the purpose of the legislation.

not increased participation or trust in government, or impacted upon the decision-making process.

Requests for information must be made in writing, and the recipient must respond within twenty days. Public authorities are not obliged to disclose all information that is requested.[3] Certain classes of information are subject to an absolute exemption (including, for example, information concerning the formulation of government policy (s. 35), or information relating to security matters (s. 23)). The Act also exempts other kinds of information if disclosure is likely to prejudice specified interests (this includes information which may prejudice the economy, law enforcement and criminal investigations). Further, a request may be refused on the grounds that the information is, or will be, available by other means (ss. 21–22), or if the cost of providing the information is excessive (s. 11).

The Act is overseen by the Information Commissioner, who will adjudicate any appeal against a decision to refuse a request for disclosure. The Information Commissioner can issue an enforcement notice, and decisions of the Information Commissioner are subject to appeal either by the person making the request, or the body which holds the information.

The Act has been utilised to a limited extent by Parliament as a mechanism for obtaining information held by government.[4] Worthy and Hazell have found that parliamentary questions remain the primary method for MPs to obtain information; with approximately five times more tabled questions than freedom of information requests in any session. Nevertheless, the Act has provided a means to obtain information where the answers to questions have been unsatisfactory or evasive. For example, the All Party Parliamentary Group on Extraordinary Rendition sought data regarding the movement of individuals across boundaries, following perceived reticence in response to parliamentary questions.[5]

The most extensive use of the Act has been by journalists, who represent the vast majority of requesters. It is well known that the MPs' expenses scandal of 2009 was triggered by freedom of information requests made by an investigative journalist, Heather Brooke. It should be noted, however, that the utility of the Act is undermined by the procedure attendant on making a request. The 20-day response time may well mean that by the time information is

[3] The question asks for discussion of the effect of the legislation. It is necessary to demonstrate understanding of how the law operates but this can be done in a brief paragraph.

[4] Many answers will focus on the use of the Act by members of the public (and journalists), but a recognition of the potential use by Parliament recognises the constitutional position of the legislature in ensuring government accountability.

[5] When dealing with an area of legislation that has not generated a great deal of case law, it is important to make sure that illustrative examples of the law in operation are included.

[6] This is a key point in the argument that is being developed, suggesting that the impact of the Act is, in fact, fairly minimal.

[7] This shows a fairly detailed level of current awareness and also suggests that the Act is not as significant as is sometimes suggested which helps point towards the eventual conclusion.

[8] There is very little case law in this area, so there will be credit given to an answer that demonstrates knowledge of any available authorities.

received, the currency of an issue has faded so that it is no longer newsworthy.[6] This is magnified when the initial response is a refusal to release the information; necessitating a lengthy appeal process. Heather Brooke made her first request for information regarding receipts in 2005. Her investigations certainly generated considerable publicity for the issue, and the release of limited information, but the scandal finally broke when the full details of the claims for additional costs allowance was leaked from a Whitehall source.[7] More recently, the Court of Appeal has overturned a refusal of a request made in 2005 (**BBC v Sugar** [2010] EWCA Civ 715).[8] This gives some support to an assertion made by a number of respondents in the study conducted by Hazell *et al.* that the appeals process is utilised by public bodies to delay the release of information and, indeed, deter some from pursuing an action. A report by the Campaign for Freedom of Information (Frankel and Gunderson, 2009) states that the average request takes almost 20 months to be concluded. The cost of legal action is feasibly a real bar to members of the general public.

It can be seen, then, that the Act has allowed access to a broad range of information, and has led to a degree of increased transparency and accountability. The limitations on the types of available information and the lengthy nature of the process have meant that the impact is perhaps less than was anticipated.[9]

[9] At this point, having discussed the effect of the Act on transparency, it is appropriate to draw a 'partial' conclusion before moving on to a different part of the argument.

[10] The quote in the question raises the issue of the decision-making process, so a good answer will consider not only access to information, but the effect of the legislation on how government operates.

One of the aims of the Act was to increase public participation in the process of government. It is difficult to see how this has been achieved. Relatively few requests are made by members of the general public. It may be that the release of information obtained by the media has increased public awareness of government issues; however, the White Paper also indicated that the decision-making process would be improved.[10] Conversely, a concern expressed by ministers during the passage of the legislation was that the decision-making process would be impaired. It was suggested that the fear of having to disclose information would deter civil servants from providing information to ministers, thus hindering the process of full and frank debate. In the event, sections 35–36 restrict access to all information regarding the formulation of policy and other information is subject to the harm test. Thus, it seems clear that the Act has had no impact on the manner in which government decisions are made.

It was also hoped that public trust in the process of government would be improved. Given the scale of the public anger following the release of information regarding expenses, it is clear to see that this objective has not been achieved. Rather, the efforts made to obstruct access to the information led to a perception of secrecy; this was not assisted by the parliamentary time given to a Private Member's Bill proposing amendments to the Act which would have excluded much of the detail regarding individual MPs' expenses.

[11] The conclusion can be brief as it simply summarises points made throughout the answer as the argument developed.

The Freedom of Information Act has allowed details regarding the machinery of government to be obtained. It cannot be said, however, that the Act has led to open government, as a result of restricted access to much information and the unwieldy appeals process.[11]

 Make your answer stand out

- By referring to a broad range of illustrative examples. As the law is fairly recent, there is not a great deal of case law authority to draw on. A really good source of information (where much of the material referred to here can be found) is the work of the Constitution Unit at UCL, headed by Professor Robert Hazell. Publications can be found online at www.ucl.ac.uk/constitution-unit.
- By using what case law there is to support your arguments. A good starting point is the discussion of the topic in Bradley, A. and Ewing, K. (2010), *Constitutional and Administrative Law* (15th edn) London: Pearson, pp. 283–8, which outlines the key authorities to date. This will show your examiner that you have a good knowledge of this developing area of law.

! **Don't be tempted to . . .**

- Simply set out the legislative provisions in detail. The bulk of the marks here are awarded for analysing the impact of the law on the operation of government. You do need to show that you understand the key provisions of the Act, and, in particular, the existence of exemptions. Try to provide a brief summary or overview so that your answer can then address the central topic.
- Ignore the wording of the quotation provided. The question requires you to consider the impact of the Freedom of Information Act on the workings of government, but the quote also suggests that openness leads to better decision-making and you should address this aspect of the question. This can be a small point, as in this answer, which states quite briefly that the decision-making process is unaffected.

❓ Question 5

Julian is the editor of an internet magazine that publishes stories and photographs in a monthly, online edition, available on subscription. One month, the magazine includes a 'photo-story' involving a group of nuns engaging in sexual acts in a church. Mrs Greenhouse has a 19-year-old son who subscribes to the magazine, and she finds the story on the family computer. Mrs Greenhouse, a devout Christian, is outraged, and also concerned that her younger children could have read the material.

The matter is reported to the police, and Julian is arrested and later released on bail whilst the Crown decides whether to press charges.

Mrs Greenhouse also informs the local paper, which publishes a story stating that Julian is a 'depraved pornographer' who must be imprisoned.

Consider the legal implications of these events.

Answer plan

→ Explain the relevant provisions of the Obscene Publication Act and the Criminal Justice and Public Order Act 1994.

→ Identify the fact that blasphemy is irrelevant.

→ Outline the provisions of the Contempt of Court Act 1981.

→ Discuss the effect of Art. 10 on domestic provisions.

Diagram plan

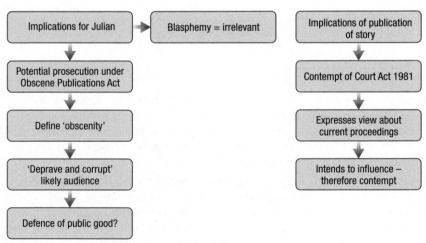

A printable version of this diagram plan is available from www.pearsoned.co.uk/lawexpressqa

Answer

Freedom of expression is protected under Art. 10 of the European Convention of Human Rights. The right to freedom of expression is qualified, and therefore restrictions are permitted in domestic law.[1] There are numerous restrictions on speech and expression in the United Kingdom; of relevance here are those concerning the dissemination of obscene material, and the reporting of court proceedings. Julian may be subject to criminal proceedings under the Obscene Publications Act 1959. The editor of the newspaper may be found to be in contempt of court.

The Obscene Publications Act 1959 makes it an offence to publish an obscene article. The Criminal Justice and Public Order Act 1994 makes it clear that 'publication' incorporates the electronic distribution of material.[2] The online magazine will be considered to have been published. Julian may, therefore, be subject to prosecution for an offence under section 1 of the 1959 Act. First, it will need to be determined whether or not the material is 'obscene' within the terms of the Act. If the jury feel that it is, Julian may wish to argue that notwithstanding its obscene nature, publication is justifiable.[3]

Section 1(1) provides that an article is obscene if it will tend to 'deprave and corrupt persons who are likely, having regard to all relevant circumstances, to read, see or hear the matter contained or embodied in it'. This definition is rather imprecise. It is clear that the fact the material may be shocking, disgusting, or 'loathsome' is not sufficient to satisfy the definition (*R v Anderson* [1972] 1 QB 304). It must be shown that the material is likely to 'deprave and corrupt', as confirmed in *R v Martin Secker and Warburg* [1954] 2 All ER 683.[4] The fact that Mrs Greenhouse found the material shocking and offensive is not, then, enough to render it obscene. The test will be whether or not a significant number of people who come across the article would be depraved, and corrupted.[5] The intended and actual audience for the online magazine may well be relevant. From the facts provided it seems that the material is restricted by the need to subscribe to see the content of the magazine,[6] which may assist as it does not appear to be aimed at children, as was the case with the infamous 'Oz' magazine (the subject of the matter of *R v Anderson*). It would not, however, be a defence for Julian to argue that the

---

[1] Although the question is focused on domestic law, any discussion of freedom of expression must take account of Convention law. A brief explanation of the qualified right at the outset demonstrates an awareness of the appropriate context for the discussion.

[2] This is a small point, but shows detailed knowledge of a range of legislation.

[3] A brief summary of how the law will be applied to the facts of the scenario is useful, and helps to ensure the answer remains focused on the problem.

[4] There are numerous cases concerned with the definition of obscenity; the answer needs to include at least one to demonstrate that mere offensiveness is not sufficient.

[5] Here, the answer demonstrates an understanding that 'obscenity' is dependent not just on content, but how it is received.

[6] All the facts given in a problem scenario will be relevant, and marks will be awarded for recognising why the information regarding subscription was included.

intended audience are already regularly exposed to similar material (**Shaw v DPP** [1962] AC 220), or even that the intended audience are already corrupt (**DPP v Whyte** [1972] AC 489). Mrs Greenhouse fears that her younger children could have seen the material but, given the need to subscribe to view content, it seems likely that the jury would find that children are not the intended, or likely, audience. Whether or not the material is obscene will be a question of fact for the jury to determine.[7]

If the story is deemed to be obscene, Julian may wish to claim that the publication is for the 'public good'; a defence under section 4 of the Act.[8] It is permissible for expert evidence to be called regarding the artistic or literary merits of the work, as occurred in the (unreported) trial regarding *Lady Chatterley's Lover*. Again, following the evidence, this is a question for the jury to decide; however, the defence of 'public good' will be interpreted narrowly. In the case of **DPP v Jordan** [1977] AC 699, it was argued that the publication of pornography was for the 'public good' due to the supposed therapeutic benefits of such material. The judge did not allow the argument and confirmed that the 'public good' is confined to art, literature and science.

It is stated that Mrs Greenhouse is a Catholic, and it may be that the religious content of the story is one of the reasons for her outrage. The Criminal Justice and Immigration Act 2008 (s. 79) abolished the offence of blasphemy, so there can be no action taken in respect of this element of the story.[9]

Julian may, then, be the subject of prosecution. He will not be able to argue that the Obscene Publication Act 1959 is an infringement of his Art. 10 rights. This point was settled in **Handyside v UK** (1976) 1 EHRR 737. The right is qualified, and Article 10(2) permits restriction for the protection of 'public health and morals'. The European Court of Human Rights (ECtHR) will afford the domestic state a wide margin of appreciation in determining what constitutes 'morals', even if the material is readily available in other jurisdictions.[10]

The publication of the story in the newspaper could make the editor liable for an action for contempt of court.[11] The Contempt of Court Act 1981 prohibits the publication of material that would tend to interfere with the course of justice in particular legal proceedings

[7] The answer must keep referring to the facts of the scenario and here an effort is made to draw some conclusions about how the law that has been outlined may be applied.

[8] A good answer will explore not only the possible charges, but also any defences; this is required for a full evaluation of the legal implications.

[9] The question expressly mentions religion, so this point needs to be mentioned but don't waste time explaining law that is no longer relevant.

[10] There are issues raised here regarding the feasibility of restricting access to material in the United Kingdom that is available on the internet, but it is not possible to deal with them in the time allowed and therefore the focus of the answer remains on obscenity law.

[11] A comprehensive answer must consider the issues raised by publication of the newspaper article, even though the bulk of the problem is focused on Julian's liability.

(s. 1). The proceedings must be 'active' (s. 2), which would be the case here as Julian has been arrested in connection with an offence. The court would consider whether the reporting created a 'substantial risk of prejudice' to the case (***Re Lonhro plc and Observer Ltd*** [1989] 2 All ER 1100). The courts have to balance the risk of prejudice to the right to a fair trial, against the right to freedom of expression. The purpose of this article would appear to be to express opprobrium about Julian's behaviour, which would appear to be prejudging the outcome of the case, and therefore, contempt. It would be possible to avoid liability if the editor were able to demonstrate the story formed part of a discussion in 'good faith' of matters of public interest (Contempt of Court Act, s. 5) but this does not appear to be the case from the facts given here.[12]

[12] The facts given are quite clear, and therefore a confident answer will briefly acknowledge the potential defence before dismissing it.

It seems that both Julian and the editor of the newspaper are likely to face proceedings. The outcome of Julian's case will depend upon the view taken by the jury and without more detail about the material, it is hard to estimate the verdict. It would seem, however, that the editor will be liable for contempt of court.

✓ Make your answer stand out

- By analysing the approach of the ECtHR in addressing freedom of expression, and exploring in more detail how the margin of appreciation is applied. There is a useful discussion of the approach of Strasbourg in Fenwick, H. and Phillipson, G. (2006) *Media Law.* Oxford: Oxford University Press, pp. 462–7.

- By incorporating reference to the case of *R* v *Perrin* [2002] EWCA Crim 747, in which it was confirmed in the domestic courts that the test for obscenity is sufficiently precise for the purpose of Art. 10(2). This shows your examiner that you are familiar with a broad range of cases, and the effect that this may have upon the persons in the scenario.

- By considering whether or not Julian would have any action in defamation in respect of the comments made about him in the newspaper. You could deal with this fairly succinctly and should make the point that if Julian is convicted of an obscenity offence, the paper may well be able to claim the defence of truth in any libel action.

> ! **Don't be tempted to . . .**
>
> ■ Explain in detail the 'old' law relating to blasphemy. You are asked to address the legal implications of these facts, and there are no marks available for exploring principles which will no longer have any impact on the parties. The question specifically mentions Mrs Greenhouse's religion and, as all facts in a scenario are mentioned for a reason, you are being invited to mention blasphemy. You will be rewarded for having the confidence to assert that it is not relevant.
>
> ■ Fail to address the legal implications which may arise for the paper. Weaker students will fail to recognise that the examiner has asked for all implications to be addressed, and will concentrate on possible actions against Julian. It is important to ensure that you consider the impact of the events on all the parties.
>
> ■ Concentrate only on obscenity law. This question highlights the danger of 'topic spotting' as a revision technique. Students who have concentrated on the Obscene Publications Act, but have failed to revise the Contempt of Court Act will be unable to advise all the parties here.

📝 Question 6

'Free speech includes not only the inoffensive but the irritating, the contentious, the eccentric, the heretical, the unwelcome and the provocative provided it does not tend to provoke violence. Freedom only to speak inoffensively is not worth having.' (Lord Justice Sedley, *Redmond-Bate* v *DPP* [1999] EWHC Admin 333).

To what extent are the courts willing to protect individuals from offence?

Answer plan

➡ Explain the qualifications upon Art. 10.

➡ Consider prosecutions of individuals engaged in protest.

➡ Discuss social media prosecutions.

➡ Analyse the relationship between public opinion and judicial decisions.

Diagram plan

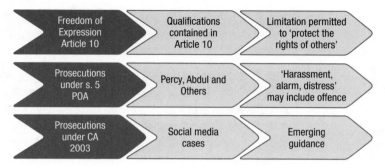

A printable version of this diagram plan is available from www.pearsoned.co.uk/lawexpressqa

Answer

Article 10 of the European Convention on Human Rights (ECHR) obliges signatory states to protect freedom of expression. Freedom of expression is, however, a qualified right, meaning that it can be restricted for one of the purposes specified in Art. 10(2). In the United Kingdom, there are a number of statutory controls upon freedom of speech. Many of these are arguably uncontroversial, such as the criminalisation of the incitement to racial or religious hatred (Racial and Religious Hatred Act 2006) which is a limitation that can be justified under Art. 10(2) as necessary for the prevention of crime. It is legitimate for the state to limit freedom of expression in order to protect the rights of others, which leads us to ask whether or not this incorporates a right to be protected from material that they find offensive.[1] This issue has been the focus of considerable media and judicial attention in a series of cases involving either public protest, or the use of social media.[2]

Section 5 of the Public Order Act 1986 (POA) criminalises behaviour likely to cause harassment, alarm or distress in a public place.[3] In **_Percy_ v _DPP_** [2001] EWHC 1125, the High Court overturned the appellant's conviction under section 5 where the behaviour in question was defacing an American flag during a protest at an American air base. In doing so, it was held that disrespectful or contemptuous conduct during an otherwise lawful protest is not prohibited; only behaviour that is intentionally or recklessly abusive, threatening or

[1] This introduction is effective, because it succinctly explains that the key legal issue is the interpretation of 'rights of others' in the ECHR.

[2] Here, the answer indicates the particular area that will be the focus for the discussion. It is a good idea to set these parameters in the introduction.

[3] You must give the definition, because the decisions in the cases you are discussing turn on the word 'distress'.

insulting. Although the conviction was quashed on the basis that the District Judge had approached the balancing exercise incorrectly, it should be noted that Mrs Justice Hallett accepted the lower court's finding that it was legitimate to claim the service personnel should be protected from actions denigrating their flag.[4]

[4] This is a really important point to make to develop your argument that the judiciary are now prepared to curtail actions that cause offence.

This somewhat tentative acceptance that 'harassment, alarm or distress' includes 'offence' has been reinforced by the more assertive judgment in **Abdul v DPP** [2011] EWHC 247.[5] The defendants in that case staged a protest against military action in Afghanistan and Iraq during a parade of British soldiers, and shouted phrases such as 'British Soldiers Murderers' and 'Go to Hell'. In this case, the convictions under section 5 were upheld by the High Court, rejecting the appellants' claim that their Art. 10 rights had been infringed. Khan (2012) has pointed out that the regiment submitted evidence confirming that they had not been offended by the protest, but the court nevertheless held that the 'citizens and public of Luton' could constitute a category of persons whose rights could legitimately be protected.

[5] Do not be afraid to offer your evaluation of a judgment: this shows that you have read the cases and are confident enough with the subject to draw inferences from the words used about the development of the law.

Whether or not this argument is accepted, there is a distinction to be made between speech or actions directed at an identifiable person or group during a public protest, and comments made on social media about a person or group which are not directed to, or even necessarily seen, by them.[6] The Communications Act 2003 prohibits the use of the 'public electronic communications' network for sending messages that are either 'grossly offensive' or of an 'indecent, obscene or menacing character' (s. 127(1)). In **Chambers v DPP** [2012] EWHC 2157 the court stated that internet social media sites such as Twitter should be considered to be part of the public communications network for the purposes of the Act.[7] It is fair to say, however, that the growth of social media has created new challenges for the state in determining when to prosecute under an Act which (as was noted in Chambers) was drafted at a time when few could have predicted the impact of such sites. In the summer of 2012, the Director of Public Prosecutions decided not to prosecute an individual who posted an offensive message regarding the Olympic diver, Tom Daley.[8] In a statement about the decision, he stated that the message had been intended as a joke aimed at family and friends and was not part of any campaign against Daley (available at http://blog.cps.gov.uk/2012/09/dpp-statement-on-tom-daley-case-and-social-media-prosecutions.html). The statement acknowledged the need

[6] You do need to make it clear why social media prosecutions are particularly contentious.

[7] There is no need to consider the facts of this case as it focused on a message said to be 'menacing'. The question has clearly directed you to discuss the narrower issue of 'offensive' speech. No marks would be available for analysing the factual background of this case; it is only included to explain why social media prosecutions are brought under this Act.

[8] Reference to this statement demonstrates that the student has read around the set texts, and as a result, can draw on very current sources.

to consider Art. 10, and conceded that the CPS are working in largely 'uncharted' territory, reaching decisions on a case-by-case basis.

Such an ad hoc approach to the issue results in contradictory decisions, as there have been prosecutions in cases that cannot objectively be said to concern statements substantially different to those in the Daley case.[9] Matthew Woods pleaded guilty to an offence under section 127(1) and was sentenced to twelve weeks in custody in October 2012 in respect of offensive comments posted on Facebook concerning the highly publicised disappearance of a young child. Azar Ahmed was convicted at trial in respect of messages he posted on Facebook stating that soldiers should die and go to hell. This message contained no specific threat and was not directed at any particular individual, but two persons complained to the police. The decisions to prosecute Woods and Ahmed appears to fly in the face of both the DPP's recent statement and a line of judicial authorities reflecting the opinion expressed by Lord Justice Sedley that the courts should protect freedom of speech even where the speech in question is unpalatable to many. The announcement of the DPP in October 2012 that consultation meetings will be held with a view to issuing guidelines regarding social media prosecutions is welcome and it is to be hoped some clarity is provided.

The ECHR does not contain any specific protection for the 'right not to be offended'. What, then, could the basis be for judicial determinations that restrictions on offensive speech fall within the ambit of Art. 10(2) protection of the 'rights of others'?[10] Khan (2012) dismisses the notion that such a right is incorporated into Art. 8 as an aspect of individual autonomy, pointing out that even if that were to be accepted, the speaker would be equally entitled to protection (p. 197). Despite this, the cases noted above do demonstrate a willingness by the judiciary to accept that freedom of expression can legitimately be restricted to prevent offence even where there is no other criminal activity.[11] This should be a matter of concern, as it does appear that prosecutors and members of the judiciary have been responsive to public opinion rather than the legal principles underpinning the convention. No cases concerning the use of social media have reached the Court of Appeal or the Supreme Court so it may well be that in due course senior members of the judiciary will reassert the need for robust protection of Art. 10 rights. At the present time, however, it seems that the courts are willing to take steps to protect citizens from offence.

[9] This part of the answer shows how a breadth of knowledge enables you to engage in critical analysis of the topic.

[10] This is an important point to make because it shows how the 'right', if it exists, is a creation of interpretation.

[11] At the outset, the answer acknowledged that speech can be restricted to prevent crime. It is a point worth reinforcing in conclusion to make clear that you recognise the distinction between offensive and criminal forms of expression.

✓ **Make your answer stand out**

- By showing an awareness of recent academic commentary. At the time of writing, the issue of social media prosecutions is still fairly new, but if you check journals regularly you will be able to find new articles when they are published. Criminal law journals are a useful source for comment on recent cases.

- By being prepared to engage with the discussion of Art. 8 and autonomy alluded to in the answer. This is quite a complex area but the Khan (2012) article is a good starting point. Cited in that article is the work by Mead, D. (2010) *The New Law of Peaceful Protest: Rights and Regulations in the Human Rights Act Era*. Oxford: Hart Publishing. Mead sets out the argument that Art. 8 may involve personal autonomy, and the book is itself a useful resource (although note that this a rapidly changing area and the law has developed since publication).

- By considering the relationship between Strasbourg and the domestic courts. In particular, you could consider the fairly broad margin of appreciation generally afforded to signatory states to deal with these kinds of issues. This deference may result in a lack of robust protection for freedom of speech in the domestic arena.

! **Don't be tempted to . . .**

- Ignore the importance of the qualifications upon Art. 10. A successful response to this question will depend upon recognising the need to assess the validity of restrictions designed to protect the rights of others. You will need to be able to give a clear explanation of the operation of qualified rights.

- Simply describe the key cases. You must use your knowledge of the facts of these cases to draw some conclusions about the direction that the developing law is taking. This is the kind of question which demands that you articulate an opinion.

❓ Question 7

Miranda works for a local newspaper *The Daily Grind* as a crime correspondent. She also maintains a 'Twitter Account' detailing her life as a reporter, and a blog.

The editor, who usually decides what stories to use, goes away for two weeks.

On the first day of the editor's holiday, Miranda is delighted to be assigned to cover a breaking story concerning the gruesome murder of a college lecturer. One of her police contacts tells her that one of the victim's colleagues, Sally, a criminal law lecturer, has been arrested. Miranda begins to research what she can about Sally. She speaks to some of Sally's ex-students, and gets detail about the kind of things that she taught. She writes her 'exclusive' which appears on the front page of *The Daily Grind* the next day. The headline reads: 'Ghoulish tutor obsessed with death and gore'. Within the article, Miranda notes that homicide took up about half of the lecture programme that Sally delivered.

Sally is released without charge the day after the story appears, and a second person, Tim, is arrested a few days later. He is charged with murder, and appears in the magistrates' court, where a trial date is set, and the matter is committed to the Crown Court for trial. That day, Miranda blogs:

'From my seat in the press gallery I am sure I was looking into the eyes of a cold-blooded killer, there is no doubt whatsoever, this man is a monster. The Crown referred to a DNA match found on the victim's clothing, so guilt looks like a foregone conclusion'.

She sends a Twitter message that states:

'The accused says nothing apart from his name'.

Miranda is surprised when she arrives at work the next day to see a furious email from the editor of the paper, as he says her actions may result in the paper facing court action.

Advise Miranda of the legal consequences that may arise from the newspaper article and the blog entry.

Answer plan

→ Explain the tension between various Convention rights.

→ Outline the elements of a contempt of court.

→ Assess whether or not the article and the blog could be contempt.

→ Consider whether or not the position is different regarding the Tweet.

Diagram plan

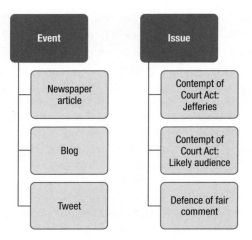

A printable version of this diagram plan is available from www.pearsoned.co.uk/lawexpressqa

Answer

The freedom of the press to report upon court proceedings has long been recognised as a key component of open justice, and is now protected by Arts. 6 and 10 of the European Convention on Human Rights.[1] Article 10 protects freedom of expression and the right to receive information, and Art. 6 makes it clear that a public hearing is one of the requirements of a fair trial. Both of these rights, however, are qualified and permit restrictions to be made where necessary to protect the rights of others. Reporting of court proceedings can be viewed as a way of protecting Art. 6 rights, but equally, coverage that is biased can make it impossible to secure a fair trial, particularly in criminal cases where a jury may be influenced by material seen in the media. Limitations can be placed upon the reporting of criminal proceedings to prevent prejudicing the defendant's right to a fair trial, and failure to respect these can be a contempt of court (now governed by the Contempt of Court Act 1981 (CCA). Miranda (and the newspaper) faces the possibility of prosecution in respect of each part of the scenario.

Contempt of court is a matter of strict liability (s. 1), and can apply to any publication aimed at the public at large (or a section of it)

[1] Surprisingly, the fact that reporting court proceedings engages Art. 6 is one that is often missed, so inclusion of this point will be rewarded.

which creates a substantial risk of prejudice or impediment in live proceedings.[2] Contempt cases are brought by the Attorney General, and there has been a sharp increase in the number of such cases under the current incumbent, Dominic Grieve.

The publication of the story concerning Sally may well be an actionable contempt, and is analogous to the facts surrounding **Attorney General v MGN Ltd and another** [2011] EWHC 2074. That case concerned the publication of stories about Christopher Jefferies, who was arrested in connection with a high profile murder case, but never charged with any offence. The court held that 'proceedings' do not begin at the point of charge, and in fact, are 'live' from the point of arrest.[3] In this case, proceedings would be brought against the newspaper, not the individual journalist. **Attorney General v MGN Limited and Others** [1997] 1 All ER 456 set out key principles for consideration in cases of contempt. When considering the 'substantial risk' of prejudice, it is not necessary to consider the actual effect of the article, only the position at the time it was published. It will not, then, be possible for the newspaper to claim that the course of justice was not impeded as Sally was never actually charged. The court would have to find that the material was likely to be seen by a potential juror, and, crucially, that it would be capable of prejudicing a juror by the time of the trial.[4] The newspaper could try to argue that, had Sally been charged, there would have been a significant delay before trial and that the risks would have been minimal by that point. Given the ruling in the Jefferies case, this is unlikely to be successful as the material here could be held to be similarly serious.[5]

Clearly, when Tim appears in court, there are live proceedings.[6] In dealing with the blog entry, at first glance, it seems that the comments clearly create a risk of prejudice as Miranda has made it clear that she believes him to be guilty. She may, however, wish to argue that the blog is not a publication that creates a substantial risk. Jurors are now customarily warned to refrain from looking at the internet, and therefore Miranda could argue that any juror reading the blog during the trial would be disobeying judicial instructions. The facts here could be distinguished from those in **Attorney General v Associated Newspapers Ltd and another** [2011] EWHC 418.[7] In that instance the court felt that a warning against internet research may not have prevented jurors seeing prejudicial material on newspapers websites, as they were advised they could read daily

[2] The answer will need to consider whether or not there has been contempt in three, separate, instances. You can avoid unnecessary repetition by setting out the elements of liability at the outset.

[3] The facts of this case are fairly well known, but take care to set out the key legal issue that the court had to determine, rather than being sidetracked by describing the content of the stories published about Jefferies.

[4] Never forget that you are being asked to advise Miranda, so do ensure that you relate all your legal points to the facts given in the scenario.

[5] Sometimes, students do not mention the legal arguments that they have considered and discounted. It is far better to show your examiner how and why you have reached your conclusions.

[6] As you have set out the matters that need to be proved at the outset, and dealt with the issue of 'live' proceedings earlier, you can deal with this aspect of liability regarding the blog in a single sentence.

[7] Here, the answer demonstrates the ability to consider the application of authorities.

news reports and this could be confusing for jurors who read news online. A blog, however, is not in that category. The difficulty with this is that, unlike the case cited above, no jurors have yet been selected, and a potential juror may come across the material in the mean time. Miranda could argue that, if the readership of the blog is modest, the risk of prejudice could not be said to be 'substantial' as the likelihood of a potential juror reading it would be slim. Alternatively, she could argue that the material is unlikely to be prejudicial as any jury would focus on the evidence presented to them, and would not be swayed by the obviously subjective view of the defendant's appearance in the blog.[8] These arguments may assist in respect of the first part of the statement, but reference to evidence presented is clearly prohibited. The Judicial Studies Board guidance of 2009 makes it clear that restrictions apply to the reporting of all preliminary hearings,[9] and only brief factual details about the defendant, the trial listing date and matters relating to bail can be published. The only other matter to consider is whether or not it would be Miranda or the newspaper who would be held liable here.[10] This would depend upon whether the blog was part of the newspaper's own online presence. If it is not linked to, or promoted by, the newspaper's own website, it is likely that she would be personally liable.[11]

The use of Twitter and other social media has created new challenges in seeking to prevent prejudice due to the difficulties in monitoring and policing usage. It is quite clear that a Tweet can be a 'publication' as defined by section 2 of the CCA. The Attorney General suggested that contempt proceedings could be brought against users of Twitter who revealed the identity of a person protected by a so-called 'super-injunction'.[12] Individuals working in media or other public roles often make it clear in their profile that views expressed are theirs and not their employers. If Miranda has done this, the paper would not be liable. In any event, the content of the Tweet is not prohibited and would be considered no more than a 'fair and accurate' account of proceedings, and therefore not actionable (s. 4).

In summary,[13] it appears that the newspaper would be liable for contempt in respect of the story published relating to Sally if proceedings were brought. If either the paper, or Miranda, faced action in respect of the blog, the statements may be found to be sufficiently prejudicial to amount to a contempt. There can be no action in respect of the Tweet.

[8] There are a number of possible ways to view the risk of prejudice here, and you will be rewarded for recognising these.

[9] By recognising the specific considerations which apply to the particular hearing, this answer demonstrates a really detailed knowledge of the topic.

[10] The question specifically referred to the email from the editor fearing action against the paper. Although you are directed to consider all possible consequences, it would be useful to draw a distinction between two issues.

[11] It does not matter which conclusion is reached on this point, as long as you explain the thinking behind it.

[12] There is no need to give details about the injunction matter, the only relevance is the fact that use of social media can be a contempt.

[13] It can be difficult to conclude a problem scenario: a brief summary of the advice will suffice.

Make your answer stand out

■ By expanding the discussion about the decision in the *Jefferies* case. Comments made in the judgment indicated that it was a possibility that coverage could have prejudiced the trial of the person eventually tried for the murder, making his conviction less likely. This, it is suggested, points towards something of an extension of the principles governing contempt as the 'proceedings' prejudiced may be separate to those concerning the individual subject of reports.

■ By considering the issues raised by the use of social media in more detail, in particular, concerns surrounding the ability of jury members to conduct internet research.

■ By utilising some additional academic comment on the area. You could look at the research by Thomas, C. (2010) commissioned by the Ministry of Justice: *Are Juries Fair?* and Murdoch, C. (2012) The Oath and the Internet, *Criminal Law and Justice Weekly*, vol 176, March, contains more recent comment on the issue of jury use of the internet.

 Don't be tempted to . . .

■ Spend time speculating about whether or not prejudice was caused by these events. This is unnecessary and misunderstands the aim and purpose of the CCA.

■ Make unsupported statements of opinion about Miranda's conduct. You must take care to find authorities that help you to see what conclusions are likely to be drawn by the courts dealing with these events.

www.pearsoned.co.uk/lawexpressqa

Go online to access more revision support including additional essay and problem questions with diagram plans, You be the marker questions, and download all diagrams from the book.

Police powers
and terrorism

How this topic may come up in exams

Problem scenarios are a common way to examine this area of the syllabus. You will need to ensure that you are familiar with the major provisions of PACE, and the associated codes of practice. You will need to know something about the special powers relating to the investigation of terrorism. You should also be able to outline the possible consequences of police misconduct, and explain the means by which evidence can be excluded from a criminal trial. Essay questions may require evaluation of the safeguards against the misuse of discretionary powers. This area of the syllabus may overlap with human rights, and you should be prepared to evaluate the compatibility of police powers with Convention rights (particularly Arts. 5, 6, and 8).

Attack the question

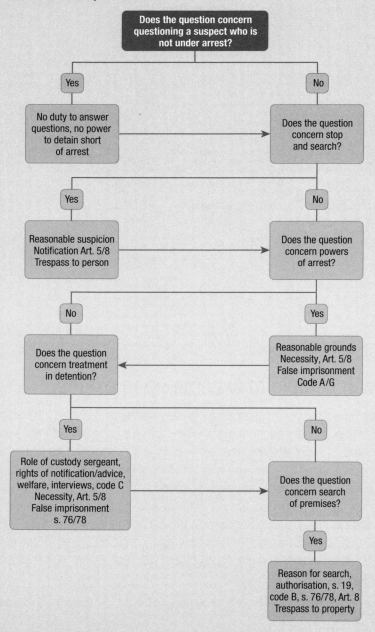

A printable version of this diagram is available from www.pearsoned.co.uk/lawexpressqa

 # Question 1

The approach taken by the courts in applying sections 76 and 78 of PACE arguably endorses unlawful behaviour on the part of the police, and provides no remedy for the suspect who is treated unlawfully.

Discuss.

Answer plan

➔ Explain the meaning of sections 76 and 78, and highlight the distinction between the sections.

➔ Outline the circumstances in which section 76 is applied, and assess the effect of section 76(4).

➔ Analyse the exercise of the discretion under section 78 with reference to case law.

➔ Identify alternative remedies for the suspect.

➔ Draw a conclusion about the approach taken by the judiciary.

Diagram plan

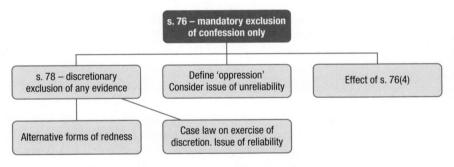

A printable version of this diagram plan is available from www.pearsoned.co.uk/lawexpressqa

Answer

The Police and Criminal Evidence Act 1984 (PACE) regulates the use of police powers to investigate crime. Sections 76 and 78 set out circumstances in which the court may exclude evidence from criminal trial as a result of conduct during the investigation. Section 76 deals with the exclusion of confession evidence, whilst section 78 is broader and can be invoked to exclude confession or non-confession evidence. Case law suggests that, in exercising discretion, the primary concern of the court is the reliability of evidence, rather than the

223

conduct of officers.[1] It will be suggested that this is the correct approach, and suspects can seek redress through other channels.

Section 76 imposes an obligation on the court to exclude confession evidence in one of two circumstances. Firstly, the court must exclude the evidence if the confession was obtained by oppression. Secondly, the evidence must be excluded if it was obtained as a result of things said or done which, in the circumstances existing at the time, render the confession unreliable. Exclusion is mandatory if either of these conditions are met. Section 76(8) states that 'oppression' in this context includes torture, inhuman or degrading treatment, and the use or threat of violence. In *R v Fulling* [1987] QB 426, the court held that the use of the word 'includes' demonstrates that this list is not exhaustive,[2] and provided a broader definition; including the exercise of authority in a 'burdensome' or 'harsh' manner as well as 'unreasonable or unjust burdens'.[3] Whilst, as Fenwick (2007) argues, it would be possible to interpret 'wrongful' in this context as 'unlawful', the courts will not exclude confession evidence simply because there has been a breach of the codes of conduct. It is clear that for exclusion under this head it must be shown that the misconduct was serious, and that there was bad faith. Even though some might maintain the bar is set too high, arguably the section does firmly discourage the police from obtaining confessions by oppressive or intimidating means; to do so could jeopardise prospects of conviction if the evidence is kept from the jury. However, as Bradley and Ewing note (2010, p. 470), section 76(4) provides that any evidence discovered as a result of the confession can still be admitted and, further, the confession itself can be admitted if it is relevant to demonstrate that the defendant expresses himself in a particular way.[4] Perhaps then, as Bradley and Ewing state '[t]he fruit of the poison tree appears to be edible in English Law'.[5]

Section 78 allows the exclusion of any evidence in a criminal trial where the court considers that 'having regard to all the circumstances, including the circumstances in which it was obtained' admission would have an adverse effect on the fairness of the proceedings. Here, the court acts at its own discretion.[6] On the face of it, the powers conferred by provision are wider; the legislation applies to all types of evidence and, in considering fairness, there is no requirement to show bad faith.[7] Confession evidence which cannot be excluded under section 76 could theoretically be excluded under section 78.

---

[1] This part of the introduction reassures the examiner that the answer will take an analytical approach to the subject.

[2] *Fulling* is an important authority that clarifies the meaning of the statute, and it should be included.

[3] Although there is no need to include quotations, inclusion of words from the judgment is a quick and simple way to illustrate what was meant by the decision.

[4] It is important to make reference to section 76(4), as it shows how the exclusionary provisions are limited.

[5] If you are able to include a memorable phrase such as this, the answer will seem very confident.

[6] You do need to make the point that exclusions under section 78 are discretionary; this demonstrates a thorough knowledge of the difference between the two sections.

[7] The answer should set out the differences between the two provisions.

However, case law demonstrates that the courts seldom invoke the power to exclude physical evidence even where the circumstances in which it was obtained amount to serious illegality by the police. The leading authority comes from the case of *R v Khan* [1997] AC 558. The prosecution case rested on evidence obtained by illegal surveillance.[8] The House of Lords held it was proper to admit the evidence even though the police actions were probably in breach of the defendant's Art. 8 rights. Other examples of evidence being admitted despite unlawful behaviour by the police include secretly recorded incriminating statements (*R v Chalkey* [1997] EWCA Crim 3416), and evidence obtained from illegally retained DNA (*A-G's Reference* (No. 3 of 1999) [2000] UKHL 63).[9] In the case of *R v Keenan* [1989] 3 All ER 598, it was held that, where there has been a breach of the rules under PACE, the court should consider first whether the breach was 'substantial or significant',[10] and only then continue to assess the impact of the breach in the particular circumstances of the case.

It may appear the courts do indeed send a signal to the police which endorses unlawful behaviour whilst investigating criminality, through the reluctance to exercise their discretion. It could be suggested that the courts, as an emanation of the state, must insist on due process.[11] On this view, the courts have a duty to maintain the standards expected of the police, and to punish those who fail to meet them by making sure they cannot benefit from illegal behaviour. Undoubtedly, though, there is a difficult balance to be struck. PACE was implemented to provide safeguards for the public by setting down clear standards of conduct, and sections 76 and 78 were intended to form part of the protection against the abuse of police power. However, the courts are wary of endorsing an acquittal where there is clear evidence pointing to guilt. The courts have sought to strike the balance by focusing primarily not upon the manner in which the evidence was collected, but on whether or not as a result the evidence has been rendered unreliable.[12] The first concern of the court, then, is to determine the guilt or innocence of the accused, and it is not part of the judicial role to police the police. If, however, the police conduct has led to evidence that could result in a miscarriage of justice, then the courts will not countenance reliance upon it. This position is understandable. It would be disturbing if in a case such as *A-G's Reference* (No. 3 of 1999), a rapist had been allowed to walk free despite DNA evidence proving guilt.

[8] *Khan* should be included. When outlining these cases, you should highlight the conduct of the police but avoid lengthy explanations of the facts.

[9] There are lots of cases that could be used to demonstrate that the courts often admit evidence obtained illegally. You should try to use a few examples to reinforce the argument, but, apart from *Khan*, it doesn't really matter which cases you cite.

[10] *Keenan* deals with a slightly different aspect of the point, as it is specific to breaches of the codes of conduct. It should be cited, as the 'significant and substantial' test is important.

[11] The introduction set out a very clear position. The answer should acknowledge that there is a different view that could be taken.

[12] This is the crux of the argument that is being advanced, and needs to be carefully explained.

Sections 76 and 78 are not the only safeguards against unlawful treatment. Where breaches of PACE or the codes of conduct have occurred, complaint can be made to the IPCC. In the most serious cases, this could result in criminal prosecution of the officer(s) involved. Alternatively, where police behaviour constitutes a tortious wrong, redress can be sought in the civil courts.[13] In conclusion, it is right to say the courts have not used sections 76 or 78 as a means of punishing police misconduct or providing remedies for the citizen. The provisions exist to ensure that miscarriages of justice do not occur, and to allow the courts to insist on reliable evidence.

[13] You should highlight the mechanisms that are available to obtain redress, but do not spend time explaining these as this is not the focus of the question.

✓ Make your answer stand out

- By referring to ECtHR decisions in this area. Consider *Schenk* v *Switzerland* [1988] 13 (EHRR) 242 in which it was held that it was for the national courts to determine admissibility of evidence. Admission of illegally obtained evidence does not necessarily breach Art. 6.

- By expanding the discussion of the procedure which applies to section 76. The case of *R* v *Bhavna Dhorajiwala* [2010] EWCA Crim 1237 confirms that, once a representation is made to the court that a confession *may* have resulted from oppression, then it shall not be admitted unless the Crown can prove that it did not. You should use this point to reinforce the distinction between section 76 and section 78. This would show detailed knowledge of PACE, and an ability to keep abreast of case law.

- By reinforcing the point that the role of the court is not to police the police. You could cite *R* v *Smurthwaite and Gill* [1994] 1 All ER 898, in which Lord Diplock stressed that the criminal court is not there to exercise a disciplinary role over the police.

! Don't be tempted to . . .

- Include general information about PACE, or the codes. That is not relevant here. There is no need to demonstrate that you know the different aspects of procedure governed by the codes, for example.

- Explain in detail the facts of the cases referred to. You do need to highlight how evidence was obtained to illustrate the argument about the courts' reluctance to use section 78, but that is all.

❓ Question 2

PC Binner is on foot patrol when he sees a group of three youths standing on a street corner. He instinctively feels that they look suspicious. He approaches the youths, and asks what they are up to. One of the youths, Silvio, begins to walk away.

PC Binner takes hold of Silvio by the elbow and says 'we'll see about that when I search you'. Silvio punches the officer in the chest. PC Binner uses his radio to call for assistance, and handcuffs Silvio. He then goes through Silvio's pockets, and finds a tablet loose in his trouser pocket. A police car arrives and PC Binner places Silvio in the back of the car, and Silvio is taken to the police station.

On arrival, the custody sergeant books Silvio into custody at 9pm. Silvio asks 'why am I here?' PC Binner tells Silvio he has been arrested for dealing drugs. Silvio immediately asks for a lawyer and is told this will be arranged. He is placed in a cell.

PC Binner asks the custody sergeant for permission to search Silvio's address. The custody sergeant calls for the duty inspector, who authorises the search. PC Binner and a colleague search Silvio's flat. No drugs are found, but a large quantity of car radios are seized.

At midnight, Silvio is told he can wait for a lawyer, or be interviewed immediately. He decides to be interviewed. In interview he is asked to explain about the car radios, and admits that he stole them. He insists that the tablet found is an aspirin.

Silvio is charged with assaulting a police officer and with theft. However, a friend of his who is studying law has told him that he will be able to have the case thrown out because of PC Binner's actions.

Advise Silvio.

Answer plan

→ Consider the legality of asking questions in the street.

→ Outline the requirements of sections 1–3 of PACE and consider legality of the search.

→ Assess the legality of the arrest, and consider if this provides a defence.

→ Briefly consider the search of premises.

→ Consider the applicability of section 78.

Diagram plan

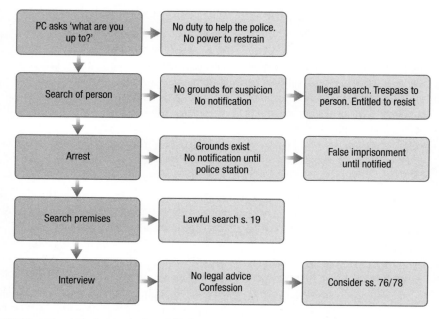

| PC asks 'what are you up to?' | → | No duty to help the police. No power to restrain |

| Search of person | → | No grounds for suspicion No notification | → | Illegal search. Trespass to person. Entitled to resist |

| Arrest | → | Grounds exist No notification until police station | → | False imprisonment until notified |

| Search premises | → | Lawful search s. 19 |

| Interview | → | No legal advice Confession | → | Consider ss. 76/78 |

A printable version of this diagram plan is available from www.pearsoned.co.uk/lawexpressqa

Answer

The validity of the police actions needs to be assessed in order to advise Silvio of any options available to him. It appears that the stop and search and initial arrest were unlawful. This may provide Silvio with a defence to the charge of assaulting a police constable. It is unlikely that he will be able to avoid the consequences of the theft as the interview is likely to be admissible.[1]

On being approached and questioned by PC Binner, Silvio is lawfully entitled to walk away. It is a long-established principle that, as stated in **Rice v Connolly** [1966] 2 All ER 649, there is no general duty to assist the police.[2] Therefore, unless the circumstances are covered by a specific statutory provision (for example, the duty to give details under the Road Traffic Acts), the police have no power to detain a person for questioning falling short of the power to arrest. Accordingly, Silvio should be advised that the officer has no lawful authority to

[1] The introduction avoids repeating the facts of the scenario, and instead, demonstrates that the key issues have been understood.

[2] *Rice* v *Connolly* is the leading authority here and it is important to include the case.

[3] The answer must use the authorities to provide specific advice regarding the facts of the scenario.

[4] You should note the similarity with *Collins* v *Wilcock* but you don't need to rehearse the facts. It is useful to remember the wording from the judgment which stresses the minimal degree of contact required for the offence.

[5] Take care not to be diverted into a discussion regarding criminal law. There is no need to consider the elements of private defence in any detail here.

[6] The facts of the scenario are very clear, and credit will be given for providing unambiguous advice in these circumstances as it shows confidence.

[7] Again, it is possible to give very definite advice here.

[8] Despite the fact that section 28, PACE deals with the same issue, the case remains good law, and is usually cited.

[9] It is important to consider any remedies that Silvio may have, as this would form part of the advice to a client.

take hold of him by the elbow, and that this may constitute a battery at common law.[3] The facts of **Collins v Wilcock** [1984] 3 All ER 374 were similar, and are authority for the proposition that 'the slightest touch can constitute a battery'.[4] Therefore, arguably, Silvio is entitled to use force to defend himself from the unwarranted interference with his person. **Kenlin v Gardiner** [1967] 2 WLR 129 confirms that a person can resist an unlawful detention. However, Silvio should be advised that the level of force used here may not be proportionate.[5]

PC Binner states his intention to search Silvio. There are no grounds disclosed in the scenario that would give rise to the power to search. Section 1 of the Police and Criminal Evidence Act (PACE) authorises a police officer to stop and search if he has reasonable grounds to suspect that the person is in possession of one of the specified items (stolen goods, offensive weapons, fireworks, or items made or adapted for use in criminal damage). We are not told whether or not PC Binner suspects that Silvio is in possession of such articles, however, the facts do not disclose any reasonable grounds for any such suspicion. The Codes of Practice, Code A 2.2, makes it clear that suspicion must be based on objective factors, and cannot arise purely on the basis of personal factors such as age, appearance or previous convictions. We are not told of any objective basis for the officer's concerns. The subsequent search is illegal as it is not justified, and in addition, the notification requirements of sections 2 and 3 do not appear to have been complied with.[6]

The initial arrest is unlawful, as PC Binner does not advise Silvio of either the fact of, or the grounds for arrest as required by section 28 PACE.[7] The case of **Christie v Leachinskey** [1947] 1 All ER 567 made it clear that failure to inform a person of the fact and reason for arrest renders it illegal.[8] The more recent case of **Lewis v Chief Constable of the South Wales Constabulary** [1991] 1 All ER 206 demonstrates that an illegality can, in effect, be 'corrected' when the detainee is properly notified. It seems that Silvio is notified once at the police station. Although detention after unlawful arrest constitutes an actionable false imprisonment, any claim would be limited to the time period prior to notification as from that point, the detention is rendered lawful.[9]

Once in custody, Silvio's treatment is governed by statutory provisions and Code C. The custody sergeant is responsible for ensuring that Silvio's detention is necessary, and for ensuring that his welfare and his rights are protected. It is his responsibility to ensure that Silvio is advised of his rights, including the right to have someone notified of his arrest (s. 56, PACE) and of his right to free legal advice (s. 58). We are not told whether or not the sergeant complies with this, only that Silvio makes a request for legal representation. Equally, it is not clear whether or not a lawyer is ever contacted. If this has not occurred then this will be a clear, and potentially significant, breach of PACE.[10]

[10] The answer should not make assumptions where the facts are silent or unclear.

Before considering the effect of such a breach, it is worth noting that the search of premises appears to be lawful. Section 18 of PACE provides for the search of premises occupied or controlled by a person in custody for evidence connected with the offence for which he has been arrested.[11] Although the extent of the search must be limited to that which is necessary for the nature of the items sought, section 19 (as amended) makes it clear that it is permissible for the officers to seize any items discovered in the course of the search that they reasonably believe are connected with any offence. The seizure of the car radios is, therefore, legitimate.[12]

[11] The answer should deal with the search as it is mentioned in the scenario. As it is clearly lawful, this issue should be dealt with briefly.

[12] It is important to note the effect of section 19, as this is often overlooked by students.

During the course of the interview, Silvio admits the offence of theft. He may seek to have the confession evidence excluded at any subsequent trial,[13] under either section 76 or section 78 of PACE. Section 76 provides for such exclusion if the confession was obtained by oppression, or if it was obtained in consequence of things said or done which, in all the circumstances, would render it unfair if admitted. On the facts provided, neither of these conditions appears to be met. Section 78 allows for the exclusion of any evidence (including confessions) if, having regard to all the circumstances in which it was obtained, it would be unfair to admit it. In this case, Silvio may seek to argue that either the initial illegal stop and search, or the denial of legal advice would render the confession unfair. Whilst both these breaches are serious, the authorities suggest that the courts are unwilling to exclude evidence unless it appears to be unreliable (see, for example, **R v Khan** [1997] AC 558.[14] Therefore, Silvio should be advised that an application under section 78 is unlikely to succeed and that therefore, contrary to the advice of his friend, the case will proceed.

[13] The reference to 'having the case thrown out' should be a clear signal that the answer needs to address the possibility of excluding evidence.

[14] When considering section 78, the leading case of *Khan* should be cited.

In summary, it appears that the police have acted unlawfully. Silvio may wish to consider claims in tort for trespass to the person, and

[15] The conclusion should summarise the advice provided.

false imprisonment.[15] The illegal search and arrest may afford Silvio a defence to the charge of assaulting a police constable. It is doubtful that confession evidence would be excluded in this instance, as it would seem the reliability of the evidence is unaffected.

 Make your answer stand out

- By including additional authorities in the answer. You could cite *DPP* v *Blake* [1989] 1 WLR 432 as part of the discussion regarding the illegal search, or any number of cases concerning the application of section 78. Whilst you should only include authorities where they are relevant, you will certainly be rewarded if you can provide an authority for as many propositions of law as you can.

- By using recent case law to reinforce the fact that Silvio is likely to have a defence to the charge of assault PC. You could cite *R (Michaels)* v *Highbury Corner Magistrates' Court* [2010] Crim LR 506, in which the Divisional Court stressed that the notification requirement of section 2 will be strictly enforced. In that case, a conviction for obstructing a police officer was set aside. You could demonstrate an ability to use analogous cases to form conclusions about the outcome of a scenario.

- By discussing the potential remedies in more detail; in particular, the answer does not address the potential for a formal complaint through the IPCC. It would be useful to show that you are aware of this procedure, as it would demonstrate that you are familiar with all aspects of this topic.

❗ Don't be tempted to . . .

- Show the examiner that you have revised all aspects of PACE. For example, many students will give detail about how and when powers to search premises may arise under section 17 or section 32. More credit will be given for demonstrating an ability to recognise that section 18 is the one which is relevant here.

- Discuss the requirements of the criminal law. It is fairly common for students to make the mistake of thinking it is helpful to outline what the Crown would have to prove to obtain a conviction for theft. There are no marks available for demonstrating knowledge of the components of criminal liability. You must ensure your answer focuses on the public law aspects of the scenario.

Question 3

'This is not an argument about whether we respect civil liberties or not; but whose take priority.' (Tony Blair, 2006)

To what extent do current legislative measures seeking to prevent terrorist activity achieve a fair balance between individual liberty and public safety?

Answer plan

→ Identify terrorist prevention investigation measures (TPIMs) as focus of discussion.

→ Explain criticism of control orders.

→ Assess the extent to which TPIMs meet these criticisms.

→ Consider whether or not TPIMs achieve a more appropriate balance.

Diagram plan

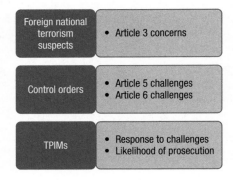

A printable version of this diagram plan is available from www.pearsoned.co.uk/lawexpressqa

Answer

The threat posed by international terrorism creates unique challenges for the state in seeking to ensure that the public are protected. Since 2000, there have been several major pieces of legislation attempting to contain the threat by criminalising conduct that may support or encourage terrorism, granting enhanced powers to investigative bodies and creating civil orders to limit the activities of persons suspected of involvement in terrorist offences.[1] The Home Office first produced the CONTEST strategy in 2003. The third draft was

[1] There is no need to list every counter-terrorism measure here, but as you intend to focus on a single issue, it is worth demonstrating that you are aware of the broader picture.

published in 2011, and promised an ongoing review of counter-terrorism measures to ensure they are effective and proportionate (Home Office 2011). The strategy also explicitly prioritises prosecution as the preferred objective.[2] The Coalition government abolished the control order regime which had been criticised for being disproportionate and of limited value in achieving prosecutions. This essay will consider Terrorism Prevention and Investigation Measures (TPIMs) which replaced control orders, and ask whether or not they are a successful restoration of the balance between individual liberty and national security.

[2] Drawing out these strands from *CONTEST* is useful, because it establishes the parameters that will be used to evaluate TPIMs throughout the answer.

Fenwick (2007) has characterised the state response to terrorism in the twenty-first century as proactive rather than reactive. Whereas the vast bulk of criminal law penalises conduct which has taken place (which may also be said to have a deterrent effect), anti-terrorist strategies seek to contain activity before it occurs.[3] In some instances this has been achieved by drafting new offences criminalising activities that encourage or prepare for terrorist attacks. The claim of the last government, and of the Coalition, is that there are a number of foreign nationals resident in the UK who pose a significant threat but cannot be prosecuted for such offences without compromising the activities of the intelligence services.[4] Obligations under the European Convention on Human Rights prevent the deportation of individuals to countries where they face a significant risk of torture or inhuman and degrading treatment (Art. 3). The control order system was introduced following the repeal of measures enabling the indefinite detention without charge of persons who could not be deported or, it was said, prosecuted.[5] Control orders were civil orders imposing a variety of conditions upon those subject to them. Conditions varied between subjects but included geographical restrictions, a bar on visitors who had not obtained home office approval, night time curfews and no access to communications equipment.

[3] You do need to explain this point carefully as the argument considers the effectiveness of the use of civil orders rather than criminal prosecutions.

[4] The question asks you to consider current legislative measures. However, in order to do this, it is necessary to set out some of the background. It is important to do this as briefly as possible in order to make sure sufficient time is left for analysis of the contemporary position.

[5] There is no need to give more detail than this about the repeal of Part IV of the Anti-Terror Crime and Security Act 2001. You need to keep the background information to the bare minimum.

[6] Reference to the leading ECtHR case demonstrates an understanding of the relationship between the Convention and domestic law.

Control orders were challenged in the UK courts and the European Court of Human Rights (ECtHR). Challenges focused on Art. 5 (right to liberty) and Art. 6 (right to a fair trial). It is clear that severe restrictions on an individual's freedom of movement, association and expression engage Art. 5 and can amount to a deprivation of liberty (***Guzzardi v Italy*** (1980) 3 EHRR 333).[6] A series of cases resulted in amended orders with less restrictive conditions (for example, **Secretary of State for the Home Department v JJ** and others [2007] UKHL 45).[7] The Art. 6 challenges focused on the reliance upon closed material proceedings in hearings concerning the orders. In **A v UK** [2009] ECHR 3455/05 the ECtHR held that an individual must always be informed of sufficient evidence against them to allow them to provide instructions and, without this, the Special Advocate procedure was not sufficient to ensure compliance with Art. 6.[8] **Secretary of State for the Home Department v AF** (No 3) [2009] UKHL 28 followed and upheld the Strasbourg decision. Dissenting, Lord Hoffman argued that the decision was wrong and would lead to the collapse of the control order system, which he saw as a key part of the nation's defences against terrorism.

Lord Hoffman was proved right. Shortly after election, the Coalition government announced an urgent review of the control order system as part of a broader reconsideration of anti-terrorism measures to 'restore the balance of civil liberties'[9] (Home Office (2010)). The Terrorism Prevention and Investigation Measures Act 2011 abolished control orders and replaced them with a new form of civil order (TPIMs). The changes made aimed to remove objections under Art. 5.

Although Liberty dismissed TPIMs as a form of 'control-order lite' there are some significant differences.[10] TPIMs can be made for a maximum of two years although a fresh order can be made at the end of that period provided there is new evidence of terrorist activity. The range of conditions that may be imposed are now limited to those set out in Schedule 1 of the Act. A person cannot now be required to relocate to an area where they have no residence or connection and some restricted access to communications equipment is permitted.

The legislation imposes a duty on the Home Secretary to keep any order under review with the aim being to seek a prosecution where possible (s. 10). This supports the current CONTEST strategy which emphasises that prosecution should be the primary objective wherever possible.[11] Critics of the control order scheme argued that it rendered a prosecution unlikely as individuals under such extensive surveillance with no access to communications were unlikely to be able to engage in any activity that would provide evidence to support criminal charges (Macdonald (2011)).

[8] Similarly, here, you do not need to explain the Special Advocate procedure. The reference made clearly demonstrates that you understand the issue, but it should not be the key focus of your argument.

[9] This is a good quote to use here because it uses the same terms as those in the question and reassures the examiner that all the material included is being used to address that central issue.

[10] There is no need to list every difference but it is important to show that you do know the significant alterations that have been made.

[11] Here, the answer shows that the argument is well structured by referring back to the point made in the introduction.

It is too early to see whether or not TPIMs will be subject to challenges under the European Convention on Human Rights, but it should be noted that the new legislation will have been carefully drafted in the light of previous judicial decisions. It seems likely, therefore, that the current measures would be considered to be an appropriate way of striking the balance between liberty and security as Lord Carlile (2011) maintained. Nevertheless, some commentators note that despite ministerial claims, the Act will do little to increase the likelihood of prosecution as the focus is on disruption rather than investigation (Walker and Horne (2012)). Inevitably this will mean that a number of individuals continue to be subject to significant restrictions upon their civil liberties which will keep them outside the criminal justice system. It appears that this is a price which all the main political parties consider to be a fair one to pay in order to preserve public safety.[12]

[12] Your conclusion should provide a direct answer to the question.

Make your answer stand out

- By considering the Enhanced Terrorism Protection and Investigation Measures (ETPIM) Bill 2012 which, at the time of writing, was in the process of being scrutinised by the Joint Select Committee of the House of Commons and the House of Lords. If enacted, the Bill would enable a more rigorous system of measures to be introduced if an emergency situation required this. This is quite controversial, as it could be argued that this would be a mechanism for keeping the draconian restrictions permitted by control orders in the statute book.

- In order to consider the ETPIM Bill, you could refer to the evidence given to the Committee. This is a useful resource, as witnesses included the Head of Metropolitan Police Counter-Terrorism Committee, the current and former independent reviewers of terrorism legislation, leading academics and members of Liberty. Taken together, their evidence provides an excellent summary of the range of opinions dealing with both control orders and TPIMs. You can access the evidence at http://www.parliament.uk/business/committees/committees-a-z/joint-select/terrorism-prevention-and-investigation-measures-bill/publications/

- Incorporating further academic comment to broaden the debate. You might consider the work of Campbell, D. (2009), The threat of terror and the plausibility of positivism *Public Law* 501, which argues that it was wrong to classify the detention of terrorist suspects at Belmarsh as discriminatory. This would demonstrate that you have the ability to engage with a range of views.

> **!** **Don't be tempted to . . .**
>
> - Include statements of opinion that you cannot support with evidence. The examples could be relevant political events, case law or academic opinion. Sometimes students attempt a broad question like this and submit weak answers that are vague and lack content. It is important to be able to express a point of view, but remember, as a lawyer, there must always be evidence provided to persuade the examiner that the point is valid.
> - Simply describe legislative provisions and outline the rights affected. The answer must address how effective the law has been in combating terrorism and, therefore, you do need to be able to draw on some factual source material in relation to, say, the number of control orders, or prosecutions for terrorist offences.

？ Question 4

Shamila is a young woman aged nineteen who suffers from anxiety. She is extremely claustrophobic and has panic attacks in confined spaces.

One evening, she is waiting for a bus when a fight breaks out. The police arrive on the scene quickly. Someone points towards Shamila, saying 'she started it'. Shamila is immediately arrested for affray and is taken to the police station.

She is booked into custody and the custody officer asks her if she would like anyone to be notified of her detention. She nominates her father. She declines legal advice. When she is told she will have to go into a cell, she becomes very distressed, explaining her claustrophobia. The custody officer assures her it will only be for a few minutes. He then telephones her father who asks to attend the interview. The custody officer states this is not possible because Shamila is an adult.

Officers investigating the fight watch the CCTV footage of the incident, which is unclear but shows a woman throwing a bottle. It is believed this resulted in serious injury to someone.

At midnight, an officer takes Shamila into a small interview room. At the start of the tape-recorded interview, she is told she is being further arrested for an offence of causing GBH (s. 18 of the Offences Against the Person Act 1861). She is properly cautioned. During the interview, she is shown the CCTV footage and the interviewing officer says: 'It is definitely you here, throwing that bottle. If you don't admit what you've done you'll be in a cell for years, not just a couple of hours'. Shamila continues to deny the offence whilst the officer repeats the assertion that she threw the bottle. When he does so for the twentieth time, she begins to cry and admits it was her.

She is charged with an offence under section 18 of the Offences Against the Person Act.

Advise Shamila of the legalities of the police conduct and the possible consequences.

Answer plan

→ Consider whether the arrest is lawful.
→ Identify the issues raised by the custody officer's conduct.
→ Assess the legality of the interview.
→ Discuss any remedies available.

Diagram plan

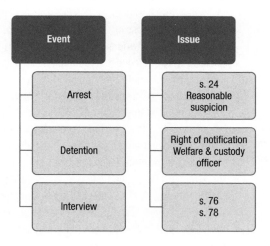

Event	Issue
Arrest	s. 24 Reasonable suspicion
Detention	Right of notification Welfare & custody officer
Interview	s. 76 s. 78

A printable version of this diagram plan is available from www.pearsoned.co.uk/lawexpressqa

Answer

The police are granted extensive powers over the citizen to facilitate prevention and investigation of crime. Many powers are exercised with the authority of a judicial warrant. There are a large number of steps, however, that can be used without warrant. It is important that such powers are carefully regulated as, inevitably, officers will need to interfere with the liberties of citizens in order to carry out their work. In this scenario, all of the officers concerned should be exercising powers regulated by the Police and Criminal Evidence Act 1984 (PACE) and the associated Codes of Practice. It appears that the custody officer and the interviewing officer have failed to carry out their functions in accordance with PACE so Shamila will need to be advised of the potential ramifications of this.[1]

[1] A general introduction to the topic is helpful, but make sure to set out the key issues that are raised in the problem.

The power of arrest exercised in this scenario is governed by section 24 of PACE (as amended by the Serious Organised Crime and Police Act 2005).[2] Officers present can lawfully arrest Shamila if they reasonably suspect that she has committed an offence (s. 24(2)). The courts have, on a number of occasions, considered what is meant by 'reasonable suspicion'. The leading case is **Castorina v Chief Constable of Surrey** [1988] NLJ 180 which set out a three-part test. Firstly, the officer must suspect that the person is guilty of an offence. Secondly, this must be based on reasonable grounds and, lastly, the arrest should be assessed in accordance with the principles used to assess irrationality in **Associated Provincial Picture Houses Ltd v Wednesbury Corporation** [1948] 1 KB 223. A decision will be 'Wednesbury unreasonable' if it is one no reasonable decision maker could have reached on the same facts. As Zander (1995) has noted, this is not 'a very exacting standard'. In this case, the purported identification of Shamila by a person at the scene would almost certainly be held to meet the requirements.[3] In addition to the grounds for arrest, the officer must also believe that it is necessary for one of the reasons specified in section 24(5). In this case, the arrest will be justified as necessary to allow prompt investigation of the offence and to prevent the disappearance of a suspect (s. 24(5)(e), (f)). It is not clear whether or not Shamila has been properly informed of the fact of, and grounds for, her arrest (s. 28).[4] If these requirements have been met, the arrest will be lawful.

The custody officer is responsible for Shamila whilst she is detained at the police station. He must decide whether to authorise her detention or, alternatively, release her without charge, or on bail, or charge her with an offence. In this case, the decision to authorise detention is unlikely to be challenged as section 37(2) states that a reason to do so will be to preserve and secure evidence.[5]

The custody officer also takes responsibility for Shamila's welfare; he must ensure her rights are protected and the conditions of detention meet the standards set out in Code C of PACE. The immediate requirement is to inform her of her right to legal advice, to have someone notified of her detention and to read the Codes of Practice (Code C Para. 3.1). The facts do not state whether or not she was informed of her right to read the Codes, but she is correctly offered legal advice and to have her nominated person informed.[6]

[2] Most students fail to note that not every arrest is authorised by PACE. You do not need to outline alternative powers as PACE does govern this arrest, but you will be rewarded for showing you are aware of this.

[3] The quote from Zander here provides support for the assertion that the arrest will be considered lawful.

[4] Ensure that you do provide statutory authority for every point made here rather than simply referring to 'section 24'.

[5] Where you are certain that an action is lawful, or unlawful, do not be afraid to confidently state your position (as long as you can explain your reason).

[6] Do not make assumptions about facts that are not stated; instead, point out the areas that require more investigation.

As Shamila is over eighteen, she will not be treated as a juvenile in police custody. However, the custody officer is required to take steps to protect a vulnerable adult in custody (Code C Para. 1). Here, there are clearly grounds that should have led him to treat her as such: her visible distress in the custody area and the fact she informs him of her claustrophobia. It is not a breach of PACE to place her in a cell in these circumstances, but he should have considered obtaining an appropriate adult to support her whilst in custody and during the interview. He would not have been obliged to allow her father to carry out the role if he felt a qualified person would be more appropriate, but there is no suggestion that this has been considered.[7]

[7] This is the sort of detail that demonstrates familiarity with the Codes of Practice that goes beyond a surface reading of the text books.

When Shamila is interviewed, the procedure appears to have initially complied with the requirements of PACE and the Codes. She is properly cautioned and the interview is tape recorded in accordance with section 60. It is not clear whether or not she was reminded of her right to legal advice. The questioning, however, appears to be a clear breach of Code C which precludes the use of oppression, or of attempting to elicit information by indicating what is likely to happen to the detainee dependent upon their answer (Para. 11.5). Repeated assertions of guilt coupled with the threat of a prison sentence are, therefore, a serious breach of the Codes of Practice.[8]

[8] Again, as this is such a clear breach, it can be stated to be so unequivocally.

The custody officer and the interviewing officer have breached the Codes of Practice during Shamila's detention. This can give Shamila grounds to make a formal complaint to either the local police force or the Independent Police Complaints Commission.[9] The misconduct will also have implications for any subsequent trial for the section 18 offence, as it appears likely that some or all of the evidence obtained in the interview will be inadmissible. Section 76 of PACE imposes a mandatory duty on the court to exclude evidence of a confession if it is obtained through oppression or in circumstances which render it unreliable. In **R v Fulling** [1987] 85 Cr App R 136 the court found that although 'oppression' would almost certainly involve impropriety by the police, it should not be defined restrictively. It is certainly arguable that the questioning here was oppressive. Even if this is not accepted, the combined effect of Shamila's vulnerable state and the form of questions used render the confession unreliable. The court may well exercise its discretion to exclude the interview in its entirety (rather than just the part containing the confession).[10] Section 78 of PACE allows any evidence to be excluded if, in all the circumstances,

[9] Although this is relevant, there is no need to enter into a detailed discussion of the complaints system because the issues surrounding the exclusion of evidence are more important.

[10] This point is often missed: the whole interview is part of the evidence and will not necessarily be covered by section 76.

it would be unfair to admit it. It is clear that the courts approach the question of 'fairness' in this context as an assessment of the reliability of the evidence rather than an opportunity to punish police misconduct (**R v Khan** [1996] 3 All ER 289). It seems that this is a case in which exclusion of evidence would be appropriate.

[11] There is no need for a lengthy conclusion to the answer as a clear decision has been set out at each point.

Although the initial arrest was lawful, police misconduct during detention will assist Shamila in defending the charge she faces. She may also have grounds to lodge a formal complaint.[11]

✓ Make your answer stand out

■ By discussing the applicability of Art. 6 to this case, and addressing some of the case law concerning the impact of sections 34–37 Criminal Justice and Public Order Act 1994 on procedural fairness. Consider, for example, *Condron* v *UK* (2001) 31 EHRR 1. This would show the examiner that you can set the facts of the scenario in the broader context of human rights law.

■ By explaining the available remedies in more detail and highlighting the fact that breaches of the Codes of Practice cannot, in and of themselves, give rise to an action in tort (s. 67(10) PACE), as this will demonstrate that you have detailed knowledge of the relevant statutory provisions. Remedies are an aspect of police powers that are often overlooked.

■ By incorporating a discussion of the efficacy of the Independent Police Complaints Commission. You could note that Liberty (2009) have raised concerns regarding complainants who lack mental capacity, which is clearly relevant to this scenario.

! Don't be tempted to . . .

■ Speculate whether or not the confession would have been made if an appropriate adult had been present. The facts give no indication of this, and therefore you should only consider whether or not there are grounds to exclude it. Often, students are diverted into discussing hypothetical situations which are not highlighted in the scenario. It is important to focus on the information that has been provided.

■ Confuse the provisions of the Codes with those in the statute. A common mistake is to say that the police have the power to arrest under Code G. This is incorrect: the statute gives the power, and the Code stipulates the manner in which it should be exercised.

❓ Question 5

PC Tomlin has been asked to investigate reports of a young woman with short blonde hair approaching pedestrians in the city centre and obtaining money by deception, by pretending she needs the train fare home. PC Tomlin is on duty in plain clothes, when he sees a young woman whose hair is hidden by a hat. The young woman approaches an old lady and tries to speak, but the old lady continues walking. PC Tomlin suspects this may be the person he is looking for, and decides to arrest her. He approaches her, saying, 'Right, you, you've got some explaining to do.'

The young woman, Penny, says 'get lost' and starts to walk away. PC Tomlin takes hold of her arms. She begins to struggle violently and strikes PC Tomlin before he is able to restrain her. He then tells her she is under arrest for assaulting a police constable in the lawful execution of his duty, and attempting to obtain property by deception.

Once at the police station, the custody officer on duty agrees that PC Tomlin can search her home address for evidence relating to the deception offence. In the breadbin, PC Tomlin discovers a bag containing a small amount of powder which later tests positive as cocaine. Penny is later charged with possession of a class A drug, and with assaulting a police constable.

As she is leaving the station, she tells PC Tomlin that she intends to take legal action against him.

Advise PC Tomlin of the legality of his actions and the likely outcome of proceedings against Penny.

Answer plan

→ Outline the issues raised: arrest, and search of premises.

→ Discuss the initial arrest, and the possible consequences for PC Tomlin and Penny.

→ Consider the legality of the search of premises and in particular the effect of this on future proceedings.

→ Conclude by summarising the implications for PC Tomlin, and the likely outcome for Penny.

Diagram plan

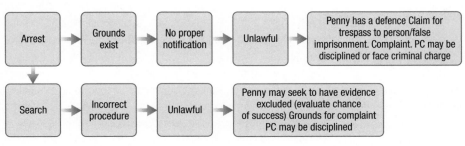

A printable version of this diagram plan is available from www.pearsoned.co.uk/lawexpressqa

Answer

The police are empowered to interfere with the liberty of the citizen for the purpose of preventing and detecting crime, and to keep the peace. Police powers are mainly governed by the Police and Criminal Evidence Act (PACE), as amended, and the associated Codes of Practice. If PC Tomlin has exceeded his powers, then this may lead to a complaint or even tortious action. In addition, there may be implications for any charges that Penny faces.[1]

[1] This question requires the answer to advise the police officer as well as the suspect, so the introduction should reassure the examiner that this will be done.

PACE (as amended by the Serious Organised Crime and Police Act 2005) sets out the circumstances in which a police officer is able to arrest an individual without a warrant. Section 24 authorises an arrest in circumstances where the officer has reasonable grounds to suspect that an individual has committed an offence, provided that the arrest is necessary. From the facts provided, PC Tomlin may well be able to demonstrate that he had the requisite level of suspicion.[2] The Codes of Practice give some guidance on the issue. Code A, Paragraph 2.2 makes it clear that there must be some objective basis, and at 2.3 sets out that there need not always be specific intelligence as an individual's conduct may give rise to suspicion.[3] The authorities suggest that it will not be particularly difficult for an officer to establish reasonable grounds for suspicion. The leading case (prior to the Human Rights Act), ***Castorina v Chief Constable of Surrey*** [1988] NLJ 180, confirmed the need for some objective basis, although this could be slight. The European Court of Human Rights has, in a number of judgments, stressed the need for reasonable grounds as protection against arbitrary arrest (see, for example, ***O'Hara v UK*** (2002) 34 EHRR 32). Post-HRA, it was held in ***Cumming v Chief Constable of the Northumbria Police*** [2003] EWCA Civ 1844 that the officer must consider the reasonableness of arrest in light of the importance of Art. 5 rights but, nonetheless, the test still relies on the concept of ***Wednesbury*** irrationality; therefore the court will only question the exercise of discretion where the decision is one that no officer could have arrived at.[4] Penny's conduct, observed in light of the information regarding the crimes committed, is likely to justify reasonable suspicion. The arrest must also be 'necessary' for a purpose specified at section 24(5). It is likely that PC Tomlin will be able to claim that in this case, there was a need to arrest to facilitate prompt and effective investigation of the offence.[5]

[2] The answer should note that a lawful arrest requires both grounds and necessity, and these issues must each be addressed.

[3] This is an important part of the Code to note, given the facts of this particular problem in which it appears that it is Penny's conduct that is the basis for suspicion.

[4] This case should be cited, and the test will need to be explained in order to demonstrate the basis for deciding that the officer is justified here.

[5] As this is straightforward, the issue can be dealt with briefly.

Although PC Tomlin may justify the arrest, it is, nevertheless, likely to be considered to be unlawful. Section 28 of PACE states that an individual must be informed of both the fact of arrest and the reason for it.[6] No particular form of words is required (**R v Brosch** [1988] Crim LR 743),[7] but it must be clear to the suspect that they have been arrested. Even if PC Tomlin had been in uniform and therefore identifiable as an officer, it is submitted that the words used are not an unambiguous explanation that an arrest is taking place.[8] This can only be compounded by the fact he is in plain clothes and seemingly makes no attempt to identify himself. Further, Penny is not informed of the grounds for arrest. **Fox, Campbell and Hartley v United Kingdom** [1990] 13 EHRR 157 stressed the importance of the requirement, as an individual must know the reason for detention in order to be able to challenge it.

PC Tomlin's conduct means that Penny has a defence to the charge of assaulting a police officer in the execution of his duty. As the arrest is unlawful, the use of force to restrain Penny is also illegal. She is entitled to use proportionate force to defend herself against an unjustified threat.[9]

Penny states that she intends to take legal action, and it would appear that there are grounds for a civil claim for trespass to person and false imprisonment.[10] If successful, damages could be awarded. Following **Thompson v Commissioner of Police for the Metropolis** [1997] 2 All ER 762, aggravated damages may be awarded if the arrest occurred in 'humiliating' circumstances. Although PC Tomlin would not be personally liable, a finding against the force would almost certainly result in disciplinary proceedings.[11] Penny may also consider making a complaint either to the Chief Superintendent, the Police Authority, or the Independent Police Complaints Commission. Complaints are now governed by the Police Reform Act 2002. PC Tomlin should be advised that an investigation could result in disciplinary actions, and the matter could be referred to the Department of Public Prosecutions to consider whether criminal charges are appropriate.

If the arrest and subsequent detention are unlawful, this has further implications for the legality of the search. Section 18 of PACE confers a power to search, without warrant, any premises occupied or controlled by a person who is under arrest. The search must be for

[6] Credit will be given for noting that a lawful arrest must be procedurally correct as well as justifiable.

[7] Students generally cite *Christie* v *Leachinskey* when discussing the requirement to be informed of arrest. This is a better authority to use here, to support the contention that there is a problem with the words used.

[8] You have outlined the legal requirements in some detail, but you must go on to apply the law to the facts of this scenario.

[9] There is no need to engage in a detailed discussion of the principles of criminal law: simply noting that police misconduct may give rise to the possibility of a defence is sufficient.

[10] As well as recognising areas of police misconduct, the answer must address the potential consequences as this is specifically required by the question.

[11] You should explain what the possible implications for the officer might be.

evidence in relation to the offence in question. Authorisation is required by an officer of the rank of inspector or above. The custody sergeant is not able to give permission. The search of Penny's flat would have been unlawful even if the initial arrest had been conducted properly.[12] The evidence against her in respect of the cocaine has, then, been obtained as a result of an unlawful search. Penny will doubtless seek to have that evidence excluded at trial. Section 78 of PACE gives the court discretion to exclude any evidence if, in all the circumstances, including those in which it was obtained, admission would have an adverse effect on the fairness of proceedings. Whilst 'significant and substantial' breaches of PACE and the Codes may justify exclusion (*R v Keenan* [1989] 3 All ER 598), the authorities seem to suggest that the court will be more concerned with the reliability of the evidence. This was confirmed in *R v Khan* [1996] 3 All ER 289, in which evidence obtained as a result of unlawful surveillance was admitted.[13] It is submitted that the evidence is unlikely to be excluded here, as the fact of the illegal search will not prevent Penny accounting for the presence of the drugs if she is able to do so.

[12] It is important to note the procedural requirements of section 18: the need for proper authorisation is often overlooked.

[13] This is a very important point to note. *Khan* is the key authority to cite here as it gives a clear indication that the evidence is unlikely to be excluded.

To conclude, Penny will have a defence to the charge of assaulting a police constable. She is unlikely to be successful in an application to exclude the evidence obtained as a result of an illegal search. PC Tomlin should be aware that she has a number of potential claims in tort: trespass to person and property, and false imprisonment. She may make a formal complaint. He may face disciplinary actions, and even criminal charges in respect of the use of force.[14]

[14] The conclusion should summarise the key points that answer the questions asked.

 Make your answer stand out

- By considering the search in more detail, and addressing section 19 of PACE, which would authorise seizure of items not the subject of the initial search. The point could be made that this is a broad power, which makes it difficult to argue that section 78 will be used to exclude evidence obtained during the search. This would show your examiner that you have detailed knowledge of the law in this area.

- By referring to some academic comment in your answer. An excellent text dealing with the search of premises is Stone, R. (2005), *The Law of Entry, Search and Seizure* (5th edn). Oxford: Oxford University Press.

> **!** **Don't be tempted to . . .**
>
> - Explain irrelevant law. A clear example would be the reasons why an arrest may be necessary at section 24(5). There is no need to list them all, it is better to highlight the one which is applicable to the facts. Students sometimes feel it necessary to demonstrate that they have learnt substantial amounts of law, when in fact marks are given for the ability to identify and utilise only the relevant provisions.
> - Ignore the instructions which have been given to you in the question. Here, you have been specifically advised to consider not only whether the officer has behaved lawfully, but the likely outcome of proceedings against Penny. A word of caution: this is not an invitation to write about the elements of the criminal offences charged.

? Question 6

Frank and Martha are students. One day, Martha asks Frank to do her a favour and he agrees. She asks him to take a USB stick to the student library and upload the contents to a web address that she writes down for him. Frank does not look at the web address but puts it in his pocket with the USB stick and sets off. As he reaches the library, he is approached by uniformed police officers who ask to search him. He asks why and is told no reason is needed 'because of terrorism'. When they find the items Martha gave to him, Frank is arrested under section 58 of the Terrorism Act 2000.

Once at the police station, he is booked into custody and asks to be allowed to speak to his solicitor. He is told this will not be possible and he is placed in a cell for 24 hours. At the end of that time, he is interviewed. In the course of the interview, he explains that he had no idea of the contents of either the USB stick or the material on the website. He is charged with the offence.

Martha is arrested under section 59 of the Terrorism Act 2000, as the police believe that she is responsible for the website, which makes extreme material available for download including how to construct bombs, and videos of terrorist atrocities. The website advocates attacks on American and British forces overseas. She is told that she can speak to a solicitor, but a police superintendent remains in the room throughout the consultation. In total, she remains in detention at the police station for 11 days before being charged with the offence.

Advise Martha and Frank of the legality of police actions and any human rights implications which may arise.

Answer plan

→ Explain the special powers given to the police by terrorism legislation.

→ Consider whether or not the police have the power to search and detain Frank.

→ Consider whether or not the police have the power to arrest and detain Martha.

→ Assess whether either party could make a claim in respect of a breach of human rights.

Diagram plan

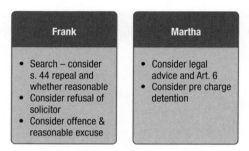

Frank	Martha
• Search – consider s. 44 repeal and whether reasonable • Consider refusal of solicitor • Consider offence & reasonable excuse	• Consider legal advice and Art. 6 • Consider pre charge detention

A printable version of this diagram plan is available from www.pearsoned.co.uk/lawexpressqa

Answer

The threat posed by international terrorism has resulted in a number of statutory provisions giving the police enhanced powers to facilitate the investigation and prevention of terrorist activity. The exercise of such powers can be contentious as they may allow officers to place significant restrictions on individual liberty and can have ramifications for the fairness of the trial process.[1] This scenario requires consideration of powers granted to the police by the Terrorism Act 2000 (as amended) as well as the particular offences which trigger the arrests.[2] It will be necessary to consider the relationship between the Terrorism Act (TA) and the European Convention on Human Rights and Fundamental Freedoms (ECHR), with reference to decisions of both the domestic courts and the European Court of Human Rights in Strasbourg (ECtHR). The first issue to consider is the search which takes place outside the library. Section 44 of the Terrorism Act conferred a power on the police to stop and search any person within a designated area, with no requirement to suspect the individual of

[1] This shows that you have identified the relevant Convention rights that will be discussed.

[2] This is a confident introduction that demonstrates the ability to select which piece of legislation applies to the facts of the scenario.

any particular offence. In ***Gillan and Quinton v UK*** [2009] ECHR 28 it was held that these broad powers infringed Art. 8 rights to respect for a private and family life. The Protection of Freedoms Act 2012 repealed the power.[3] It is still possible for a senior officer to authorise searches of any person or vehicle within a designated area whether or not they are suspected of a particular offence (s. 47[A](5)) but there are stricter limitations on the grant of such authorisation.[4] In this case, the officer's comment may imply that such an authorisation is in force.[5] This could be the case if specific intelligence led a senior officer to reasonably suspect an act of terrorism could take place and reasonably considers the authorisation is necessary to prevent it.

Initially, Frank is arrested on suspicion of the offence of collecting or making a record of information likely to be of assistance to terrorists. Section 58(1)(b) specifies that it is an offence to possess any document or record of information of that kind. The statute does contain a defence of 'reasonable excuse' for possession, placing the evidential burden upon the defendant. Frank may wish to argue that he did not realise that the USB stick contained the information, but that may not assist him. ***R v G*** [2009] UKHL 13 provides that if he raises the possibility of possession for a non-terrorist reason, the Crown do not have to prove any terrorist intention, only that the reason is not objectively reasonable: a case which led Mackie (2009) to comment that the offence 'lurches towards strict liability'. It seems highly unlikely that taking the material as a favour to a flatmate will meet that objective test.

Once in custody, Frank is denied access to legal advice. Schedule 8 of the Terrorism Act 2000 permits an officer of at least the rank of superintendent to delay access to legal advice for up to 48 hours if it is felt that the exercise of the right may lead to one of the consequences outlined[6] (Para. 8(4)). These largely mirror the grounds for delay permissible in respect of non-terrorist offences in section 56 of the Police and Criminal Evidence Act. It should be remembered, however, that the denial of legal advice during interview is a serious step that could potentially render the use of evidence gathered a breach of Art. 6 of the ECHR. It is not clear, here, what reason the police have for the denial. If the concerns relate to the specific solicitor Frank has nominated, it would not be a breach of Art. 6 as long as he were allowed access to a different solicitor (***R (Malik)***

[3] The words used by the officer in the problem scenario should alert you to the need to explain the repeal of section 44.

[4] Many students will note the repeal of section 44, but not recognise the powers that have replaced it. It is important to consider these, because they may well mean that this search is lawful.

[5] You must take care not to make assumptions about whether or not there is an authorisation in place, so ensure that you make it clear that more information is needed.

[6] You do not need to list these.

v Chief Constable for Greater Manchester [2007] EWHC 2936).[7] The denial of legal advice in this case, then, may have ramifications for the fairness of any subsequent trial. The ECHR considered the effect of the denial of legal advice in **Murray (John) v UK** (1996) 22 EHRR 29 and **Averill v UK** (2000) 31 EHRR 839. In both cases, the question was whether or not inferences could be drawn from silence in an interview conducted without legal advice. Although permitting the jury to draw inferences from silence was considered to be acceptable, the refusal of access to advice was held to be a breach of Art. 6. The issue here can be distinguished from that case because Frank does provide an account, but the authorities suggest that if he wished to amend or alter his account at trial no direction could be given to the jury that would permit inferences to be drawn from this inconsistency.[8]

[8] This is a good point that shows an ability to consider how the authorities would be applied in cases with different facts.

Martha has been arrested for inciting terrorist activities overseas. It is not necessary for the Crown to demonstrate that the material on the website led to any specific criminal activity. The main issues arising here relate to the length of her detention in police custody and the denial of a confidential consultation with a solicitor.[9] Schedule 8 Para. 9 of the TA authorises for a consultation to take place within the hearing of a senior officer who is not connected to the investigation. This provision has not yet been tested in the courts, but use of a similar power under earlier legislation was considered in **Brennan v UK** (2002) 34 EHRR 18. It was held that, whilst a denial of access to private legal advice would not necessarily be a breach of Art. 6, it could be if in circumstances where the defendant was inhibited from speaking frankly to his solicitor as a result. It may well be the case, then, that Martha could seek to argue that the use of evidence gained whilst in police custody should be excluded from a subsequent trial as inclusion would be unfair.[10]

[9] There is no need to consider Martha's liability for the offence.

[10] It is important that you do explain the impact of any potential breaches of Convention rights, as the question requires you to consider the implications.

Martha is unlikely to be able to claim that the length of pre-charge detention is in breach of Art. 5, providing that the necessary judicial authorisation has been obtained. The Protection of Freedoms Act 2012 amended the Terrorism Act, reducing the maximum period of detention in police custody from 28 to 14 days.[11] After 48 hours, application must be to court for a warrant of further detention. Article 5(3) requires a detainee to be brought 'promptly' before a judge, and an appearance for the purpose of authorising detention would meet this requirement.[12]

[11] You will be rewarded for knowing the relevant amending legislation.

[12] This part of the scenario is straightforward, so you can deal with it fairly briefly.

It seems that the actions taken by the police are likely to be a lawful exercise of the powers granted by the Terrorism Act 2000 (although some questions must be asked to ascertain that all necessary authorisations were made). However, both parties may seek to argue that their right to a fair trial has been compromised by the denial of confidential legal advice whilst in custody.

 Make your answer stand out

- By considering some of the powers available to the state to seize property and freeze assets of those suspected of terrorism. Although the question will lead most students to concentrate on possible offences, there is no reason why you should not touch on these powers as well, as theoretically this could affect either Martha or Frank.

- By incorporating additional academic comment in support of the propositions you make. For example, there is some helpful discussion of the courts' construction of 'reasonable' excuses in respect of sections 57 and 58 in Middleton, B. (2009). Sections 57 and 58 of the Terrorism Act 2000: Interpretation update *Journal of Criminal Law*, 73: 203–6.

- By considering additional relevant case law. In particular, more time could be spent examining the effect of questioning without legal advice. You may want to consider the Strasbourg authority *Salduz* v *Turkey* (2008) 49 EHRR 1.

Don't be tempted to . . .

- Speculate about whether or not Martha is likely to be convicted of any offence. This is not a criminal law question, and therefore you are not being tested on your ability to evaluate liability.

- Discuss the background to the repeal of section 44 search provisions in detail. Although you will have to explain that they were repealed, you need to remember that in a problem scenario you should apply the current law. Any description of the evolving law should be the bare minimum that allows the examiner to see you understand the issues relevant to these facts.

www.pearsoned.co.uk/lawexpressqa

 Go online to access more revision support including additional essay and problem questions with diagram plans, You be the marker questions, and download all diagrams from the book.

Bibliography

Allan, T.R.S. (2001) *Constitutional Justice: A Liberal Theory of the Rule of Law*. Oxford: Oxford University Press.

Bagehot, W. (1963) *The English Constitution*. London: Fontana.
Bamforth, N. (2001) The True 'Horizontal Effect' of the Human Rights Act 1998 117 *LQR* 34.
Barber, N. (2009) Laws and constitutional conventions *LQR* 125.
Blackburn, R. (2004) Monarchy and the Personal Prerogatives *Public Law* 546.
Blackstone, W. (1787) *Commentaries on the Laws of England* (10th edn).
Bondy, V. and Sunkin, M. (2009) *The Dynamics of Judicial Review Litigation: The Resolution of Public Law Challenges before Final Hearing*. London: Public Law Project, www.publiclawproject.org.uk/documents/TheDynamicsofJudicialReviewLitigation.pdf.
Bradley, A. (2011) The sovereignty of parliament – form or substance? in J. Jowell and D. Oliver (eds.) *The Changing Constitution* (7th edn). Oxford: Oxford University Press.
Bradley, A. (2012) The Damian Green affair – all's well that ends well? *Public Law* Jul 396–407.
Bradley, A. and Ewing, K. (2010) *Constitutional and Administrative Law* (15th edn). London: Pearson.
Brazier, R. (1999) *Constitutional Practice* (3rd edn). Oxford: Oxford University Press.
Brazier, R. (2008) *Constitutional and Administrative Law* (8th edn). London: Penguin.
Brighton Declaration (2012) High Level Conference on the Future of the European Court of Human Rights, http://hub.coe.int/20120419-brighton-declaration.

Cabinet Office (2010) *Cabinet Manual*, www.cabinetoffice.gov.uk/sites/default/files/resources/cabinet-manual.pdf.
Cameron, D. and Clegg, N. (2011) Foreword to the Draft House of Lords Reform Bill, www.official-documents.gov.uk/document/cm80/8077/8077.pdf.
Campbell, D. (2009) The threat of terror and the plausibility of positivism *Public Law* 501.
Campbell, D. and Young, J. (2002) The metric martyrs and the entrenchment jurisprudence of Lord Justice Laws *Public Law* 399.
Campbell, M. (2010) *Police Searches on the Parliamentary Estate* HC 62, www.publications.parliament.uk/pa/cm200910/cmselect/cmisspriv/62/62.pdf.
Cane, P. (1995) Standing up for the public *Public Law* 276.

BIBLIOGRAPHY

Carlile, Lord (2011) Sixth Report of the Independent Reviewer pursuant to section 14(3) of the Prevention of Terrorism Act 2005. London: Home Office, www.homeoffice.gov.uk/publications/counter-terrorism/independent-reviews/lord-carlile-sixth-report?view=Binary.

Chamberlain, N. (2009a) Special Advocates and Procedural Fairness in Closed Proceedings 28 *CJQ* 314.

Chamberlain, N. (2009b) Update on Special Advocates and Procedural Fairness in Closed Proceedings *CJQ*, 28: 448.

Craig, P. (1992) Legitimate expectations: a conceptual analysis *LQR*, 108: 79.

Craig, P. (1997) Formal and substantive conceptions of the Rule of Law: an analytical framework *Public Law* 467.

de Smith, S. and Brazier, R. (2008) *Constitutional and Administrative Law* (8th edn). London: Penguin.

Dewan, T. and Dowding, K. (2005) The Corrective Effect of Ministerial Resignations on Government Popularity, *American Journal of Political Science* 49: 46–56.

Dicey, A. (1885) *The Law of the Constitution*. London: Macmillan.

Elliot, M. (2007) Bicameralism, Sovereignty and the Unwritten Constitution *Int'l J Const L*, 5: 370.

Ewing, K.D. and Tham, J. (2008) The continuing futility of the Human Rights Act *Public Law* 668.

Feldman, D. (2002) *Civil Liberties and Human Rights in England and Wales*. Oxford: Oxford University Press.

Fenwick, H. (2007) *Civil Liberties and Human Rights* (4th edn). London: Routledge-Cavendish.

Fenwick, H. (2009) Marginalising Human Rights: Breach of the peace, 'kettling', the Human Rights Act and public protest *Public Law* 737.

Fenwick, H. and Phillipson, G. (2006) *Media Law*. Oxford: Oxford University Press.

Fox, R. (2009) Engagement and Participation: What the Public Want and How our Politicians Need to Respond *Parliamentary Affairs* 62(4), 673.

Frankel, M. and Gunderson, K. (2009) Delays in Investigating Freedom of Information Complaints, www.cfoi.org.uk/pdf/foidelaysreport.pdf.

Gay, O. and Powell, T. (2004) *Individual Ministerial Responsibility – Issues and Examples*, Research Paper 04/31, House of Commons Library, www.parliament.uk/documents/commons/lib/research/rp2004/rp04-082.pdf.

Geddis, A. (2004) Free speech martyrs or unreasonable threats to social peace – Insulting expression and section 5 of the Public Order Act 1986 *Public Law* 853.

Hart, H.L.A. (1994) *The Concept of Law* (2nd edn) Oxford: Oxford University Press.

Hickman, T. (2008) The courts and politics after the Human Rights Act: a comment *Public Law* 84.

Home Office (1997) *Your Right to Know: White Paper on Freedom of Information* (Cm 3818). London: HMSO.

Home Office (2010) Rapid review of counter-terrorism powers press release 13 July, www.homeoffice.gov.uk/media-centre/press-releases/counter-powers.

Home Office (2011) *CONTEST: The United Kingdom's Strategy for Countering Terrorism*, www.homeoffice.gov.uk/publications/counter-terrorism/counter-terrorism-strategy/contest-summary?view=Binary.

House of Lords Constitution Committee (2006) *Waging War: Parliament's Role and Responsibility*, 15th Report Session 2005–2006, www.publications.parliament.uk/pa/ld200506/ldselect/ldconst/236/23602.htm.

House of Lords Constitution Committee (2007) *Waging War: Parliament's Role and Responsibility*, 3rd Report Session 2006–2007, www.publications.parliament.uk/pa/ld200607/ldselect/ldconst/51/5102.htm.

Human Rights Joint Committee (2010) *Counter-Terrorism Policy and Human Rights (16th Report): Annual Review of Control Orders Legislation.*

Jaconelli, J. (2005) Do constitutional conventions bind? *CLJ*, 64(1): 149.

Jennings, I. (1959a) *The Law and the Constitution* (5th edn). London: Hodder and Stoughton.

Jennings, I. (1959b) *Cabinet Government* (3rd edn). Cambridge: Cambridge University Press.

Joint Committee on the Draft Enhanced Terrorism Prevention and Investigation Measures Bill (2012) *Report* www.parliament.uk/business/committees/committees-a-z/joint-select/terrorism-prevention-and-investigation-measures-bill/publications/.

Joint Committee on Human Rights (2005) Sixth Report, www.publications.parliament.uk/pa/jt200506/jtselect/jtrights/96/9602.htm.

Joint Committee on Human Rights (2006) 23rd Report, www.publications.parliament.uk/pa/jt200506/jtselect/jtrights/239/23902.htm.

Jowell, J. (2000) Beyond the rule of law: towards constitutional judicial review *Public Law* 671.

Jowell, J. and Oliver, D. (eds.) (2000) *The Changing Constitution* (4th edn). Oxford: Oxford University Press.

Khan, A. (2012) A 'right not to be offended' under Article 10(2) ECHR? Concerns in the construction of the 'rights of others' *EHRLR* 191–204.

Knight, C.J.S. (2009) Expectations in transition: recent developments in legitimate expectations *Public Law* 15.

Law Commission (2010) Report, *Administrative Redress: Public Bodies and the Citizen* (No. 322). www.lawcom.gov.uk/docsAc322.pdf.

Leopold, P.M. (1999) Report of the Joint Committee on Parliamentary Privilege *Public Law* 604.

Lever, A. (2007) Is judicial review undemocratic? *Public Law* 280.

Liberty (2009) *Liberty's response to the Independent Police Complaints Commission Consultation on the IPCC's proposed Statutory Guidance for the Police Service 2009*, www.liberty-human-rights.org.uk/pdfs/policy09/liberty-s-response-to-the-consultation-on-the-ipcc-s-proposed-statutory-guid.pdf.

BIBLIOGRAPHY

Liberty (2011) *Progress on stop and search but control orders by any other name* available on their web site at http://liberty-human-rights.org.uk/media/press/2011/progress-on-stop-and-search-but-control-orders-by-any-ot.php.

Loveland, I. (2012) *Constitutional Law, Administrative Law, and Human Rights: A Critical Introduction* (6th edn). Oxford: Oxford University Press.

Macdonald, Lord (2011) *Review of Counter-Terrorism and Security Powers* (Cm 8003). www.homeoffice.gov.uk/publications/counter-terrorism/review-of-ct-security-powers/report-by-lord-mcdonald?view=Binary.

McKeever, D. (2010) The HRA and anti-terrorism in the UK: one great leap forward by Parliament but are the courts able to slow the steady retreat that has followed? *Public Law* 100.

McKeown, M. and Thomson, S. (2010) The role of the House of Lords in a hung parliament *Scots Law Times*, 19: 99.

Mackie, J. (2009) Being Unreasonable *SJ* 153/12.

Maer, L. (2010) *Hung Parliaments* SN/PC/04951, www.parliament.uk/documents/commons/lib/research/briefings/snpc-04951.pdf.

Marshall, G. (1971) *Constitutional Theory.* Oxford: Cavendish Press.

Marshall, G. (2002) The Crown and Bagehot's dubious death warrant *Public Law* Spring 4–8.

Mead, D. (2009) Of kettles, cordon and crowd control – Austin, Commissioner of Police for the Metropolis and the meaning of 'deprivation of liberty' *EHRLR* 376.

Mead, D. (2010) *The New Law of Peaceful Protest: Rights and Regulations in the Human Rights Act Era.* Oxford: Hart Publishing.

Middleton, B. (2009) Sections 57 and 58 of the Terrorism Act 2000: Interpretation update, *Journal of Criminal Law*, 73: 203.

Millar, D. (2011) *Erskine May's Parliamentary Practice* (23rd edn). London: Lexis-Nexis Butterworth.

Ministerial Code of Conduct (2010) www.cabinetoffice.gov.uk/sites/default/files/resources/ministerial-code-may-2010.pdf.

Montesquieu, C. (1989) *The Spirit of the Laws.* Cambridge: Cambridge University Press.

Murdoch, C. (2012) The Oath and the Internet *Criminal Law and Justice Weekly* 176, March.

Neuberger, Lord (2011a) Open Justice Unbound? Judicial Studies Board Annual Lecture 2011, www.judiciary.gov.uk/Resources/JCO/Documents/Speeches/mr-speech-jsb-lecture-march-2011.pdf.

Neuberger, Lord (2011b) *Report of the Committee on Superinjunctions: Superinjunctions, Anonymised Injunctions and Open Justice*, www.judiciary.gov.uk/Resources/JCO/Documents/Reports/super-injunction-report-20052011.pdf.

Otty, T. (2012) The slow creep of complacency and the soul of justice: observations on the proposal for English courts to adopt 'closed material procedures' for the trial of civil damages claims *EHRLR* 3, 267.

Parpworth, N. (2010) The Parliamentary Standards Act 2009: A Constitutional Dangerous Dogs Measure? *MLR*, 73(2): 262.

Phillipson, G. (2009) Max Mosley goes to Strasbourg; Article 8, claimant notification and interim injunctions *Journal of Media Law*, 1: 73.

Phillipson, G. (2004) 'The Greatest Quango of Them All', 'A Rival Chamber' or 'A Hybrid Nonsense'? Solving the Second Chamber Paradox *Public Law* 352.

Public Administration Select Committee (2002) *The Second Chamber: Continuing the Reform, Fifth Report of Session 2001–02*, HC 494-I, www.publications.parliament.uk/pa/cm200102/cmselect/cmpubadm/494/49402.htm.

Public Administration Select Committee (2004) 4th Report Session 2003–2004, www.publications.parliament.uk/pa/cm200304/cmselect/cmpubadm/422/42202.htm.

Raz, J. (1979) *The Authority of Law*. Oxford: Oxford University Press.

Russell, M. (2011) 'Never allow a crisis to go to waste': the Wright Committee Reforms to strengthen the House of Commons *Parliamentary Affairs*, 64(4): 612.

Schaeffer, A. (2004) Reasons and rationalisations: late reasons in judicial review *JR* 151.

Scott, A. (2010) Prior notification in privacy case: a reply to Professor Phillipson *Journal of Media Law*, 2(1): 49.

Stone, R. (2001) Breach of the peace: the case for abolition 2 *WebJCLI*.

Stone, R. (2005) *The Law of Entry, Search and Seizure* (5th edn). Oxford: Oxford University Press.

Stone, R. (2012) *Textbook on Civil Liberties and Human Rights* (9th edn). Oxford: Oxford University Press.

Straw, J. (1994) Abolish the Royal Prerogative in A. Barnett (ed.), *Power and the Throne: The Monarchy Debate*. London: Vintage.

Sumption, J. (2011) Judicial and Political Decision-making: The Uncertain Boundary The F.A. Mann Lecture, www.legalweek.com/digital_assets/3704/MANNLECTURE_final.pdf.

Sunkin, M. (2010) Remedies available in judicial review proceedings, in D. Feldman (ed.), *English Public Law* (2nd edn). Oxford: Oxford University Press.

Thomas, C. (2010) *Are Juries Fair?*, London: Ministry of Justice, www.justice.gov.uk/downloads/publications/research-and-analysis/moj-research/are-juries-fair-research.pdf.

Vile, L. (1998) *Constitutionalism and the Separation of Powers* (2nd edn) Indianapolis: Liberty Fund Inc.

Wade, H.W.R. (1955) The basis of legal sovereignty, *Cambridge LJ* 172.

Wade, H.W.R. (1996) Sovereignty – Revolution or Evolution? *LQR*, 112: 568.

Wakeham, Lord (2000) *A House for the Future* (Cm 4534), www.archive.official-documents.co.uk/document/cm45/4534/4534.htm.

Waldron, J. (1990) *The Law*. London: Routledge.

Waldron, J. (2006) The core of the case against judicial review *Yale Law Journal*, 115: 1346.

BIBLIOGRAPHY

Walker, C. (2010) The threat of terrorism and the fate of control orders *Public Law* 4.
Walker, C. and Horne, A. (2012) The Terrorism Prevention and Investigations Measures Act 2011: one thing but not much the other?, Crim LR, 6: 421–438.
Wheare, K.C. (1966) *Modern Constitutions* (2nd edn). Oxford: Oxford University Press.
White Paper (1997) *Your Right to Know* (Cm. 3818). London: HMSO, www.official-documents.gov.uk/document/cm38/3818/3818.pdf.
Woolf, Lord (1996) *Access to Justice*, webarchive.nationalarchives.gov.uk/+www.dca.gov.uk/civil/final/index.htm.
Worthy, B. and Hazell, R. (2010) Assessing the performance of freedom of information, *Government Information Quarterly*, 27(4): 352.

Zander, M. (1995) *The Police and Criminal Evidence Act 1984* (3rd edn). London: Sweet & Maxwell.

Index

INDEX